Praise for Toni Morrison's

The Source of Self-Regard

"Profoundly insightful. . . . Speaks to today's social and political moment as directly as this morning's headlines." —NPR

"Moving. . . . Magnificent. . . . It's a large, rich, heterogeneous book, and hallelujah. . . . With this book, one is tempted to quote at length from her words: her acuity and moral clarity are dazzling, but so is her vision for how we might find our way towards a less unjust, less hateful future." —*The Guardian*

"Her critical mind is as original as her literary vision. . . . Morrison's style is, for the most part, stately, not so much ornate as complex, not so much stentorian as insistent, authoritative, often fierce. . . . Morrison is not simply a narrative spellbinder. . . . She is also a thundering prophet for our time." —*Commonweal*

"*The Source of Self-Regard* is a must-read." —*Essence*

"Altogether fantastic . . . one of the deepest seers of our time." —*Brain Pickings*

"Give[s] insight into Morrison not just as a master of American folklore and the novel but also as a keen observer of humankind." —*Vogue*

Toni Morrison

The Source of Self-Regard

Toni Morrison is the author of eleven novels, from *The Bluest Eye* (1970) to *God Help the Child* (2015). She received the National Book Critics Circle Award and the Pulitzer Prize, and in 1993 she was awarded the Nobel Prize in Literature. She died in 2019.

www.tonimorrisonsociety.org

INTERNATIONAL

The Source of Self-Regard

The Source
of Self-Regard

Selected Essays, Speeches, and Meditations

TONI MORRISON

VINTAGE INTERNATIONAL
VINTAGE BOOKS
A DIVISION OF PENGUIN RANDOM HOUSE LLC
NEW YORK

FIRST VINTAGE INTERNATIONAL EDITION, JANUARY 2020

Copyright © 2019 by Toni Morrison

All rights reserved. Published in the United States by Vintage Books,
a division of Penguin Random House LLC, New York, and distributed in
Canada by Penguin Random House Canada Limited, Toronto. Originally
published in hardcover in the United States by Alfred A. Knopf, a division
of Penguin Random House LLC, New York, in 2019.

Vintage is a registered trademark and Vintage International
and colophon are trademarks of Penguin Random House LLC.

The Library of Congress has cataloged the Knopf edition as follows:
Names: Morrison, Toni, author.
Title: The source of self-regard : selected essays, speeches, and meditations /
Toni Morrison.
Description: First edition. | New York : Alfred A. Knopf, 2019.
Identifiers: LCCN 2018023690 (print) | LCCN 2018024415 (ebook)
Classification: LCC PS3563.O8749 (ebook) | LCC PS3563.O8749 A6 2019
(print) | DDC 814/.6—dc23
LC record available at https://lccn.loc.gov/2018023690

Vintage International Trade Paperback ISBN: 978-0-525-56279-5
eBook ISBN: 978-0-525-52111-2

Book design by Cassandra J. Pappas

www.vintagebooks.com

Printed in the United States of America

10 9

Contents

Peril

Authoritarian regimes, dictators, despots are often, but not always, fools. But none is foolish enough to give perceptive, dissident writers free range to publish their judgments or follow their creative instincts. They know they do so at their own peril. They are not stupid enough to abandon control (overt or insidious) over media. Their methods include surveillance, censorship, arrest, even slaughter of those writers informing and disturbing the public. Writers who are unsettling, calling into question, taking another, deeper look. Writers—journalists, essayists, bloggers, poets, playwrights—can disturb the social oppression that functions like a coma on the population, a coma despots call peace, and they stanch the blood flow of war that hawks and profiteers thrill to.

That is their peril.

Ours is of another sort.

How bleak, unlivable, insufferable existence becomes when we are deprived of artwork. That the life and work of writers facing peril must be protected is urgent, but along with that urgency we should remind ourselves that their absence, the choking off of a writer's work, its cruel amputation, is of equal peril to us. The rescue we extend to them is a generosity to ourselves.

We all know nations that can be identified by the flight of writers from their shores. These are regimes whose fear of unmonitored writing is justified because truth is trouble. It is trouble for the warmonger, the torturer, the corporate thief, the political hack, the corrupt justice system, and for a comatose public. Unpersecuted, unjailed, unharassed writers are trouble for the ignorant bully, the sly racist, and the predators feeding off the world's resources. The alarm, the disquiet, writers raise is instructive because it is open and vulnerable, because if unpoliced it is threatening. Therefore the historical suppression of writers is the earliest harbinger of the steady peeling away of additional rights and liberties that will follow. The history of persecuted writers is as long as the history of literature itself. And the efforts to censor, starve, regulate, and annihilate us are clear signs that something important has taken place. Cultural and political forces can sweep clean all but the "safe," all but state-approved art.

I have been told that there are two human responses to the perception of chaos: naming and violence. When the chaos is simply the unknown, the naming can be accomplished effortlessly—a new species, star, formula, equation, prognosis. There is also mapping, charting, or devising proper nouns for unnamed or stripped-of-names geography, landscape, or population. When chaos resists, either by reforming itself or by rebelling against imposed order, violence is understood to be the most frequent response and the most rational when confronting the unknown, the catastrophic, the wild, wanton, or incorrigible. Rational responses may be censure; incarceration in holding camps, prisons; or death, singly or in war. There is, however, a third response to chaos, which I have not heard about, which is stillness. Such stillness can be passivity and dumbfoundedness; it can be paralytic fear. But it can also be art. Those writers plying their craft near to or far from the throne of raw power, of military power, of empire building and countinghouses, writers who construct meaning in the face of chaos must be nurtured, protected. And it is right that such protection be initiated by other writers. And it is imperative not only to save the besieged writers but to save ourselves. The thought that leads me to contemplate with dread the erasure of other voices, of unwritten novels, poems whispered or swallowed for fear of being overheard by the wrong people, outlawed languages flourishing underground, essayists' questions challenging authority never being posed, unstaged plays, canceled films—that thought is a nightmare. As though a whole universe is being described in invisible ink.

Certain kinds of trauma visited on peoples are so deep, so cruel, that unlike money, unlike vengeance, even unlike justice, or rights, or the goodwill of others, only writers can translate such trauma and turn sorrow into meaning, sharpening the moral imagination.

A writer's life and work are not a gift to mankind; they are its necessity.

The Foreigner's Home

The Dead of September 11

Some have God's words; others have songs of comfort for the bereaved. If I can pluck up courage here, I would like to speak directly to the dead—the September dead. Those children of ancestors born in every continent on the planet: Asia, Europe, Africa, the Americas; born of ancestors who wore kilts, obis, saris, geles, wide straw hats, yarmulkes, goatskin, wooden shoes, feathers, and cloths to cover their hair. But I would not say a word until I could set aside all I know or believe about nations, war, leaders, the governed and ungovernable; all I suspect about armor and entrails. First I would freshen my tongue, abandon sentences crafted to know evil—wanton or studied; explosive or quietly sinister; whether born of a sated appetite or hunger; of vengeance or the simple compulsion to stand up before falling down. I would purge my language of hyperbole, of its eagerness to analyze the levels of wickedness; ranking them, calculating their higher or lower status among others of its kind.

Speaking to the broken and the dead is too difficult for a mouth full of blood. Too holy an act for impure thoughts. Because the dead are free, absolute; they cannot be seduced by blitz.

To speak to you, the dead of September, I must not claim false intimacy or summon an overheated heart glazed just in time for a camera. I must be steady and I must be clear, knowing all the time that I have nothing to say—no words stronger than the steel that pressed you into itself; no scripture older or more elegant than the ancient atoms you have become.

And I have nothing to give either—except this gesture, this thread thrown between your humanity and mine: *I want to hold you in my arms* and as your soul got shot of its box of flesh to understand, as you have done, the wit of eternity: its gift of unhinged release tearing through the darkness of its knell.

The Foreigner's Home

EXCLUDING THE HEIGHT of the slave trade in the nineteenth century, the mass movement of peoples in the latter half of the twentieth century and the beginning of the twenty-first is greater now than it has ever been. It is a movement of workers, intellectuals, refugees, armies crossing oceans, continents, immigrants through custom offices and hidden routes, speaking multiple languages of trade, of political intervention, of persecution, exile, violence, and poverty. There is little doubt that the redistribution (voluntary or involuntary) of people all over the globe tops the agenda of the state, the boardrooms, the neighborhoods, the street. Political maneuvers to control this movement are not limited to monitoring the dispossessed. While much of this exodus can be described as the journey of the colonized to the seat of the colonizers (slaves, as it were, abandoning the plantation for the planters' home), and while more of it is the flight of war refugees, the relocation and transplantation of the management and diplomatic class to globalization's outposts, as well as the deployment of fresh military units and bases, feature prominently in legislative attempts to control the constant flow of people.

The spectacle of mass movement draws attention inevitably to the borders, the porous places, the vulnerable points where one's concept of home is seen as being menaced by foreigners. Much of the alarm hovering at the borders, the gates, is stoked, it seems to me, by (1) both the threat and the promise of globalism and (2) an uneasy relationship with our own foreignness, our own rapidly disintegrating sense of belonging.

Let me begin with globalization. In our current understanding, globalization is not a version of the nineteenth-century "Britannia rules" format—although postcolonial upheavals reflect and are reminiscent of the domination one nation had over most others. The term does not have the "workers of the world unite" agenda of the old internationalism, although that was the very word—"internationalism"—that the president of the AFL-CIO used at the executive council of union presidents. Nor is the globalism the postwar appetite for "one world," the rhetoric that stirred and bedeviled the fifties and launched the United Nations. Nor is it the "universalism" of the sixties and seventies—either as a plea for world peace or an insistence on cultural hegemony. "Empire," "internationalism," "one world," "universal"—all seem less like categories of historical trends than yearnings. Yearnings to corral the earth into some semblance of unity and some measure of control, to conceive of the planet's human destiny as flowing from one constellation of nations' ideology. Globalism has the same desires and yearnings as its predecessors. It too understands itself as historically progressive, enhancing, destined, unifying, utopian. Narrowly defined, it is meant to mean instant movement of capital and the rapid distribution of data and products operating within a politically neutral environment shaped by multinational corporate demands. Its larger connotations, however, are less innocent, encompassing as they do not only the demonization of embargoed states or the trivialization cum negotiation with warlords, but also the collapse of nation-states under the weight of transnational economies, capital, and labor; the preeminence of Western culture and economy; the Americanization of the developed and developing world through the penetration of U.S. culture into others as well as the marketing of third-world cultures to the West as fashion, film settings, and cuisine.

Globalization, hailed with the same vigor as was manifest destiny, internationalism, etc., has reached a level of majesty in our imagination. For all its claims of fostering freedom, globalism's dispensations are royal, for it can bestow much. In matters of reach (across frontiers); in terms of mass (of populations affected and engaged); and in terms of riches (limitless fields to mine for resources and services to offer). Yet as much as globalism is adored as near messianic, it is also reviled as an evil courting a dangerous dystopia. Its disregard of borders, national infrastructures, local bureaucracies, internet censors, tariffs, laws, and languages; its disregard of margins and the marginal people who live there; its formidable, engulfing properties accelerating erasure, a flattening out of difference, of specificity for marketing purposes. An abhorrence of diversity. We imagine indistinguishability, the elimination of minority languages, minority cultures in its wake. We speculate with horror on what could be the irrevocable, enfeebling alteration of major languages, major cultures in its sweep. Even if those dreaded consequences are not made completely manifest, they nevertheless cancel out globalism's assurances of better life by issuing dire warnings of premature cultural death.

Other dangers globalism poses are the distortion of the public and the destruction of the private. We glean what is public primarily, but not exclusively, from media. We are asked to abandon much of what was once private to the data-collecting requirements of governmental, political, market, and now security needs. Part of the anxiety about the porous divide between public and private domains certainly stems from reckless applications of the terms. There is the privatization of prisons, which is the private corporate control of a public facility. There is the privatization of public schools. There is also private life—claims to which can be given up freely on talk shows, or negotiated in the courts by celebrities, "public" figures, and privacy rights cases. There is private space (atriums, gardens, etc.) open to the public. And public space (parks, playgrounds, and beaches in certain neighborhoods) limited to private use. There is the looking-glass phenomenon of the "play" of the public in our private, interior lives. Interiors of our houses look like store displays (along with shelf after shelf of "collections") and store displays are arranged as house interiors; young people's behavior is said to be an echo of what the screen offers; the screen is said to echo, represent, youthful interests and behavior—not create them. Since the space in which both civic and private life is lived has become so indistinguishable from inner and outer, from inside/outside, these two realms have been compressed into a ubiquitous blur, a rattling of our concept of home.

It is this rattling I believe that affects the second point: our uneasiness with our own feelings of foreignness, our own rapidly fraying sense of belonging. To what do we pay greatest allegiance? Family, language group, culture, country, gender? Religion, race? And if none of these matter, are we urbane, cosmopolitan, or simply lonely? In other words, how do we decide where we belong? What convinces us that we do? Or put another way, what is the matter with foreignness?

I have chosen to comment on a novel written in the fifties by a Ghanaian author as a means of addressing this dilemma—the inside/outside blur that can enshrine frontiers, and borders real, metaphorical, and psychological, as we wrestle with definitions of nationalism, citizenship, race, ideology, and the so-called clash of cultures in our search to belong.

African and African American writers are not alone in coming to terms with these problems, but they do have a long and singular history of confronting them. Of not being at home in one's homeland; of being exiled in the place one belongs.

Before I discuss this novel, I want to describe what preceded my reading of African literature and compelled my excursion into what troubles contemporary definitions of the foreign.

Velvet-lined offering plates were passed down the pews on Sunday. The last one was the smallest and the one most likely to be empty. Its position and size signaled the dutiful but limited expectations that characterized most everything in the thirties. The coins, never bills, sprinkled there were mostly from children encouraged to give up their pennies and nickels for the charitable work so necessary for the redemption of Africa. Although the sound of the name, "Africa," was beautiful it was riven by the complicated emotions with which it was associated. Unlike starving China, Africa was both ours and theirs; intimately connected to us and profoundly foreign. A huge needy homeland to which we were said to belong but that none of us had seen or cared to see, inhabited by people with whom we maintained a delicate relationship of mutual ignorance and disdain, and with whom we shared a mythology of passive, traumatized otherness cultivated by textbooks, film, cartoons, and the hostile name-calling children learn to love.

Later, when I began to read fiction set in Africa, I found that, with no exceptions that I knew of, each narrative elaborated on and enhanced the very mythology that accompanied those velvet plates floating between the pews. For Joyce Cary, Elspeth Huxley, H. Rider Haggard, Africa was precisely what the missionary collection implied: a dark continent in desperate need of light. The light of Christianity, of civilization, of development. The light of charity switched on by simple goodheartedness. It was an idea of Africa fraught with the assumptions of a complex intimacy coupled with an acknowledgment of unmediated estrangement. This conundrum of foreign ownership alienating the local population, of the dispossession of native speakers from their home, the exile of indigenous peoples within their home contributed a surreal glow to these narratives, enticing the writers to project a metaphysically void Africa ripe for invention. With one or two exceptions, literary Africa was an inexhaustible playground for tourists and foreigners. In the work of Joseph Conrad, Isak Dinesen, Saul Bellow, Ernest Hemingway, whether imbued with or struggling against conventional Western views of benighted Africa, their protagonists found the continent to be as empty as that collection plate—a vessel waiting for whatever copper and silver imagination was pleased to place there. As grist for Western mills, accommodatingly mute, conveniently blank, Africa could be made to support a wide variety of literary and/or ideological requirements. It could stand back as scenery for any exploit or leap forward and obsess itself with the woes of any foreigner; it could contort itself into frightening malignant shapes upon which Westerners could contemplate evil; or it could kneel and accept elementary lessons from its betters. For those who made that literal or imaginative voyage, contact with Africa offered thrilling opportunities to experience life in its primitive, formative, inchoate state, the consequence of which experience was self-enlightenment— a wisdom that confirmed the benefits of European proprietorship free of the responsibility of gathering overly much actual intelligence about the African culture that stimulated the enlightenment. So big-hearted was this literary Africa, only a little geography, lots of climate, a few customs and anecdotes sufficed as the canvas upon which a portrait of a wiser or sadder or fully reconciled self could be painted. In Western novels published up to and throughout the fifties, Africa was itself Camus's *l'étranger,* offering the occasion for knowledge but keeping its own unknowableness intact. Like Marlow's "white patch for a boy to dream gloriously over, mapped since his boyhood with "rivers and lakes and names, [it] had ceased to be a blank space of delightful mystery. . . . It had become a place of darkness." What little could be known was enigmatic, repugnant, or hopelessly contradic-tory. Imaginary Africa was a cornucopia of imponderables that like the monstrous Grendel in *Beowulf* resisted explanation. Thus, a plethora of incompatible metaphors can be gleaned from the literature. As the original locus of the human race, Africa is ancient, yet, being under colonial control, it is also infantile. A kind of old fetus always waiting to be born but confounding all midwives. In novel after novel, short story after short story, Africa is simultaneously innocent and corrupt-ing, savage and pure, irrational and wise.

In that racially charged literary context, coming upon Camara Laye's *Le Regard du Roi,* known in English as *The Radiance of the King,* was shocking. Suddenly the clichéd journey into storybook Afri-can darkness either to bring light or find it is reimagined. The novel not only summons a sophisticated, wholly African imagistic vocabu-lary from which to launch a discursive negotiation with the West, it exploits the images of homelessness that the conqueror imposes on the native population: the disorder of Joyce Cary's *Mister Johnson;* the obsession with smells in Elspeth Huxley's *The Flame Trees of Thika;* the European fixation on the meaning of nakedness as in H. Rider Haggard, or Joseph Conrad, or virtually all travel writing.

Camara Laye's narrative is, briefly, this: Clarence, a European, has come to Africa for reasons he cannot articulate. There, he has gambled, lost, and heavily in debt to his white compatriots, is hiding among the indigenous population in a dirty inn. Already evicted from the colonists' hotel, about to be evicted by the African innkeeper, Clarence decides the solution to his pennilessness is to be taken into the service of the king. He is prevented by a solid crowd of villagers from approaching the king, and his mission is greeted with scorn. He meets a pair of mischief-loving teenagers and a cunning beggar who agree to help him. Under their guidance he travels south, where the king is expected to appear next. By way of his journey, not wholly unlike a pilgrim's progress, the author is able to trace and parody the parallel sensibilities of Europe and Africa.

The literary tropes of Africa are exact replicas of perceptions of foreignness: (1) threatening, (2) depraved, (3) incomprehensible. And it is fascinating to observe Camara Laye's adroit handling of those perceptions.

1. Threatening. Clarence, his protagonist, is stupefied with fear. In spite of noting that the "forests [are] devoted to the wine industry"; that the landscape is "cultivated"; that the people living there give him a "cordial welcome," he sees only inaccessibility, "common hostility." The order and clarity of the landscape are at odds with the menacing jungle in his head.

2. Depraved. It is Clarence who descends into depravity, enacting the full horror of what Westerners imagine as "going native": the "unclean and cloying weakness" that imperils masculinity. Clarence's blatant enjoyment of and feminine submission to continuous cohabitation reflect his own appetites and his own willful ignorance. As mulatto children crowd the village, Clarence, the only white in the region, continues to wonder where they came from. He refuses to believe the obvious—that he has been sold as stud for the harem.

3. Incomprehensible. Camara Laye's Africa is not dark; it is suffused with light: the watery green light of the forest; the ruby-red tints of the houses and soil; the sky's "unbearable . . . azure brilliance"; even the scales of the fish women "glimmered like robes of dying moonlight." Understanding the motives, the sensibilities of the Africans—both wicked and benign—require only a suspension of belief in an unbreachable difference between humans.

Unpacking the hobbled idioms of the foreigner usurping one's home, of delegitimizing the native, of reversing claims of belonging, the novel allows us to experience a white man emigrating to Africa, alone, without a job, without authority, without resources or even a family name. But he has one asset that always works, can only work, in third-world countries. He is white, he says, and therefore suited in some ineffable way to be advisor to the king whom he has never seen, in a country he does not know, among people he neither understands nor wishes to. What begins as a quest for a position of authority, for escape from the contempt of his own countrymen becomes a searing process of reeducation. What counts as intelligence among these Africans is not prejudice, but nuance and the ability and willingness to see, to surmise. The European's refusal to meditate cogently on any event except the ones that concern his comfort or survival dooms him. When insight finally seeps through, he feels annihilated by it. This fictional investigation allows us to see the deracing of a Westerner experiencing Africa without European support, protection, or command. Allows us to rediscover or imagine anew what it feels like to be marginal, ignored, superfluous; to have one's name never uttered; to be stripped of history or representation; to be sold or exploited labor for the benefit of a presiding family, a shrewd entrepreneur, a local regime.

It is a disturbing encounter that may help us deal with the destabilizing pressures of the transglobal tread of peoples. Pressure that can make us cling or discredit other cultures, other languages; make us rank evil according to the fashion of the day; make us legislate, expel, conform, purge, and pledge allegiance to ghosts and fantasy. Most of all this pressure can make us deny the foreigner in ourselves and make us resist to the death the commonness of humanity.

After many trials, enlightenment slowly surfaces in Camara Laye's Westerner: Clarence gets his wish to meet the king. But by then he and his purpose have altered. Against the advice of the local people, Clarence crawls naked to the throne. When he finally sees the king, who is a mere boy laden with gold, the "terrifying void that is within [him]," the void that he has been protecting from disclosure, opens to receive the royal gaze. It is this openness, this crumbling of cultural armor maintained out of fear, this act of unprecedented courage that is the beginning of Clarence's salvation, his bliss and his freedom. Wrapped in the boy king's embrace, feeling the beat of his young heart, Clarence hears him murmur these exquisite words of authentic belonging, words welcoming him to the human race: "Did you not know that I was waiting for you?"

Racism and Fascism

L ET US BE REMINDED that before there is a final solution, there must be a first solution, a second one, even a third. The move toward a final solution is not a jump. It takes one step, then another, then another. Something, perhaps, like this:

1. Construct an internal enemy, as both focus and diversion.
2. Isolate and demonize that enemy by unleashing and protecting the utterance of overt and coded name-calling and verbal abuse. Employ ad hominem attacks as legitimate charges against that enemy.
3. Enlist and create sources and distributors of information who are willing to reinforce the demonizing process because it is profitable, because it grants power, and because it works.
4. Palisade all art forms; monitor, discredit, or expel those that challenge or destabilize processes of demonization and deification.
5. Subvert and malign all representatives of and sympathizers with this constructed enemy.
6. Solicit, from among the enemy, collaborators who agree with and can sanitize the dispossession process.
7. Pathologize the enemy in scholarly and popular mediums; recycle, for example, scientific racism and the myths of racial superiority in order to naturalize the pathology.

8. Criminalize the enemy. Then prepare, budget for, and rationalize the building of holding arenas for the enemy— especially its males and absolutely its children.

9. Reward mindlessness and apathy with monumentalized entertainments and with little pleasures, tiny seductions: a few minutes on television, a few lines in the press; a little pseudo-success; the illusion of power and influence; a little fun, a little style, a little consequence.

10. Maintain, at all costs, silence.

In 1995 racism may wear a new dress, buy a new pair of boots, but neither it nor its succubus twin fascism is new or can make anything new. It can only reproduce the environment that supports its own health: fear, denial, and an atmosphere in which its victims have lost the will to fight.

The forces interested in fascist solutions to national problems are not to be found in one political party or another, or in one or another wing of any single political party. Democrats have no unsullied history of egalitarianism. Nor are liberals free of domination agendas. Republicans have housed abolitionists and white supremacists. Conservative, moderate, liberal; right, left, hard left, far right; religious, secular, socialist—we must not be blindsided by these Pepsi-Cola, Coca-Cola labels because the genius of fascism is that any political structure can host the virus and virtually any developed country can become a suitable home. Fascism talks ideology, but it is really just marketing—marketing for power.

It is recognizable by its need to purge, by the strategies it uses to purge, and by its terror of truly democratic agendas. It is recognizable by its determination to convert all public services to private entrepreneurship, all nonprofit organizations to profit-making ones—so that the narrow but protective chasm between governance and business disappears. It changes citizens into taxpayers—so individuals become angry at even the notion of the public good. It changes neighbors into consumers—so the measure of our value as humans is not our humanity or our compassion or our generosity but what we own. It changes parenting into panicking—so that we vote against the interests of our own children; against *their* health care, *their* education, *their* safety from weapons. And in effecting these changes it produces the perfect capitalist, one who is willing to kill a human being for a product (a pair of sneakers, a jacket, a car) or kill generations for control of products (oil, drugs, fruit, gold).

When our fears have all been serialized, our creativity censured, our ideas "marketplaced," our rights sold, our intelligence sloganized, our strength downsized, our privacy auctioned; when the theatricality, the entertainment value, the marketing of life is complete, we will find ourselves living not in a nation but in a consortium of industries, and wholly unintelligible to ourselves except for what we see as through a screen darkly.

Home

L AST YEAR a colleague of mine asked me where I had gone to
school when a child. I told her, Lorain, Ohio. Then she questioned me: Were your schools desegregated then? I said, What?
They were never segregated in the thirties and forties—so why would
they be desegregated. Besides, we had one high school and four junior
high schools. Then I recalled that she herself was around forty years
old when that term "desegregated" was alive everywhere. Obviously I
was in a time warp and obviously the early diverse population of the
town I grew up in was not the way of the country. Before I left Lorain
for Washington, D.C., then Texas, then Ithaca, then New York City,
I thought every place was more or less like it, except in size. Nothing
could be further from the truth. In any case her questions made me
think anew about this area of Ohio and my recollections of home.
This region (Lorain, Elyria, Oberlin) is not like it was when I lived
here, but in a way it doesn't matter because home is memory and companions and/or friends who share the memory. But equally important
as the memory and place and people of one's personal home is the very
idea of home. What do we mean when we say "home"?

It is a virtual question because the destiny of the twenty-first century will be shaped by the possibility or the collapse of a shareable
world. The question of cultural apartheid and/or cultural integration
is at the heart of all governments and informs our perception of the
ways in which governance and culture compel the exoduses of peoples

(voluntarily or driven) and raises complex questions of dispossession, recovery, and the reinforcement of siege mentalities. How do individuals resist or become complicit in the process of alienizing others' demonization—a process that can infect the foreigner's geographical sanctuary with the country's xenophobia? By welcoming immigrants, or importing slaves into their midst for economic reasons and relegating their children to a modern version of the "undead." Or by reducing an entire native population, some with a history hundreds, even thousands of years long, into despised foreigners in their own country. Or by the privileged indifference of a government watching an almost biblical flood destroy a city because its citizens were surplus black or poor people without transportation, water, food, help and left to their own devices to swim, slog, or die in fetid water, attics, hospitals, jails, boulevards, and holding pens. Such are the consequences of persistent demonization; such is the harvest of shame.

Clearly, the movement of peoples under duress at, beyond, and across borders is not new. Forced or eager exodus into strange territory (psychological or geographical) is indelible in the history of every quadrant of the known world, from the trek of Africans into China and Australia; to military interventions by Romans, Ottomans, Europeans; to merchant forays fulfilling the desires of a plethora of regimes, monarchies, and republics. From Venice to Virginia, from Liverpool to Hong Kong. All these and more have transferred the riches and art they found into other realms. And all these left that foreign soil stained with their blood and/or transplanted into the veins of the conquered. While in their wake the languages of conquered and conqueror swell with condemnation of the other.

The reconfiguration of political and economic alliances and the almost instant reparsing of nation-states encourage and repel the relocation of large numbers of peoples. Excluding the height of the slave trade, this mass movement of peoples is greater now than it has ever been. It involves the distribution of workers, intellectuals, refugees, traders, immigrants, and armies all crossing oceans and continents, through custom offices and via hidden routes, with multiple narratives spoken in multiple languages of commerce, of military intervention, political persecution, exile, violence, poverty, death, and shame. There is little doubt that the voluntary or involuntary displacement of people all over the globe tops the agenda of the state, the boardrooms, the neighborhoods, the streets. Political maneuvers to control this movement are not limited to monitoring the dispossessed. The transplantation of management and diplomatic classes to globalization's outposts, as well as the deployment of military units and bases, feature prominently in legislative attempts to exert authority over the constant flow of people. This slide of people has freighted the concept of citizenship and altered our perceptions of space—public and private. The strain has been marked by a plethora of hyphenated designations of national identity. In press descriptions, place of origin has become more telling than citizenship, and persons are identified as "a German citizen of such and such origin" or "a British citizen of such and such origin." All this while a new cosmopolitanism, a kind of multilayered cultural citizenship, is simultaneously being hailed. The relocation of peoples has ignited and disrupted the idea of home and expanded the focus of identity beyond definitions of citizenship to clarifications of foreignness. Who is the foreigner? is a question that leads us to the perception of an implicit and heightened threat within "difference." We see it in the defense of the local against the outsider; personal discomfort with one's own sense of belonging (Am I the foreigner in my own home?); of unwanted intimacy instead of safe distance. It may be that the most defining characteristic of our times is that, again, walls and weapons feature as prominently now as they once did in medieval times. Porous borders are understood in some quarters to be areas of threat and certain chaos, and whether real or imagined, enforced separation is posited as the solution. Walls, ammunition—they do work. For a while. But they are major failures over time, as the occupants of casual, unmarked, and mass grave sites haunt the entire history of civilization.

Consider another consequence of the blatant, violent uses to which foreignness is put—ethnic cleansing. We would be not merely remiss but irrelevant if we did not address the doom currently faced by millions of people reduced to animal, insect, or polluted status by nations with unmitigated, unrepentant power to decide who is a stranger and whether they live or die at, or far from, home. I mentioned earlier that the expulsion and slaughter of "enemies" are as old as history. But there is something new and soul destroying about this last and current century. At no other period have we witnessed such a myriad of aggression against people designated as "not us." Now, as you have seen over the last two years, the central political question was, Who or what is an American?

From what I gather from those who have studied the history of genocide—its definition and application—there seems to be a pattern. Nation-states, governments seeking legitimacy and identity, seem able and determined to shape themselves by the destruction of a collective "other." When European nations were in thrall to royal consolidation, they were able to act out this slaughter in other countries—African, South American, Asian. Australia and the United States, self-declared republics, required the annihilation of all indigenous peoples if not the usurpation of their land to create their new, democratic state. The fall of communism created a bouquet of new or reinvented nations who measured their statehood by "cleansing" communities. Whether the targets were of different religions, races, cultures—whatever—reasons were found first to demonize then to expel or murder them. For an assumed safety, hegemony, or pure land grabs, foreigners were constructed as the sum total of the putative nation's ills. If these scholars are right, we will see more and more illogical waves of war—designed for the grasp of control by the leaders of such states. Laws cannot stop them, nor can any god. Interventions merely provoke.

Wartalk

I N TRYING to come to terms with the benefits and challenges of globalism, it has become necessary to recognize that the term suffers from its own history. It is not imperialism, internationalism, or even universalism. Certainly a major distinction between globalism and its predecessors is how much it is marked by speed: the rapid reconfiguration of political and economic alliances, and the almost instant reparsing of nation-states. Both of these remappings encourage and repel the relocation of large numbers of peoples. Excluding the height of the slave trade, this mass movement of peoples is greater now than it has ever been. It involves the distribution of workers, intellectuals, refugees, traders, immigrants, and armies crossing oceans, continents, through custom offices and via hidden routes, speaking multiple languages of commerce, or political intervention, of persecution, exile, violence, and defiling poverty. There is little doubt that the voluntary or involuntary displacement of people all over the globe tops the agenda of the state, the boardrooms, the neighborhoods, the streets. Political maneuvers to control this movement are not limited to monitoring the dispossessed. The transplantation of management and diplomatic classes to globalization's outposts, as well as the deployment of fresh military units and bases, feature prominently in legislative attempts to exert authority over the constant flow of people.

This slide of people across the globe has altered and freighted the concept of citizenship. The strain has been marked by a plethora of hyphenated designations of national identity in the United States, by press descriptions where origin is of more significance than citizenship. People are described as "German citizen of 'fill-in-the-blank' origin" or "British citizen of 'blank' origin," all this while a new cosmopolitanism, a kind of cultural citizenship, is simultaneously being hailed. The relocation of peoples that globalism ignites has disrupted and *sullied* the idea of home and has expanded the focus of identity beyond definitions of citizenship to clarifications of foreignness. Who is the foreigner? is a question that leads us to the perception of an implicit threat within "difference." The interests of global markets, however, can absorb all these questions, thrive in fact on a multiplicity of differences, the finer, the more exceptional the better, since each "difference" is a more specific, identifiable consumer cluster. This market can reconstitute itself endlessly to any broadened definition of citizenship, to ever-narrowing, proliferating identities, as well as to the disruptions of planetary war. But unease creeps into the conversation about this beneficial morphing ability when the flip side of citizenship is addressed. The chameleon-like characteristic of global economy provokes the defense of the local and raises newer questions of foreignness—a foreignness that suggests intimacy rather than distance (Is he my neighbor?) and a deep personal discomfort with our own sense of belonging (Is he us? Am I the foreigner?). These questions complicate the concept of belonging, of home, and are telling in the alarm apparent in many quarters regarding official, prohibited, unpoliced, protected, and subversive languages.

There is some gasping at what North Africans may have done or are capable of doing to French; of what Turkish people have made of German; of the refusal of some Catalan speakers to read or even speak Spanish. The insistence on Celtic in schools; the academic study of Ojibwe; the poetic evolution of Newyorican. Even some feeble (and I think misguided) efforts to organize something called Ebonics.

The more globalism trumps language differences—by ignoring, soliciting, or engulfing them—the more passionate these protections and usurpations become. For one's language—the one we dream in—is home.

I believe it is in the humanities, and specifically the branch of literature, where such antagonisms become rich fields of creativity and thus ameliorate the climate between cultures and itinerant people. Writers are key to this process for any number of reasons, principal among which is the writer's gift for teasing language, eliciting from its vernacular, its porous lexicon, and the hieroglyphics of the electronic screen greater meaning, more intimacy, and, not incidentally, more beauty. This work is not new for writers but the challenges are, as all languages, major and dominant, minor and protected, are reeling from the impositions of globalism.

Yet globalism's impact on language is not always deleterious. It can also create odd and accidental circumstances in which profound creativity erupts out of necessity. Let me suggest one case in point, where severe changes in public discourse have already taken place as communication floods virtually every terrain. The language of war has historically been noble, summoning the elevating quality of warrior discourse: the eloquence of grief for the dead; courage and the honor of vengeance. That heroic language, rendered by Homer, Shakespeare, in sagas and by statesmen, is rivaled for beauty and force only by religious language, with which it frequently merges. In this parade of inspiring wartalk, from BC to the twentieth century, there have been disruptions. One moment of distrust and disdain for such language occurred immediately after World War I when writers like Ernest Hemingway and Wilfred Owen, among others, questioned the paucity of terms such as "honor," "glory," "bravery," "courage" to describe the reality of war, the obscenity of those terms being associated with the carnage of 1914–1918.

As Hemingway wrote: "I was always embarrassed by the words sacred, glorious, and sacrifice and the expression in vain. We had heard them, sometimes standing in the rain almost out of earshot. . . . [A]nd I had seen nothing sacred, and the things that were glorious had no glory and the sacrifices were like the stockyards at Chicago if nothing was done with the meat except to bury it. There were many words that you could not stand to hear and finally only the names of places had dignity."

But the events of 1938 quieted those interventions and once more the language of war rose to the occasion of World War II. The glamour-coated images we carry of Roosevelt, Churchill, and other statesmen are due in part to their rousing speeches and are testimony to the strength of militant oratory. Yet something interesting happened after World War II. In the late fifties and sixties, wars continued, of course—hot and cold, north and south, big and small—more and more cataclysmic, more and more heartbreaking because so unnecessary; so wildly punitive on innocent civilians one could only drop to one's knees in sorrow. Yet the language that accompanied these recent wars became oddly diminished. The dwindling persuasiveness of combat discourse may have been due to the low requirements of commercial media: their abhorrence of complex sentences and less-known metaphors, the dominance of the visual over linguistic communication. Or perhaps it was due to the fact that all of these wars were the seething mute children of preceding ones. Whatever the cause, warrior discourse has become childlike. Puny. Vaguely prepubescent. Underneath the speeches, bulletins, punditry, essays lies the clear whine of the playground: "He hit me. I did not. Did too." "That's mine. Is not. Is too." "I hate you. I hate you."

This decline, it seems to me, this echo of passionate juvenilia affects the highest level of contemporary warrior discourse and sounds like that of the comic book or action film. "I strike for freedom!" "We must save the world!" "Houston, we have a problem." An inane, enfeebled screed has emerged to address brain-cracking political and economic problems. What is fascinating is that such language sank to its most plodding at precisely the time another language was evolving: the language of nonviolence, of peaceful resistance, of negotiation. The language of Gandhi, of Martin Luther King Jr., of Nelson Mandela, of Václav Havel. Compelling language, robust, rousing, subtle, elevating, intelligent, complex. As war's consequences became more and more dire, wartalk has become less and less credible, more infantile in its panic. A change that became obvious just at the moment when the language of resolution, of diplomacy was developing its own idiom— a moral idiom worthy of human intelligence, shedding the cloud of weakness, of appeasement, that historically has hovered above it.

I do not believe the shift is coincidental. I believe it represents a fundamental change in the concept of war—a not-so-secret conviction among various and sundry populations, both oppressed and privileged, that war is, finally, out of date; that it is truly the most inefficient method of achieving one's (long-term) aims. No matter the paid parades, the forced applause, the instigated riots, the organized protests (pro or con), self- or state censoring, the propaganda; no matter the huge opportunities for profit and gain; no matter the history of the injustice—at bottom it is impossible to escape the suspicion that the more sophisticated the weapons of war, the more antiquated the idea of war. The more transparent the power grab, the holier the justification, the more arrogant the claims, the more barbaric, the more discredited the language of war has become. Leaders who find war the sole and inevitable solution to disagreement, displacement, aggression, injustice, abasing poverty seem not only helplessly retrograde, but intellectually deficient, precisely like the empurpled comic-book language in which they express themselves.

I understand that my comments may appear disjunctive on this date in 2002 when legislatures, revolutionaries, and the inflamed do not "declare" war, but simply wage it. But I am convinced that the language that has the most force, requires the most acumen, talent, grace, genius, and, yes, beauty, can never be, will never again be found in paeans to the glory of war, or erotic rallying cries to battle. The power of this alternate language does not arise from the tiresome, wasteful art of war, but rather from the demanding, brilliant art of peace.

The War on Error

I ACCEPTED this invitation to speak at Amnesty International with instant glee. I didn't have a second thought about the opportunity to address an extraordinary community of active humanitarians whose work I so profoundly respect. The honor pleased and challenged me and I believed it would be relatively effortless to find something of consequence to say to you. Months later, however, I began to have grave reservations about my early and unthinking enthusiasm. Benumbed with news of ignited chaos, death tolls, manufactured starvation, wars of choice against disarmed countries, I became virtually speechless; startled into mute disbelief; disabled by what I understood to be the equanimity of congresses and inert parliaments going about their business of business. The irrelevance cum sensationalism of mainstream media, its strange quietude on vital issues, its publicity posing as journalism did their job and mangled my own hapless, helpless unspeakable thoughts.

Although an obvious theme for this occasion occurred to me: a rehearsal of salutations and compliments to AI, I realized at last that the time for compliments has passed—although I am amazed by the breadth and depth of AI's resiliency. I came to believe that this is no time for self-congratulation—although there is room for it; room to recall and marvel at the record AI has garnered, its impact on the lives of the forgotten, and its success in tarnishing the glitz of the mighty.

Unaligned, nobly interventionist, unbrooked by nations and political parties, private interests or public exhaustion, Amnesty International declares states, walls, borders irrelevant to its humanitarian goals, detrimental to its tasks, by summoning responsibility and refusing to accept a myopic government's own narrative of its behavior.

I can share the seethe of millions, but it won't do. Rage has limited uses and serious flaws. It cuts off reason and displaces constructive action with mindless theater. Besides, absorbing the lies, untruths, both transparent and nuanced, of governments, their hypocrisy so polished it does not even care if it is revealed, can lead to a wearied and raveled mind.

We live in a world where justice equals vengeance. Where private profit drives public policy. Where the body of civil liberties, won cell by cell, bone by bone, by the brave and the dead withers in the searing heat of "all war, all the time," and, where facing eternal war, respect for, even interest in, humanitarian solutions can dwindle. Even as the conviction that "the security of every other nation in the world be subordinate to the comfort of the United States" is, finally, being challenged, civil rights and humanitarian solutions are being steadily crushed by the imperatives of that conviction.

Let me describe a little of what is happening in my country.

Death-penalty advocates are more and more entrenched even as thousands of planned executions in Texas are forced into being reviewed because of blatant errors committed in DNA laboratories.

A so-called Clear Skies Act, designed to replace the Clean Air Act, has exactly the opposite effect. Corporations, mining companies, factories can now ignore or delay every environmental safeguard put in place by the previous administration and turn "death by breathing" into gold.

Constitutional rights are facing impoverishment and annihilation as the biggest, most undertold story in the United States is the looming disenfranchisement of the electorate. Under the "Help America Vote" Act of 2002, the new electronic voting machines are said to be unable to do what ATMs and grocery clerks do: provide a paper receipt documenting the voter's choice; this while any astute hacker can gain access, the largest manufacturer of these new machines is able to calculate (perhaps control) the results in its home office.

Withdrawal from treaties, preemption, dismantlement, mass arrests minus charges or legal representation; judges instructed by the Justice Department to impose maximum terms; whistle-blowers fired; Draconian censorship—these actions are taking place in an atmosphere of aggression, panic, greed, and malice reminiscent of the oppressive political architecture we believed we had demolished. But all this you already know. The history of your activities is the documentation of and intervention into such travesties.

It seems to me that among the several wars being waged around the planet, one is paramount and surpasses in urgency all the others. That is the War Against Error.

"War Against Error" is a phrase originated to describe the fifteenth- and sixteenth-century efforts on the part of institutional religions to correct those whose beliefs were different. In a time when and place where state religion is the norm, apostasy is literally treason. Our modern world has "inherited a fully fledged apparatus of persecution and an intellectual tradition that justified killing in the name of God." Saint Thomas Aquinas himself wrote that apostates were "to be severed from the world by death." The point, in that medieval war, was not the inherent evil of the dis- or unbelieving, but his or her refusal to acknowledge his or her mistake. The lesson to be learned was: acceptance or death. A hard education in a difficult school, the doors to which are still ajar. Freely, reverently it is pried open by unbelievers as well as the faithful, by politicians as well as Enron, Halliburton, and WorldCom.

Now that this medieval school has reopened, the old curricula are revised. Rushing to teach the lessons, administrations spin out of control, skipping between the cheating scholar's expedience and the dullard's violence; between courses on empire's fundamentalism and seminars on theocratic domination. And nations and pseudo-states assert powers that would make Caligula smile as they educate their pupils in purging, cleansing, slaughtering. Graduation parties are held where exploitation, assuming the seductive costume of globalism, dances with any willing partner. In its pursuit corporations plop themselves down in every corner of the globe selling "democracy" as though it were a brand of toothpaste, the patent to which they alone control.

I think it is time for a modern War Against Error. A deliberately heightened battle against cultivated ignorance, enforced silence, and metastasizing lies. A wider war that is fought daily by human rights organizations in journals, reports, indexes, dangerous visits, and encounters with malign oppressive forces. A hugely funded and intensified battle of rescue from the violence that is swallowing the dispossessed.

If we have progressed psychologically, scientifically, intellectually, emotionally no further than 1492, when Spain cleansed itself of Jews, to 2004, when Sudan blocks food and remains content to watch the slow starvation of its people; no further than 1572, when France saw ten thousand slaughtered on Saint Bartholomew's Day, to 2001, when thousands were blown into filament in New York City; no further than 1692, when Salem burned its own daughters and wives and mothers, to 2004, when whole cities are choked with sex tourists feeding off the bodies of young girls and boys. Then, in spite of our shiny new communication toys, our gorgeous photos of Saturn, our sophisticated organ transplants, we are studying the same old curricula that waste the lives they cannot destroy. We turn to sorcery: summoning up a brew of aliens, enemies, demons, "causes" that deflect and soothe anxieties about gates through which barbarians stroll; anxieties about language falling into the mouths of others, about authority shifting into the hands of strangers. The desire, the mantra, the motto of this ancient educational system is, Civilization in neutral, then grinding to a halt. And anyone who thinks otherwise is naïve because there is real danger in the world. Of course there is. That is precisely why a correction is in order—new curricula, containing some powerful visionary thinking about how the life of the moral mind and a free and flourishing spirit can operate in a context increasingly dangerous to their health.

No more apologies for a bleeding heart when the opposite is no heart at all. Danger of losing our humanity must be met with more humanity. Otherwise we stand meekly behind Eris, hold Nemesis's cloak, and genuflect at the feet of Thanatos.

Enjoining the work of AI is more critical today than ever before because the world is more desperate; because governing bodies more hampered, more indifferent, more distracted, more inept, more depleted of creative strategies and resources; because media are increasingly cheerful pawns on the exchange market, courtiers for corporations who have no national interests or loyalties and are committed to no public service.

What strings these social perversions together, for me, is profound error—not only the errors in questionable but unquestioned data, in distorted "official" releases, in censorship and the manipulation of the press, but also and especially faults deeply embedded in the imagination. A prime example is the inability or unwillingness to imagine future's future. The inability or unwillingness to contemplate a future that is neither afterlife nor the tenure of grandchildren. Time itself seems not to have a future that equals the length or breadth or sweep or even the fascination of its past. Infinity is now, apparently, the domain of the past. And the future becomes discoverable space, outer space, which is in fact the discovery of past time. Billions of years of it. Random outbreaks of armageddonism and persistent apocalyptic yearnings suggest that the future is already over.

Oddly enough it is in the West—where advance, progress, and change have been signatory features—where confidence in an enduring future is at its slightest. Since 1945, "world without end" has been subject to serious debate. Even our definitions of the present have prefixes pointing backward: postmodern, poststructuralist, postcolonial, post–Cold War. Our contemporary prophets look back behind themselves after what has gone on before.

There are good reasons for this rush into the past for all our answers to contemporary problems. First there is the happiness that its exploration, its revision, its deconstruction afford. One reason has to do with the secularization of culture, another to do with the theocratization of culture. In the former there will be no Messiah and afterlife is understood to be medically absurd. In the latter, the only existence that matters is the one following death. In both, sustaining human existence on this planet for another half a billion years is beyond our powers of imagination. We are cautioned against the luxury of such meditation, partly because it is the unknown, mostly because it may defer and displace contemporary issues—like missionaries who were accused of diverting their convert's attention from poverty during life to rewards following death.

I don't want to give the impression that all current discourse is unrelievedly oriented to the past and indifferent to the future. The social and natural sciences are full of promises and warnings that will affect us over very long stretches of time. Scientific applications are poised to erase hunger, annihilate pain, extend individual life spans by producing illness-resistant people and disease-resistant plants. Communication technology is making sure that virtually everyone on earth can "interact" with one another and be entertained, maybe even educated, while doing so. We are warned about global change in terrain and weather that radically alters human environment; we are warned of the consequences of maldistributed resources on human survival and warned of the impact of overdistributed humans on natural resources. We invest in the promises and sometimes act intelligently on the warnings. But the promises trouble us with ethical dilemmas and a horror of playing God blindly, while the warnings have left us less and less sure of how and which and why. The prophecies that win our attention are those with bank accounts large enough or photo ops sensational enough to force debate and outline corrective action, so we can decide which war or political debacle or environmental crisis is intolerable enough; which disease, which natural disaster, which institution, which plant, which animal, bird, or fish needs our attention most. These are obviously serious concerns. What is noteworthy among the promises and warnings is that, other than products and a little bit more personal time owing to improved health, and more resources in the form of leisure and money to consume these products and services, the future has nothing to recommend itself. We are being seduced into accepting truncated, short-term, CEO versions of the world's wholly human race.

The loudest voices are urging those already living in day-to-day dread to think of the future in military terms—as a cause for and expression of war. We are being bullied into understanding the human project as a manliness contest where women and children are the most dispensable collateral.

If scientific language is about longer individual life in exchange for an ethical one; if political agenda is the xenophobic protection of a few of our families against the catastrophic others; if religious language is discredited as contempt for the nonreligious; if secular language bridles in fear of the sacred; if market language is merely an excuse for inciting greed; if the future of knowledge is not wisdom but "upgrade," where might we look for humanity's own future? Isn't it reasonable to assume that, projecting earthly human life into the far-distant future may not be the disaster movie we have come to love, but a reconfiguration of what we are here for? To lessen suffering, to tell the truth, raise the bar? To stand one remove from timeliness, like an artist encouraging reflection, stoking imagination, mindful of the long haul and putting his or her own life on the line, to imagine work in a world worthy of life?

For a future that perhaps only the young will be able fully, purely to imagine, this new War Against Error has no guarantee of victory. Sentient life is original and very hard. A student of mine (probably twenty years old) recently gave me a piece of art. Printed, cut, and pasted within it were these lines:

> No one told me it was like this.
> It's only matter shot through with pure imagination.
> [So] rise up little souls—join the doomed army toward the meaning
>   of change.
> Fight . . . fight . . . wage the unwinnable.

He seems ready. And so are we. Yes?
Thank you.

A Race in Mind

The Press in Deed

THE VASTNESS and omnipresence of the press can easily over-shadow our mutual dependence: that which exists between the professionals in the press and its outsiders. There are not, to my knowledge, any other entities quite like a "free" press, and while I have surrounded the word "free" in quotation marks here, the presence or absence of that sign of ambivalence is also something that has been the subject of years of deliberation in the press itself. It could not even be a topic in a system in which such deliberations were closed.

But I have not come here to waste your time by flattering you, to paint in even brighter colors your portrait as both the pomp and the circumstance of democratic freedom, but to comment on what I know you understand to be serious problems in the way the press functions as mediator between the experience of life in the world and its narrative and visual representation.

The harshest critics call the press-media a "closed circuit world of spectacle that has no goal other than its spectacular self." Relying like a politician only on vested interests to critique and defend its activities, the press encourages its own journalists to explain and deplore press culpability; these critics are appalled by the sight of journalists behaving like independent experts within the spectacle they have created and have an interest in sustaining, pretending to speak for a public so remote from their lives only polls can allude to its nature, defending itself from criticism with incoherent but effective lines of defense such as "We are better than we used to be," "This story just won't go away," "We do both sides of an issue."

I can't accept so sweeping a condemnation, yet the claustrophobia one feels in the sheltering arms of the press often seems permanent and conspiratorial. Notwithstanding the promise of more choices and more channels—targeted and consumer-designed magazines, barely limited numbers of cable channels—the fear of being suffocated by eternal and eternally replenished ephemera is real; so is the fear of the complete inability of a public to engage in public discourse. This latter fear—the closing off of public debate—is palpable because there is no way to answer the systemic distortions of the press in a timely, effective fashion and because the definition of "public" is already so radically changed. Homelessness and crime have been recharacterized and redeployed so that "public space" is increasingly seen as a protected preserve open only to the law-abiding and the employed, or rather to those who appear to be. Homelessness has been recharacterized as streetlessness. Not the poor deprived of homes, but the homed being deprived of their streets. And crime is construed as principally black. Neither one of these constructions is new. But as each affects public space, each affects public discourse.

It is clear to anyone interested that when the term "public" has been appropriated as space regulated for one portion of society only, when the "poor" have no political party to represent their interests, then the concept of public service—which is your business, the business of a "free" press—gets altered as well. And has been. The public interest of minorities, farmers, labor, women, and so on have, in frequently routine political language, become "special interests." "We, the people" have become "They, the people."

I am introducing the terms "public," "crime," "homelessness," "unemployment" (meaning poverty) early in these remarks because they segue into my observations on race. Although there are other matters of equal concern to editors, the handling of race seems to me symptomatic of the general wariness, ire, and intellectual fatigue the press continues to cause among so wide a spectrum of the country.

I'd like to begin by posing two questions. First, why is race identity important in print and broadcast news at all? And second, if it is necessary, why is it so often obscured and distorted at the very moment it is enunciated?

Originally race identification was urged, even insisted upon, by African Americans to make sure our presence and our point of view were represented. That urging assumed that we had a point of view unlike the mainstream one and, certainly, had experience of life in the States different from the legendary one presented in the press. That regardless of its difference or its concurrence, the African American point of view should not be buried underneath mainstream views and taken for granted. That seemed all well and good in theory, but in practice something quite other took place, an "othering" that took two forms: (1) the encoding of race in order to perpetuate some very old stereotypes even while the stereotypes were being disassembled in the popular mind, and (2) the insistence upon underscoring racial difference at precisely those moments when it really made no difference. For example, last June a *New York Times* reporter struggled heroically with the twin demand to be accurate *and* to theatricalize race in an article on immigration in Florida. The piece was headlined "As Hispanic Presence Grows, So Does Black Anger." What could "black" possibly mean in that formulation other than the commonly accepted code word for poor or working poor or economically marginal? We could assume that the Hispanics are also poor, without jobs, homes, and so on, but that would be a mistake because the Hispanics in question are Cubans fleeing Castro for a city heavily populated with middle-class Cubans and so, unlike Haitians, have a welcome mat of social services spread out before them. But whoever they are, they are certainly competing for jobs and housing with any and all. The question becomes, Why are blacks singled out? Why are they not called Miamians or "local." ("As Hispanic Presence Grows, So Does Local Anger"?) Except when they are soldiers, blacks are never American citizens. Why? Because in media-talk we are not local, or general citizens—we are those whose financial security is fragile; those whose reactions are volatile ("anger"—not concern). If the reader knows the code, this headline's use of the term "local" (economically fragile American citizens) could very well be Miami's white working poor.

But that is dismissed at once by the knowing, because the already encoded black-versus-anything-else connotation is what we have been led and taught to believe is the real, the vital, the incendiary story. There is no printable word for "poor" that does not connote "race." Thus, under the guise of representing the interests of black citizenry, the conventional stereotypical oppositions are maintained and useful information is sacrificed in the process.

It turns out to be a very difficult piece of work for this reporter. Consider the necessary contortions language is put through to describe the impact of recent immigration of Miami's Spanish-speaking population on its English-speaking one—which is or ought to be the real point of the story. These are the labels that appear: "Cubans of both colors": "non-Hispanic whites"; "non-Hispanic blacks"; "native-born English speaking blacks"; "Hispanic whites"; "Haitian and other Caribbean blacks." What are "non-Hispanic blacks"? Africans? No. Who are "Haitian and other Caribbean blacks"? Cubans? No. Think how clear the article would have been if nationality and language had been the mark of difference. It would tell us that American citizens were nervous about the wave of immigrants who spoke little English and were after their jobs. But clarity took second place to skin color and race took pride of place over language. The result: the obfuscation of everything but racial identity. "Patterns of Immigration Followed by White Flight." Middle-class blacks out of the loop here.

Even when *within* the race, where differences of national origin *are* information, as in the Crown Heights melee, where the population is predominately Caribbeans who have no history of American black and American Jewish relations, that distinction was subsumed into generalized blackness.

So confusing are the consequences of race stress that it led a CNN reporter to wonder with deep concern if someone who spoke Haitian could be found to help a Haitian pilot who had skyjacked a plane to Miami. French never occurred to him.

Now I would like to follow those questions with one other. Since it seems important in some way to represent blacks, we need to ask ourselves what we are represented as, and why. How can the press be challenged to represent *any* point of view—white, black, neither, both—that does not evoke a pseudo-world of commodified happiness and unified agreement on what or who is the enemy? The "enemy" seems to be either a diffuse, discursive vaguely black criminal or the angry helpless poor (who are also black).

In discussing the way blacks are represented—notwithstanding the successful examples of the elimination of race bias and some extraordinarily fine reporting of race matters (Hunter-Gault, on the Zulu Nation)—and the highly volatile effects that racially biased representation has on the public, it may be of some interest to locate its sources, because although historical, race bias is not absolute, inevitable, or immutable. It has a beginning, a life, a history in scholarship, and it can have an end. It is often enough pointed out that the popularization of racism, its nationalization, as it were, was accomplished not by the press (complicit though nineteenth-century newspapers may have been) but in theater, in entertainment. Minstrelsy. These traveling shows reached all classes and regions, all cities, towns, and farms. Its obvious function was entertainment, but its less obvious one was masking and unmasking social problems. The point to remember is that minstrelsy had virtually nothing to do with the way black people really were; it was a purely white construction. Black performers who wanted to work in minstrelsy were run off the stage or forced to blacken their black faces. The form worked literally as, and only as, a black façade for whites: whites in blackface. The black mask permitted whites to say illegal, unorthodox, seditious, and sexually illicit things in public. In short, it was a kind of public pornography, the main theme of which was sexual rebellion, sexual license, poverty, and criminality. In short, all of the fears and ambivalences whites had that were otherwise hidden from public discourse could be articulated through the mouth of a black who was understood to be already outside the law and therefore serviceable. In this fashion, the black mask permitted freedom of speech and created a place for public, *national* dialogue. For whites that is. On the other hand, the mask hid more than it revealed. It hid the truth about black humanity, views, intelligence, and most importantly, it hid the true causes of social conflict by transferring that conflict to a black population. Without going into the growth, transformation, and demise of minstrelsy (a demise that was simply an enhancement in and a transfer to another site—film, for example), suffice it to say that its strategy is still useful and its residue everywhere. The spectacle of a black and signifying difference, taught to an illiterate white public (via minstrelsy) became entrenched in a literate public via the press. It was a way of transforming organic ignorance into manufactured error, so the political representation of the interests of the white poor is and remains unnecessary. Those interests need not be given serious consideration—just rhetorical alliance. My point is that African Americans are still being employed in that way: to *disappear* the white poor and unify all classes and regions, erasing the real lines of conflict.

The justifications for enslavement became accepted wisdom and a whole race of people became criminalized. This criminalization is as old as the republic and stems from, among other things, the outside-the-law status imposed on slaves—and the dishonor that accompanies enslavement. Its modern formation is the residue, the assumption of criminality flash-signaled by skin color. People who say this is not so, that there is a disproportionate percentage of crime committed by blacks, miss something: the unconscionable, immoral, and dangerous treatment of blacks by the justice system and the press. It is unconscionable because it is racist disinformation. Unless, for example, you can intelligently use the phrase "white on white crime," you cannot use the phrase "black on black crime." It has no meaning and no use other than exoticizing blacks, separating the violence blacks do to one another into some nineteenth-century anthropological racism where the "dark continent" was understood to be violent, blank, unpeopled (the people were likened to nature), an easily available site of Conrad's *Heart of Darkness* where whites went for self-realization, self-discovery, and loot. Is that white on white crime in Northern Ireland? Bosnia? World War II? (Dan Rather in Somalia.) In this mythic construct it should not be a shock, as it was to me, that the only allegedly raped victim whose face was ever shown in the newspaper and on television to my knowledge was an underage black girl. I have never seen another one. Why? Because there is no honor or privacy due black women when they claim or protest sexual misbehavior, as recent Senate deliberations regarding Clarence Thomas will support.

This treatment is immoral because it proceeds from corruption—the corruption of accuracy, information, and even truth in the interests of sensation and sales. And it is dangerous because it has nothing to do with the real world of whites or blacks. It has everything to do with mystifying the world—rendering it incomprehensible and assuring the insolubility of its real problems, such as reducing the attraction to and the means of executing crime; such as employing and educating "they, the people"; such as domestic disarmament; such as the health of our communities.

When the mystification of everyday life is complete, there is nothing new or contemporary in the news. It will be, in spite of its up-to-the-minuteness, as archaic, moribund, and unreal as a quill pen, lagging behind the future in order to enshrine deprivation—making the absence of commodities (poverty) the only despair worth discussing. If poverty and criminality can be off-loaded to blacks, then the illusion of satisfaction and the thrill of the hunt might keep the public still and obedient. But for how long? How long can news function as a palliative for despair and counter space for products? It is so frustrating and sad to open a newspaper and find the news literally at the edges, like the embroidered hem of the real subject—advertisement.

The media spectacle must not continue to direct its attention to the manufacture of consent, rather than debate with *more* than two sides, to the reinforcement of untruths, and a review of what else there is to buy. Otherwise it will be not out of commerce, but already out of business. When the spectacle becomes "public" in the narrowest sense of the word—meaning available to purchase—the world can buy you, but it can't afford you.

Now I have been talking to you as though you were a single organism that took shape and grew by some immutable natural law outside human decision-making. When in fact, you are people, human individuals with a stake in being so. You have public-spiritedness and dreams of a secure democracy, as well as prejudices that seep through and shape the tools at your disposal. Boards of directors, owners, and editorial managers are made up of people trying to get profitable, stay profitable, and increase profitability. That must be tough. But if your industry becomes socially irrelevant, it will be impossible.

I suspect that a nonracist, nonsexist, educating press is as profitable as one that is not. I suspect that clarification of difficult issues is just as entertaining as obscuring and reducing them is. But it will take more than an effort of the will to make such a press profitable; it will take imagination, invention, and a strong sense of responsibility and accountability. Without you, by ourselves we can just pull raw data off of our computers; shape it ourselves, talk to one another, question one another, argue, get it wrong, get it right. Reinvent public space, in other words, and the public dialogue that can take place within it. The generations of students that I teach (and my own sons, for that matter) do it all the time.

But, irrespective of the internet's CompuServes, nodes, bulletin boards, Lexus—whatever makes the information highway work—there is something the press can do in language that a society cannot do. You've done it before. Move us closer to participatory democracy; help us distinguish between a pseudo-experience and a living one, between an encounter and an engagement, between theme and life. Help us all try to figure out what it means to be human in the twenty-first century.

Moral Inhabitants

I N *The Historical Statistics of the United States, Colonial Times to 1957* right after "rice" and just before "tar" and "turpentine" are the humans. The rice is measured by pounds; the pitch, tar, and turpentine by the barrel weight. There was no way to measure by pound, tonnage, or barrel weight the humans. Head count served the purpose of measuring. This reference book is full of fascinating information, not the least of which is Series Z 281–303, which documents, in chronological order and by point of destination, the import and export of humans in the United States from 1619 to 1773. Every effort seems to have been made to assure the accuracy of the tables. Below the neat columns of figures, footnotes seem to apologize for the occasional lapses from complete information. "We are sorry," the Bureau of the Census seems to be saying, "that better records were not kept or available to us. The country was just getting itself together, you understand, and things were less than efficient."

One senses reasonableness and gentlemanly assertion everywhere in these pages. But it is reasonableness without the least hope of success, for the language itself cracks under the weight of its own implications. Footnote 3, for example, under "Slaves" clarifies the ambiguity of its reference with the following words: "Source also shows 72 Indian slaves imported; 231 slaves died and 103 drawn back for exportation." "Died" . . . "drawn back"—strange, violent words that could never be used to describe rice, or tar, or turpentine. Footnote 5, by far the coolest in its civilized accuracy, is as follows: "Number of Negroes shipped, not those actually arrived." There was a difference, apparently, between the number shipped and the number that arrived. The mind gallops to the first unanswered question: How many? How many were shipped? How many did not arrive? Then the mind slides toward the next question—the vital one that withers all others: Who? Who was absent at the final head count? Was there a seventeen-year-old girl there with a tree-shaped scar on her knee? And what was her name?

I do not know why it is so difficult to imagine and therefore to realize a genuinely humane society—whether the solutions lie in natural sciences, the social sciences, theology or philosophy or even belles lettres. But the fact is that the *Historical Statistics of the United States* is pretty much like what the contours of academic scholarship are now and have always been: the equating of human beings with commodity, lumping them together in alphabetical order—when even the language used to describe these acts bends and breaks under that heavy and alien responsibility. The gentle souls, those dedicated civil servants of the Census Bureau do not create facts, they simply record them. But their work, I believe, reflects the flaw that obstructs the imaginative and humane scholarship and the realization of a humane society. Such scholarship would be one in which the thrust is toward the creation of members of a society who can make humane decisions. And who do. It is a scholarship that refuses to continue to produce generation after generation of students who are trained to make distinctions between the deserving poor and the undeserving poor but not between rice and human beings. To make distinctions between an expendable life and an indispensable one, but not between slaves and turpentine. Trained to determine who shall flourish and who shall wither, but not between the weight of a barrel and the sanctity of a human head.

That is what indices are like, of course. Not the fan-shaped spread of rice bursting from a gunnysack. Not the thunder roll of barrels of turpentine cascading down a plank. And not a seventeen-year-old girl with a tree-shaped scar on her knee—and a name. History is percentiles, the thoughts of great men, and the description of eras. Does the girl know that the reason that she died in the sea or in a twenty-foot slop pit on a ship named *Jesus* is because that was her era? Or that some great men thought up her destiny for her as part of a percentage of national growth, or expansion, or manifest destiny, or colonialization of a new world? It is awkward to differ from a great man, but Tolstoy was wrong. Kings are not the slaves of history. History is the slave of kings.

The matrix out of which these powerful decisions are born is sometimes called racism, sometimes classicism, sometimes sexism. Each is an accurate term surely, but each is also misleading. The source is a deplorable inability to project, to become the "other," to imagine her or him. It is an intellectual flaw, a shortening of the imagination, and reveals an ignorance of gothic proportions as well as a truly laughable lack of curiosity. Of course historians cannot deal with rice grain by grain; they have to deal with it in bulk. But dependence on that discipline should not be so heavy that it leads us to do likewise in human relationships. One of the major signs of intelligence, after all, is the ability to make distinctions, small distinctions. We judge an intellect by the ease with which it can tell the difference between one molecule and another, one cell and another, between a 1957 Bordeaux and a 1968, between mauve and orchid, between the words "wrest" and "pry," between clabber and buttermilk, between Chanel No. 5 and Chanel No. 19. It would seem, then, that to continue to see any race of people as one single personality is an ignorance so vast, a perception so blunted, an imagination so bleak that no nuance, no subtlety, no difference among them can penetrate. Except the large differences: who shall flourish and who shall wither, who deserves state assistance and who does not. Which may explain why we are left with pretty much the same mental equipment in 1977 that we had in 1776. An intelligence so crippled that it could, as a white professor did in 1905, ask W. E. B. Du Bois "whether colored people shed tears" is also crippled enough to study the "genetic" influences on intelligence of a race so mixed that any experimental data similarly performed on mice would fall apart at the outset.

If education is about anything other than being able to earn more money (and it may not be about any other thing), that other thing is intelligent problem-solving and humans relating to one another in mutually constructive ways. But educational institutions and some of our most distinguished scholars have considered the cooperation among human beings and mutually constructive goals to be fourth- and fifth-rate concerns where they were concerns at all. The history of the country is all the proof one needs that it is so.

Now no one can fault the conqueror for writing history the way he sees it, and certainly not for digesting human events and discovering their patterns according to his point of view. But we can fault him for not owning up to what his point of view is. It might prove a useful exercise, in this regard, to look at some of the things our conquerors (our forefathers), our men of vision and power in America have actually said.

Andrew Jackson, December 3, 1833:

"Indians have neither the intelligence, the industry, the moral habits, nor the desire of improvement which are essential to any favorable change in their condition. Established in the midst of another and a superior race, and without appreciating the causes of their inferiority or seeking to control them, they must necessarily yield to the force of circumstances and ere long disappear."

Theodore Roosevelt (to Owen Wister) 1901:

"I entirely agree with you that as a race and in the mass the [blacks] are altogether inferior to the whites.

"I suppose I should be ashamed to say that I take the Western view of the Indian. I don't go so far as to think that the only good Indians are the dead Indians, but I believe nine out of every ten are, and I shouldn't like to inquire too closely into the case of the tenth. The most vicious cowboy has more moral principle than the average Indian."

General Ulysses S. Grant:

(to) General Webster
La Grange, Tenn.
November 10, 1862
"Give orders to all the conductors on the road that no Jews are to be permitted to travel on the railroad southward from any point.

They may go north and be encouraged in it; but they are such an intolerable nuisance that the department must be purged of them."

Holly Springs, Miss.
December 8, 1862
General Order
"On account of the scarcity of provisions all cotton speculators, Jews, and other vagrants having no honest means of support, except trading upon the misery of the country . . ."

Sam Houston, U.S. Senate, 1848:

"The Anglo-Saxon [must] pervade the whole southern extremity of this vast continent. . . . (The) Mexicans are no better than the Indians and I see no reason why we should not take their land."

Freeman's Journal, March 4, 1848:

"Our object is to show, once more, that Protestantism is effete, powerless, dying out though disturbed only by its proper gangrenes, and conscious that its last moment is come when it is fairly set, face to face, with Catholic truth."

Richard Pike, Boston, 1854:

"Catholicism is, and it ever has been, a bigoted, a persecuting, and a superstitious religion. There is no crime in the calendar of infamy of which it has not been guilty. There is no sin against humanity which it has not committed. There is no blasphemy against God which it has not sanctioned. It is a power which has never scrupled to break its faith solemnly plighted, wherever its interests seem to require it; which has no conscience; which spurns the control of public opinion; and which obtrudes its head among the nations of Christendom, dripping with the cruelties of millions of murders, and haggard with the debaucheries of a thousand years, always ambitious, always sanguinary, and always false."

New York Tribune, 1854

"The Chinese are uncivilized, unclean and filthy beyond all conception, without any of the higher domestic or social relations;

lustful and sensual in their dispositions; every female is a prostitute of the barest order."

General William Sherman:
"We must act with vindictive earnestness against the Sioux, even to their extermination, men, women and children. Nothing else will reach the root of this case. The more we can kill this year, the less will have to be killed the next war, for the more I see of these Indians, the more convinced I am that they will all have to be killed or be maintained as a species of pauper."

Benjamin Franklin, 1751:
"Why increase the Sons of *Africa,* by Planting them in *America,* where we have so fair an Opportunity, by excluding all Blacks and Tawneys, of increasing the lovely White and Red?"

William Byrd, Diary, Virginia, 1710–1712:
2/8/09: Jenny and Eugene were whipped.
4/17/09: Anaka was whipped.
5/13/09: Mrs. Byrd was whipped.
3/23/09: Moll was whipped.
6/10/09: Eugene [a child] was whipped for running away and had the bit put on him.
9/3/09: I beat Jenny.
9/16/09: Jenny was whipped.
9/19/09: I beat Anama.
11/30/09: Eugene and Jenny were whipped.
12/16/09: Eugene was whipped for doing nothing yesterday.
(In April I was occupied in my official capacity in assisting the investigation of slaves "arraigned for high treason"— two were hanged.)
7/1/10: The Negro woman ran away again with the bit on her mouth.
7/8/10: The Negro woman was found, and tied, but ran away again in the night.

7/15/10: My wife, against my will, caused little Jenny to be
   burned with a hot iron.
8/22/10: I had a severe quarrel with little Jenny and beat her too
   much, for which I was sorry.
8/31/10: Eugene and Jenny were beaten.
10/8/10: I whipped three slave women.
11/6/10: The Negro woman ran away again.

Its editors describe him as "Virginia's most polished and ornamental gentleman . . . a kindly master [who] inveighed in some of his
letters against brutes who mistreat their slaves."

Such is language, the vision, the memory bequeathed to us in this
society. They said other things, and they did other things—some of
which were good. But they also said, and more importantly felt, *that*.

Our past is bleak. Our future dim. But I am not reasonable. A
reasonable man adjusts to his environment. And unreasonable man
does not. All progress, therefore, depends on the unreasonable man.
I prefer not to adjust to my environment. I refuse the prison of "I"
and choose the open spaces of "we."

With such a past we cannot be optimistic about the possibility
of a humane society, in which humane decision-making is the prime
goal of educators, ever becoming imagined and therefore realized.
We cannot be optimistic, but we can be clear. We can identify the
enemy. We can begin by asking ourselves what is right rather than
what is expedient. Know the difference between fever and the disease.
Between racism and greed. We can be clear and we can be careful.
Careful to avoid the imprisonment of the mind, the spirit, and the
will of ourselves and those among whom we live. We can be careful
of tolerating second-rate goals and secondhand ideas.

We are humans. Humans who must have discovered by now what
every three-year-old can see: "how unsatisfactory and clumsy is this
whole business of reproducing and dying by the billions." We are
humans, not rice, and therefore "we have not yet encountered any god
who is as merciful as a man who flicks a beetle over on its feet. There is
not a people in the world that behaves as badly as praying mantises."

We are the moral inhabitants of the globe. To deny this, regardless of our feeble attempts to live up to it, is to lie in prison. Of course there is cruelty. Cruelty is a mystery. But if we see the world as one long brutal game, then we bump into another mystery, the mystery of beauty, of light, the canary that sings on the skull. . . . Unless all ages and all races of man have been deluded . . . there seems to be such a thing as grace, such a thing as beauty, such a thing as harmony . . . all wholly free and available to us.

The Price of Wealth,
the Cost of Care

I WANT to talk about a subject that influences and, in many cases, distresses us all. A subject that is a companion to each graduate just as it is on all campuses as well as communities all over the country, indeed the world. A subject that is an appropriate theme of a speech delivered to students during these provocative times of uncertainty.

That subject is money.

Whether we have the obligation to protect and stabilize what we already have and, perhaps, to increase it, or whether we have the task of reducing our debt in order to simply live a productive, fairly comfortable life, or whether our goal is to earn as much as possible—whatever our situation, money is the not-so-secret mistress of all our lives. And like all mistresses, you certainly know, if she has not already seduced you, she is nevertheless on your mind. None of us can read a newspaper, watch a television show, or follow political debates without being inundated with the subject of wealth. Immigration discourse, health care implementation, Social Security, employment opportunities—virtually all personal problems and government policies twist and coil around money. Nations, regimes, media, legislation all are soaked in and overwhelmed by the wealth narrative concerning its availability, its movement, its disappearance. How its absence and mismanagement topples nations at worst, distorts and manipulates them, or how wealth keeps nations safe. Austerity or stimulus? War or peace? An idle life or a productive one?

The subjects studied here—art, science, history, economics, medicine, law—are by and large constricted by or liberated by money in spite of the fact that the purpose of each of these areas of scholarship is not money at all but knowledge and its benefit to the good life. Artists want to reveal and display truth while pretending to rise above money; scientists want to discover how the world works but are limited or supported by financial resources, as are historians and economists, who need funds for their projects and research; medicine seeks to save life or at least make it livable but cannot do so without somebody else's wealth.

All that is obvious, but in case we forget, I believe it is helpful to rehearse something of the price of wealth, its history. The origins of its accumulation are bloody and profoundly cruel, involving as it always and invariably does war. Virtually no empire became one without mind-warping violence. The Spanish empire saved itself from collapse and irrelevance by the theft of gold from South America necessitating massacres and enslavement. The Roman empire became one and remained one for centuries by the conquest of land, its treasure, and the labor of slaves. More war and aggression were used to rape Africa of its resources, which, in turn, sustained and empowered a plethora of nations. Rubber, for example, was extracted by a country literally privately owned by Leopold, king of Belgium (thus its once-agreed-upon name—the Belgian Congo). Sugar, tea, spices, water, oil, opium, territory, food, ore all sustained the power of nations like the United Kingdom, like the Dutch, like ours. Here in America the slaughter of millions of bison in order to replace them with cattle required the massacre of Native Americans. Here a new agricultural nation moved quickly into the industrial period via the importation of slaves. Chinese empires destroyed legions of monks to acquire the gold and silver they used to decorate temples and representations of gods. All of this robbery was accomplished by war, which, by the way, is itself a wealth-making industry regardless of victory or defeat.

The price of wealth, historically, has been blood, annihilation, death, and despair.

But alongside that price, something interesting and definitive began to happen in the late seventeenth and early eighteenth centuries. "Noblesse oblige," which soothed the nobility by suggesting that generosity was not only honorable but in their interests and allied perhaps with their religious beliefs, morphed into a conviction that wealth could not be its own excuse for being. There was some moral impediment to the Midas effect, to the Gatsby gene, some shame attached to the idea of being more by having more, of vanity projects posing as genuine commitments to the elevation of public life.

These alterations were made more felicitous in the United States by the tax code and, in some cases, worker strikes and organizations. Instead of building transcontinental railroads with Chinese labor slaves, instead of producing sugar for rum with the constant importation of more slaves (a turnover made necessary by the quick deaths of so many of them), instead we figured out how to have electricity, roads, public hospitals, universities, et al., without searing brutality.

Citizens began to realize the costs of caring was money well spent. Foundations, government support, individual largesse, service organizations grew exponentially to improve the lives of citizens. As you well know from the creation of this university, gifts to build institutions, care for the indigent, house art and books for the public are only a few of the projects in which the costs of caring are happily assumed. The consequences of these costs are varied, of course—some were weak, some were nefarious—but it became unthinkable that no elementary services existed. Inviting compassion into the bloodstream of an institution's agenda or a scholar's purpose is more than productive, more than civilizing, more than ethical, more than humane; it's humanizing.

This powerful commitment to caring, whatever the cost, is now threatened by a force almost as cruel as the origins of wealth: that force is the movement of peoples under duress at, beyond, and across borders. This current movement is greater now than it has ever been and it costs a lot—to defend against it, to accommodate it, to contain it, protect it, control and service it. It involves the trek of workers, intellectuals, agencies, refugees, traders, immigrants, diplomats, and armies all crossing oceans and continents, through custom offices and via hidden routes, with multiple narratives spoken in multiple languages of commerce, of military intervention, political persecution, rescue, exile, violence, poverty, death, and shame. There is no doubt that the voluntary or involuntary displacement of people all over the globe tops the agenda of the state, the boardrooms, the communities, and the streets. Political maneuvers to control this movement are not limited to monitoring the dispossessed. The transplantation of management and diplomatic classes to globalization's outposts, as well as the deployment of military units and bases, feature prominently in legislative attempts to exert authority over the constant flow of peoples. This slide has freighted the concept of citizenship and altered our perceptions of space: public and private, walls and frontiers. It may be that the defining characteristic of our times is that, again, walls and weapons feature as prominently now as they once did in medieval times. Porous borders are understood in some quarters to be areas of threat and have actually become places of chaos.

All of this is going on at the same time that technology has narrowed the distances among peoples and countries. Technology has made it possible to see others, talk to, support, or agitate others anywhere in the world. Yet the fear of dispossession, the loss of citizenship remains. We see it in the plethora of hyphenated designations of national identity. In press descriptions and documents birthplace has become more telling than citizenship and persons are identified as "a German of Turkish origin" or a "British citizen of African origin" and being identified as Muslim (at least in the West) takes precedent over country of origin. At the same time a revered cosmopolitanism, a multilayered cultural citizenship, is simultaneously hailed as sophisticated, superior. There is clearly a heightened threat of "difference." We see it in the defense of the local against the outsider, of unwanted intimacy instead of safe distance.

When the unhoused remain suspect aliens, when the frightened and destitute huddle in beleaguered, garbage-strewn tent cities on land not their own, when "identity" becomes the very essence of the self, then recurring strategies of political construction are demanded. When incompetence and irrationality run roughshod over decency and continue to endanger "lesser" lives, we can anticipate a steep rise in the cost of caring. A cost to be borne if we value civilization.

The ethics of affluence insist upon civic obligations and when we assume that obligation we reveal not our solitary goodwill but our dependence on others. You, all of us, struggle to turn data into information into knowledge and, we hope, into wisdom. In that process we owe everything to others. We owe others our language, our history, our art, our survival, our neighborhood, our relationships with family and colleagues, our ability to defy social conventions as well as support those conventions. All of this we learned from others. None of us is alone; each of us is dependent on others—some of us depend on others for life itself. And it is because of the latter that I choose to share this generous lecture honorarium with Doctors Without Borders—winners of a Nobel Prize for the risks, the direct medical aid, and the determination to serve in the most dangerous places on earth and among the most shattered people.

Your opportunity here and beyond this campus is huge, demanding, and vital. You are singularly able more than previous generations; not because you are smarter (although you may be) or because you have tools your predecessors lacked, but because you have time. Time is on your side, as is a chance to fashion an amazing future. Relish it. Use it. Revel in it.

I am a writer and my faith in the world of art is intense but not irrational or naïve. Art invites us to take the journey beyond price, beyond costs into bearing witness to the world as it is and as it should be. Art invites us to know beauty and to solicit it from even the most tragic of circumstances. Art reminds us that we belong here. And if we serve, we last. My faith in art rivals my admiration for any other discourse. Its conversation with the public and among its various genres is critical to the understanding of what it means to care deeply and to be human completely. I believe.

The Habit of Art

ARTTABLE HAS complimented itself by choosing this year's winner. As prestigious as the award itself is, its gleam is located in its choices. Your selection of Toby Lewis is another of its compliments to itself as well as to her commitment to so many avenues of creative art and her special devotion to the visual arts.

It is in this latter, visual arts, that I am most impressed. Her collection at the headquarters of Progressive Insurance: there I saw for myself the fruits of her passionate hard work. How, by placing diverse, powerful, beautiful, provocative, thoughtful visual art in the workplace, where the employees encountered it at every turn, all day and responded to it with deep criticism or desperate affection, she encouraged them to begin to create for themselves their own art in their own work spaces. The intimacy she and Peter Lewis insisted upon made me understand what they understood: that art is not mere entertainment or decoration, that it has meaning, and that we both want and need to fathom that meaning—not fear, dismiss, or construct superficial responses told to us by authorities. It was a manifestation of what I believe is true and verifiable: the impulse to do and revere art is an ancient need—whether on cave walls, one's own body, a cathedral or a religious rite, we hunger for a way to articulate who we are and what we mean.

Art and access is a much-written-about, much-sermonized-upon subject. Artists and supporters alike see an abyss between elitist and popular understandings of "high" and "found" art and try to span or fathom it. The tools for making art matter to ever larger, ever more diverse populations are many: more and more creative uses of funding, free performances, individual grants, and so on. The perception that the chasm remains may be the fruit of an imaginary landscape made real by the restrictions of available resources or by fiat. It is an unconscionable, almost immoral perception.

I want to describe to you an event a young gifted writer reported:

During the years of dictatorship in Haiti, the government gangs, known as the Tonton Macoutes, roamed about the island killing dissenters, and ordinary and innocent people, at their leisure. Not content with the slaughter of one person for whatever reason, they instituted an especially cruel follow-through: no one was allowed to retrieve the dead lying in the streets or parks or in doorways. If a brother or parent or child, even a neighbor ventured out to do so, to bury the dead, honor him or her, they were themselves shot and killed. The bodies lay where they fell until a government garbage truck arrived to dispose of the corpses—emphasizing that relationship between a disposed-of human and trash. You can imagine the horror, the devastation, the trauma this practice had on the citizens. Then, one day, a local teacher gathered some people in a neighborhood to join him in a garage and put on a play. Each night they repeated the same performance. When they were observed by a gang member, the killer only saw some harmless people engaged in some harmless theatrics. But the play they were performing was *Antigone,* that ancient Greek tragedy about the moral and fatal consequences of dishonoring the unburied dead.

Make no mistake, this young writer said: art is fierce.

There is one other anecdote I want to share with you. At a conference in Strasbourg, I spoke to a woman writer from a North African country. She knew my work; I did not know hers. We chatted amiably, when suddenly she leaned in closer and whispered, "You have to help us. You have to." I was taken aback. "Help who? Help what?" I asked her. "They are shooting us down in the street," she said. "Women who write. They are murdering us." Why? Women practicing modern art was a threat to the regime.

What these anecdotes represent is the healing and the danger art provides whether classical or contemporary.

Furthermore, these awful stories are meant to impress upon you that what Toby Lewis has spent a lifetime doing, what you are celebrating today, is no small thing.

I want to say a few words about the necessity of organizations such as this one. We live in a world where justice equals vengeance. Where private profit drives public policy, where the body of civil liberties, won cell by cell, bone by bone, by the brave and the dead, withers in the searing heat of all war all the time, and where respect for and even passionate interest in great art can dwindle, can shrink to a price list. It is possible to wonder if we have progressed psychologically, intellectually, emotionally no further than 1492, when Spain cleaned itself of Jews, to 2004, when Sudan blocks food and medicine and remains content to watch the slow starvation of its people. No further than 1572, when France saw ten thousand slaughtered on Saint Bartholomew's Day, to 2001, when thousands were blown into filament in New York City. No further than 1692, when Salem burned its own daughters and wives and mothers, to 2007, when whole cities are chock-full of sex tourists feeding off the bodies of young boys and girls. It is possible to wonder whether, in spite of technical and scientific progress, we have turned to sorcery: summoning up a brew of aliens, enemies, demons, "causes" that deflects and soothes anxieties about gates through which barbarians stroll; about language falling into the mouths of others; about authority shifting into the hands of strangers. Civilization in paralyzing violence, then grinding to a halt. Don't misunderstand me. There is real danger in the world. And that is precisely why a correction is in order—new curricula containing some meaningful visionary thinking about the life of the moral mind and a free and flourishing spirit can operate in a context increasingly dangerous to its health. But if scientific language is about longer individual life in exchange for an ethical one; if political agenda is the xenophobic protection of a few of our families against the catastrophic others; if secular language bridles in fear of the sacred; if the future of knowledge is not wisdom but "upgrade," where might we look for humanity's own future? Isn't it reasonable to assume that projecting earthly human life into the future may not be the disaster movie we are constantly invited to enjoy, but a reconfiguration of what we are here for? To lessen suffering, to know the truth and tell it, to raise the bar of humane expectation. Perhaps we should stand one remove from timeliness and join the artist who encourages reflection, stokes the imagination, mindful of the long haul and putting her/his own life on the line (in Haiti or North Africa) to do the work of a world worthy of life.

This in short has been the mission of ArtTable.

One of my students gave me a painting—a collage, sort of, printed, cut, and pasted. Within it were these lines:

> *No one told me it was like this.*
> *It's only matter shot through with pure imagination.*
> *[So] rise up little souls—join the doomed army toward the meaning*
> *of change.*
> *Fight . . . fight . . . wage the unwinnable.*

The Individual Artist

I T OUGHT to be relatively easy to describe the plight of the individual artist, the importance of such a resource to the country, and to describe the nature of the commitment made to that component in the goals of the National Endowment for the Arts. But it really isn't all that easy because the phrase itself—"individual artist"—provokes all sorts of romantic images, pictures and notions of a beleaguered, solitary individual struggling against Philistines, willy-nilly, who somehow breaks through the walls of ignorance and prejudice to acclaim acceptance perhaps, by a critical few in his or her lifetime—and/or posthumous fame, if not eminence, at a time when it does the artist no good. And that picture is one we love to fondle, but it is a kind of Procrustean bed, an intellectual trap, because it's such an attractive portrait that it encourages what ought to be eliminated. We seem somehow to cut off the limbs of the individual artist to fit our short bed, and we ascribe to him or her penury and sacrifice and the notion of posthumous award. We love so much the idea of the struggling artist that we enfranchise not the artist, but the struggle. In fact, we insist on it. Our notions of quality sometimes require it. It is true, and I think we all agree, that quality equals/means/suggests that which is rare and difficult to achieve. But sometimes, the word "rare" translates into "appreciated only by the very few," and sometimes the phrase "difficult to achieve" means "had to suffer in order to do it."

I think there is some ambivalence in our perception about individual quality and individual artists. On the one hand, we can identify it *because* it is rare and limited in its appeal to a few. We know how difficult it is to execute excellence in art (although I am convinced that for the true genius the things that look difficult to us are easy and effortless for him). But while we recognize quality by its rareness, on the other hand we consistently moan about the absence of quality from the hearts and minds of the masses. We talk about a crisis in literacy; we are upset and disquieted about pop art; we talk about airport sculpture; we are unnerved, and legitimately so, about the sensational play as opposed to the sensitive one. Each of us has a group of phrases that identify for us the mediocre in an art form.

I sometimes wonder if we really and truly mean it. Do we really mean that the world is the poorer because too few appreciate the finer things? Suppose we did live in a world in which people chatted about Descartes and Kant and Lichtenstein in McDonald's. Suppose *Twelfth Night* was on the best-seller list. Would we be happy? Or would we decide that since everybody appreciated it, maybe it wasn't any good? Or maybe if the artist himself had not begged for his life—begged and struggled through poverty, perhaps on into death—perhaps his art wasn't any good. There seems to have been an enormous amount of comfort taken in some quarters (in print and in conversation) that when thousands and thousands of people stood in line to see the Picasso show, only 4 or 5 percent of the people who saw it really knew what they were seeing.

First novels shouldn't be successes—they are supposed to be read by a few. They are not supposed to be profitable—they must be limited. If a first novel "makes it," then there is some suspicion about its quality. A minority artist in this game and in this climate of ambivalence is required either to abandon his minorityhood and join the prevailing criteria, or he has to defend and defend and defend ad nauseam his right to hear and love a different drummer. That's part of the romanticism that clings to the idea of the individual artist—the artist as beggar. It keeps him begging, and when he is successful, he should feel guilty—even apologetic.

There is danger inherent in being an artist, always—the danger of failure, the danger of being misunderstood. But there are some dangers now that are not inherent; some new dangers are being imposed. Be patient with me for a moment while I describe one that is of particular interest to me in the field of literature. There is a most exciting feud and public battle going on at Cambridge University at the moment—a fight between the traditional critics and the postmodernists, or the structuralists. It is a pyrotechnic delight in issues of *The Times Literary Supplement,* and scholarly debates are continuing in full force. I will not go into the details of the nature of the fight, but in oversimplified terms, there is a core group of traditional critics who believe that "literature and life" practical criticism is the way in which to teach people how to read the great works of literature, and then there is a newer, younger group, sometimes called "pluralists" by the British, that attacks and ignores traditional British criticism. This newer group is accused of being obscure and difficult and limiting in their perception of criticism.

What's interesting about the feud to me is that in it the writer has no place at all. Structuralists and proponents of semiotics and proponents of deconstruction perceive the written work as a phenomenon—but not central to the act of criticism or "reading." It's interesting that this fight goes on in literature studies, as opposed to theology and philosophy and other areas in which it belongs, but I think there is a reason for that. In the contemporary world of art and scholarship, literature is, I think, the only discipline in which the scholars do not produce what they criticize. The chemists, the social scientists, the historians, the philosophers—all of those people produce what they teach, they produce what they question, they produce what they change. In literary criticism, the critic now produces the criticism that he teaches; he produces the discipline, and the subject of the discipline—which is the text—is peripheral to the discussion. Perhaps it is true, as someone suggested, that English teachers have always envied the mathematicians—all those little formulas they put on the wall—and that they now would like to have a group of formulae they could also put on the blackboard. But where the criticism is itself the art form—that doesn't mean it isn't an art form—but when it denigrates the sources, there is a genuine threat to the preeminence of the creative artists. And that is significant, and it is filtering down to the artists themselves, some of whom are totally isolated from the critics in a way they never were before. There was a time in fourteenth-century Germany, in eleventh-century Italy, when the great translators were the poets, when the great critics were the writers; they did both. Now it is separate; the creative artist goes one route and the critic goes another.

Because the individual artist does not manage or control, at least in literature, what is taught—not even what is produced and what is decided to be taught—the endowment plays an incomparable role in his life. With an agency like the endowment there is a place and a means for creative artists to come together and make decisions about what ought to be nurtured, and what ought to be of value, and what ought to be supported. He may not have that right in universities; he certainly has not that right in publishing institutions; he probably does not have it in the media that exist and surround him. But he does have it in a confederacy and a brotherhood and a sisterhood—in the structure as provided by the panels and the programs of the National Endowment for the Arts. The endowment assuages the guilt of a gifted person who has the "misfortune" to do something extraordinarily well the first time. The endowment says out loud and in cash, "Your needs can be met. Your early work may be worth attention, even though it is early, even though you have not hit your stride, even though this may not be the 'breakthrough' work." The endowment says, "We will give you some help now. Your problems of audience, your problems of distribution, your problems of rent and time and space and data are not fixed stars; they are not immutable. They can be solved—and if not totally solved, they can be ameliorated."

The endowment, through its panels and its programs, says, out loud and in cash, that your ethnic aesthetics *are not to be questioned* by people who don't know anything about them. It says your cultural differences are not to be denigrated, especially by people outside the culture. It says your working-class background will not keep you from the full expression of your art. For, among other reasons, this is a country founded by laborers and farmers and small businessmen and convicts and clerks and pirates—so we know about your working-class background because we are your background.

Half of all of the funding categories have a place for the express aid and guidance for support of this beleaguered, guilt-ridden, frustrated species—the individual artist whom we have perhaps inadvertently relegated to the necessity of pain and struggle.

The individual artist is by nature a questioner and a critic; that's what she does. Her questions and criticisms are her work, and she is frequently in conflict with the status quo. But the artist can't help that; if she is to have any integrity at all in her art, she can't help it. The endowment does not penalize her for the controversy her art may engender because it is, or ought to be, axiomatic with the endowment that the last things we wish to encourage are safe art and safe artists. So the endowment takes risks—takes them itself and thereby underlies and legitimatizes the necessity for risk, the necessity for innovation and criticism. And it is in that climate that individual artists develop.

I remember a time, years ago, when I sat on a literature panel; the big problem was trying to get the writers to apply. They didn't want it; they thought they were going to be censored; they thought the government was meddling in their books; they thought they couldn't say certain things. There was a taint attached to the acceptance of the fellowship grants and the direct grants, and only with persistence were the panels able to overcome it. With persistence, the panels of the endowment have become Brother Theo to little Vinnie van Gogh. They have become a friend to little Jimmy Joyce. They are a platform for that outrageous, shocking, controversial George Bernard Shaw. But, in addition, we are food, we are rent and we are medical care for that arrogant and feisty Zora Neale Hurston—who didn't have any of that at the end. We have a chance to be the audience in the performance hall for Scott Joplin—who didn't have it at the end. What we do is no small thing; it is the first of the four or, I guess, five legs upon which the endowment stands. And any kick to that leg, any break in it, is insupportable because the endowment cannot stand without it.

Now for a very personal note. I do not want to go into my old age without Social Security, but I can; I do not want to go into my old age without Medicare, but I can, I'll face it; I do not like the notion of not having a grand army to defend me, but I can face that. What I cannot face is living without my art. Like many of you here, with your own particular backgrounds, I come from a group of people who have always refused to live that way. In the fields we would not live without it. In chains we would not live without it—and we lived historically in the country without *everything,* but not without our music, not without our art. And we produced giants. We, the National Council on the Arts, the endowment, are the bastions; we will make it possible to keep individuals and artists alive and flourishing in this country.

Arts Advocacy

WHENEVER ANYONE begins to think about arts advocacy, a complex obstacle presents itself at once: artists have a very bad habit of being resilient, and it is that resilience that deceives us into believing that the best of it sort of gets done anyhow—and the "great" of that "best" sort of lasts anyhow. The public and even academic perception is that nothing, neither social nor personal devastation, stops the march and production of powerful and beautiful artworks.

Chaucer wrote in the middle of the plague.

James Joyce and Edvard Munch carried on with a blind eye and a weak one respectively.

French writers excelled in and defined an age writing in the forties under Nazi occupation.

The greatest of composers was able to continue while deaf.

Artists have fought madness, ill-health, penury, and humiliating exile—political, cultural, religious—in order to do their work.

Accustomed to their grief, their single-minded capacity for it and their astonishing perseverance in spite of it, we sometimes forget that what they do is in spite of distress—not because of it.

Last year I spoke to an extremely gifted and well-established artist who told me he vetoed a living for a fellow artist because he thought having so much money would undermine the recipient—hurt his work—and that the applicant was "too good to receive such a financial windfall." To me the shock of that revelation is that, in some quarters, it is not shocking at all. For even when there is attention turned to an artist's plight in the form of a modest living, there is at the same time a problem of perception: What constitutes a hospitable environment and what principles inform whether we provide or deny it?

It brings us, as always, to the question of how haphazard should art support be. Should it take its text from the hazard of being an artist and become itself erratic, risky? Should it examine artists' lives, note the pain in so much of them, and imitate that pain by enfranchising it—even producing it, as in the anecdote above, for the good of the artist? Should grief and penury be built into art patronage, so the marketable wares created under those limiting circumstances are folded into the equation of the work's value in the marketplace in years and eras to come?*

When all attention is withdrawn from artists, they have always been mad enough to do it anyway, so what's the fuss? Can't they depend on enlightened philanthropy when available—and look elsewhere when it isn't? Or can't they depend on the marketplace—which is to say design the art itself for the marketplace—and hope the target will not move before their work is completed? Or can't they rely on government support and trust to chance or the law of averages that their work will prove at least equal to the dollar value of the support?

Such are a few of the questions art advocacy raises. But they are critical questions, made more critical by economic decay if not catastrophe and political cunning. And they are questions begging for answers, strategies in state art organizations, educational institutions, museums, foundations, community and neighborhood groups, and so on. What all of us know, you and I, is that the situation is more than dire—it is dangerous.

All of the art of all of the past can be destroyed in a few minutes by oafish politics and/or war games. It is also true that a good deal of the art of the future can be aborted by carelessness, whimsy, and disdain among art providers and consumers. National prerequisites

* Or should as much attention be given to *why* as to how much and how long?

can sweep clean or waver; crystallize or flow. There have been times when support for new and emerging art was at floodtide, matching the support for traditional institutions; other times such support, as now, is in drought. The uncertainty can devastate whole generations of artists and deprive a nation irrevocably. There already are such nations. It will take real intelligence and foresight not to become one of them. One of the nations that rests on the passion of the artists long dead—appropriating that passion, that engagement as their own, and meanwhile daring contemporary artists to work their own way. Or one of the nations that can be defined by the number of its artists who have fled the country. If one judges a civilization, as I believe it should be judged, not by the high-mindedness with which it regards art but by the seriousness with which art regards the civilization, then it is high time we begin to address anew and with vigor certain problems that continue to signify alarm.

The public perception of the artist is frequently so at variance with the art world's perception, they can hardly speak to each other. But the effort to do so, to have unpatronizing exchanges between arts professionals and the public, between artists and audiences cannot be overemphasized. It is also possible and necessary to encourage dialogues in which the artist is not a supplicant and the art supporter is not an enforcer. It is possible to have a forum in which the citizen, the student feels he or she is welcome for more than the ticket purchased or the applause. It is important to include, even to work the student-citizen into these projects; to insist upon discussion of the problems that seem to be gripping the art world in general and that are plaguing all of us—providers, grantors, artists, teachers, organizers.

Sarah Lawrence
Commencement Address

I AM extremely pleased to have this opportunity to speak to so very special a gathering. To pay compliments to a community of teacher-scholars, teacher-administrators, parents, board members, and students in an extraordinary institution. I commend you. These last few years could not have been easy. To the parents and relatives of the graduates I extend my congratulations. That your son or daughter or relative has been graduated is cause for a splendid celebration. Quietly or with fireworks, relish it today, for in just a little while you will again feel the anxiety of her or his next step—some further penetration into the adult world you are yourselves familiar with, and, being familiar with that world, you certainly feel some apprehension. I cannot reassure you but I can remind you that youth is indelicate—managing generation after generation not only to survive and replace us, but to triumph over us.

But to you, the graduates, I would like to do more than commend and congratulate. I would like to provoke. By the reputation of your faculty and the alumni of this college, I would guess that your education here has not been idle or irrelevant; it has been serious. I would like what I say to approach the seriousness of your tenure here.

So what shall I say to the Sarah Lawrence Class of '88? The last time I did this, I believe, was 1984—a year fraught with symbolism and the tension Mr. Orwell had projected onto it. I honestly don't know what might be of value to any graduating class four years after 1984.

Obviously I must make some reference to the future—how sparkling it can be . . . provided it exists; if only the possibility of actually "killing" time was not a real one, real because, if we want it that way, we can arrange things so that there will be no one left to imagine or remember that human invention: time. Its absence (the absence of time) has been thinkable during the whole of your lives. I would talk about the future if only it were a rolled carpet you had only to kick to see it unfurl limitlessly before your feet.

Surely there must be some talk of responsibility. I am addressing, after all, bright, industrious, accomplished people who are about to shoulder the very considerable weight of educated adulthood. So there should be some mention of responsibility: the need for and the risk of assuming the burden of one's own life and, in the course of that, assuming the care of the life of another (a child, a friend, a mate, a parent, an acquaintance, even, perhaps, a stranger).

And shouldn't I also touch upon goodness? Ethical choices? I ought to, since goodness is not only better and good for you, but it is also more interesting, more complicated, more demanding, less predictable, more adventuresome than its opposite. Evil really is boring. Sensational, perhaps, but not interesting. A low-level activity that needs masses or singularity or screams or screeching headlines to even get attention for itself, while goodness needs nothing.

And how can I leave out happiness? How could I omit the secret ingredients, the combination of which will invite, if not guarantee it? A little clarity, a bit of daring, some luck, and a great deal of self-regard. Then life is bountiful and one becomes both loved and lovable.

The future, responsibility, goodness—I'd love talking about all that, but not the last one: happiness. It makes me uncomfortable. Uneasy. I am not interested in your happiness. I am not sure it's all it's cracked up to be. I know, of course, that its pursuit (if not its achievement) is a legal one amended into the Constitution. I know that whole industries are designed to help you identify, attain, and feel it. One more article of clothing, the ultimate telephone, the best-appointed boat, an instantly timeless camera taking hundreds of shots of nothing to outlast the ages, the fastest diet, the perfect ice cream with all the pleasure of sugar and cream and none of their dangers. I know, also, happiness has been the real, if covert, target of your labors here, your choices of companions, of the profession, perhaps, that you will enter. And I do want you to have it; you clearly deserve it. Everyone does. And I hope it continues, or comes, effortlessly, quickly, always. Still, I am not interested in it. Not yours, nor mine nor anybody's. I don't think we can afford it anymore. I don't think it delivers the goods. Most important, it gets in the way of everything worth doing. There was a time, for most of the history of the human race, in fact, when to contemplate and strive for happiness was critical, necessarily compelling. But I am convinced that focusing on it now has gotten quite out of hand. It has become a bankrupt idea, the vocabulary of which is frightening: money, things, protection, control, speed, and more.

I'd like to substitute something else for its search. Something urgent, something neither the world nor you can continue without. I assume you have been trained to think—to have an intelligent encounter with problem-solving. It's certainly what you will be expected to do. But I want to talk about the step before that. The preamble to problem-solving. I want to talk about the activity you were always warned against as being wasteful, impractical, hopeless. I want to talk about dreaming. Not the activity of the sleeping brain, but rather the activity of a wakened, alert one. Not idle wishful speculation, but engaged, directed daytime vision. Entrance into another's space, someone else's situation, sphere. Projection, if you like. By dreaming the self permits intimacy with the Other without the risk of being the Other. And this intimacy that comes from pointed imagining should precede our decision-making, our cause-mongering, our action. We are in a mess, you know; we have to get out, and only the archaic definition of the word "dreaming" will save us: "to envision; a series of images of *unusual vividness, clarity, order, and significance.*" Unusual, clarity, order, significance, vividness. Undertaking that kind of dreaming we avoid complicating what is simple or simplifying what is complicated, soiling instead of solving, ruining what should be revered. We avoid substituting slogans like "national will" for national intelligence and perception. National will? What kind? Informed? Uninformed? Obstinate South African national will? Nineteen forty Germany's national will? Hanging on to destructive theses simply because one developed them half a century ago? These are comic book solutions to biblical problems in nuclear times. We must do all we can to imagine the Other before we presume to solve the problems work and life demand of us.

Dream the world as it ought to be, imagine what it would feel like not to be living in a world loaded with zero-life weapons manned by people willing to loose them, develop them, or store them for money, or power, or data, but never for your life and never for mine. What would it be like to live in a world where the solution of serious, learned people to practically every big problem was not to kill somebody? Narcotics trade? Whom shall we kill—or lock up? Disease? Whom shall we let die—or lock up? Self-rule by a neighboring (or even distant) country? Whom shall we slaughter? Famine? What is an acceptable death rate? Unemployment? Homelessness? What is the tolerable starvation rate? Too many babies by all the wrong mothers? Too many people living too long? Even our goodwill is couched in killing. We are asked to give millions of dollars to "Feed the Children"—until they are fourteen, that is, at which point we are forced to pay billions to blow their brains out if they make demands in their own interests but not ours. Are their deaths not timely enough for us? They will all die anyway—as we will. All the babies, all the elderly, all the fettered and unenfranchised, the ill, the idle—just like us. Maybe after, before, or even because of us, but we will all be together by and by.

If that is the consequence of our sophisticated thinking, our expert problem-solving, then we need to step back and refine the process that precedes it: experimental, intimate, ranging daylight vision that is not ashamed to dream, to visualize the Other.

Imagine, envision what it would be like to know that your comfort, your fun, your safety are not based on the deprivation of another. It's possible. But not if we are committed to outmoded paradigms, to moribund thinking that has not been preceded or dappled by dreaming. It is possible, and now it is necessary. Necessary because if you do not feed the hungry, they will eat you, and the manner of their eating is as varied as it is *fierce*. They will eat your houses, your neighborhoods, your cities; sleep in your lobbies, your lanes, your gardens, your intersections. They will eat your revenue because there will never be enough prisons, and wards, and hospitals, and welfare hotels to accommodate them. And in their search for your kind of happiness, they will eat your children, render them stunned and terrified, desperate for the sleeping life narcotics can offer. We may already have lost the creative intelligence of two-thirds of a new generation to this poisoned, violent sleep—a torpor so brutal they cannot wake from it for fear they will remember it; a sleep of such numbed recklessness it turns our own wakefulness to dread.

It is possible to live without defending property or surrendering it, but we will never live that way unless our thinking is shot through with dreams. And it is necessary now because if you don't educate the unschooled with the very best you have, don't give them the help, the courtesy, the respect you had in becoming educated, then they will educate themselves, and the things they will teach and the things they will learn will destabilize all that you know. And by education I do not mean hobbling the mind, but liberating it; by education I do not mean passing on monologues, but engaging in dialogues. Listening, assuming sometimes that I have a history, a language, a view, an idea, a specificity. Assuming that what I know may be useful, may enhance what you know, may extend or complete it. My memory is as necessary to yours as your memory is to mine. Before we look for a "usable past" we ought to know *all* of the past. Before we start "reclaiming a legacy" we ought to know exactly what that legacy is—all of it and where it came from. In the business of education there are no minorities, only minor thinking. For if education requires tuition but no meaning, if it is to be about nothing other than careers, if it is to be about nothing other than defining and husbanding beauty or isolating goods and making sure enrichment is the privilege of the few, then it can be stopped in the sixth grade, or the sixth century, when it had been mastered. The rest is reinforcement. The function of twentieth-century education must be to produce humane human beings. To refuse to continue to produce generation after generation of people trained to make expedient decisions rather than humane ones.

Oh, what would it be like without putrefying hatred we have been told and taught was inevitable among humans? Inevitable? Natural? After five million years? After four thousand years we haven't imagined anything better than that? Which one of us was born that way? Which one of us prefers it that way? Hating, grabbing, despising? Racism is a scholarly pursuit and it always has been. It is not gravity or ocean tides. It is the invention of our minor thinkers, our minor leaders, minor scholars, and our major entrepreneurs. It can be uninvented, deconstructed, and its annihilation begins with visualizing its absence, losing it, and if it can't be lost at once or by saying so, then by behaving as if, in fact, our free life depended on it, because it does. If I spend my life despising you because of your race, or class, or religion, I become your slave. If you spend yours hating me for similar reasons, it is because you are my slave. I own your energy, your fear, your intellect. I determine where you live, how you live, what your work is, your definition of excellence, and I set limits to your ability to love. I will have shaped your life. That is the gift of your hatred; you are mine.

Well, now, you may be asking yourself: What is all this? I can't save the world. What about my life? I didn't ask to come here. I didn't ask to be born. Didn't you? I put it to you that you did. You not only asked to be born, you insisted on your life. That is why you are here. No other reason. It was too easy not to be. Now that you are here, you have to do something you respect, don't you? Your parents did not dream you up—you did. I am simply urging you to continue the dream you started. For dreaming is not irresponsible; it is first-order human business. It is not entertainment; it is work. When Martin Luther King Jr. said, "I have a dream," he was not playing; he was serious. When he imagined it, envisioned it, created it in his own mind it began to be, and we must dream it too to give it the heft and stretch and longevity it deserves. Don't let anybody, anybody convince you this is the way the world is and therefore must be. It must be the way it ought to be. Full employment is possible. Positing a workforce of 20 to 30 percent of the population of the future is yearning greed, not inevitable economics.

All public schools can be hospitable, welcoming, safe learning environments. *No one,* teachers or students, prefers mindlessness, and in some places such environments have already been built.

Appetites for self-murder can be eradicated. *No* addict or suicide wants to be one.

Enemies, races, and nations can live together. Even I in the last forty years have seen deadly national enemies become warm, mutually supporting friends, and four national friends become enemies. And it doesn't take forty years to witness it. Anybody over eight years old has witnessed the expedient, commercial, almost whimsical nature of national friendships. I have seen resources committed to the disenfranchised, the discredited, the unlucky, and before we could reap the harvest of those resources, before legislation put in place could work (twenty years?) it was disassembled. Like stopping the union in 1796 because there were problems. Building a bridge halfway and saying we can't get there from here.

That determined commitment must be redreamed, rethought, reactivated—by me and by you. Otherwise, as nationalism and racisms solidify, as coasts and villages become and remain the sources of turmoil and dispute, as eagles and doves alike hover over the remaining sources of raw wealth on this earth, as guns and gold and cocaine topple grain, technology, and medicine to win first place in world trade, we will end up with a world not worth sharing or dreaming about.

We are already life-chosen by ourselves. Humans, and as far as we know there are no others. *We* are the moral inhabitants of the galaxy. Why trash that magnificent obligation after working so hard in the womb to assume it? You will be in positions that matter. Positions in which you can decide the nature and quality of other people's lives. Your errors may be irrevocable. So when you enter those places of trust, or power, dream a little before you think, so your thoughts, your solutions, your directions, your choices about who lives and who doesn't, about who flourishes and who doesn't will be worth the very sacred life you have chosen to live. You are not helpless. You are not heartless. And you have time.

The Slavebody and the Blackbody

I N 1988, the same year James Cameron opened America's Black Holocaust Museum here in Milwaukee, I responded to an interviewer's question. Having published a novel investigating the lives of a family born into bondage, I was being asked about the need for, the purpose in articulating that unspeakable part of American history. The need for remembering the men, the women, the children who survived or did not survive the three-hundred-odd years of international commerce in which their bodies, their minds, their talents, their children, their labor were exchanged for money—money they could lay no claim to. Since the argument for shunning bad memories or sublimating them was so strong and, in some quarters, understood not only to be progressive but healthy, why would I want to disturb the scars, the keloids, that civil war, civic battle, and time itself had covered? The slavebody was dead, wasn't it? The blackbody was alive, wasn't it? Not just walking, and talking, and working, and reproducing itself, but flourishing, enjoying the benefits of full citizenship and the fruits of its own labor. The question seemed to suggest that, whatever the level of accomplishment, little good could come from writing a book that peeled away the layers of scar tissue that the blackbody had grown in order to obscure, if not annihilate, the slavebody underneath.

My answer was personal. It came from a kind of exhaustion that followed the completion of my novel. An irritability. A sorrow.

"There is no place," I said, "where you or I can go, to think about or not think about, to summon the presences of, or recollect the absences of slaves; nothing that reminds us of the ones who made the journey and of those who did not make it. There is no suitable memorial or plaque or wreath or wall or park or skyscraper lobby. There is no three-hundred-foot tower. There's no small bench by the road. There is not even a tree scored with an initial that I can visit or you can visit in Charleston or Savannah or New York or Providence or, better still, on the banks of the Mississippi."

"Somebody told me," I continued, "that there is a gentleman in Washington who makes his living by taking busloads of people around to see the monuments of the city. He has complained because there is never anything there about black people that he can show. I can't explain to you why I think it's important, but I really do. I think it would refresh. Not only that, not only for black people. It could suggest the moral clarity among white people when they were at their best, when they risked something, when they didn't have to risk and could have chosen to be silent; there's no monument for that either." Except in the names of institutions that pay homage to a white person's care, or generosity: Spingarn, General Howard, Spelman, etc. "I don't have any model in mind," I said, "or any person, or even any art form. I just have the hunger for a permanent place. It doesn't have to be a huge, monumental face cut into a mountain. It can be small, some place where you can put your feet up. It can be a tree. It doesn't have to be a statue of liberty."

As you can tell I was feeling quite bereft when I made those comments.

When I use the term "slavebody" to distinguish it from "black-body," I mean to underscore the fact that slavery and racism are two separate phenomena. The origins of slavery are not necessarily (or even ordinarily) racist. Selling, owning people is an old commerce. There are probably no people in this auditorium among whose ancestors or within whose tribe there were no slaves. If you are Christian, among your people were slaves; if you are Jewish, among your people were slaves; if you are Muslim, among your people were the enslaved. If your ancestors are European they lived under the serfdom of eastern Europe, the tenancy of feudalism in England, in Viking Europe, Visigothic Spain, or fifteenth- or sixteenth-century Venice, Genoa, and Florence. The majority population of ancient Rome and ancient Greece—all were deliberately constructed slave societies. Medieval Ghana; Songhai Mali; the Dahomey and Ashanti kingdoms. Slavery was critical to the world of Islam and systematic in the Orient, including a thousand years in Korea alone. We are all implicated in the institution. The colonists of the New World, patterning their economies on those earlier and contemporary societies that were dependent on free or forced labor, tried to enslave indigenous populations and would have imported any foreign group available, capable, and survivable. Available because highly organized African kingdoms could provide laborers to Europeans; capable because they were clever, strong, and adaptable; survivable because they were creative, spiritual, and intensely interested in their children—foreigners from Africa fit the bill.

Not only the origins but the consequences of slavery are not always racist. What is "peculiar" about New World slavery is not its existence but its conversion into the tenacity of racism. The dishonor associated with having been enslaved does not inevitably doom one's heirs to vilification, demonization, or crucifixion. What sustains these latter is racism. Much of what made New World slavery exceptional was the highly identifiable racial signs of its population in which skin color, primarily but not exclusively, interfered with the ability of subsequent generations to merge into the nonslave population. For them there was virtually no chance to hide, disguise, or elude former slave status, for a marked visibility enforced the division between former slave and nonslave (although history defies the distinction) and supported racial hierarchy. The ease, therefore, of moving from the dishonor associated with the slavebody to the contempt in which the freed blackbody was held became almost seamless because the intervening years of the Enlightenment saw a marriage of aesthetics and science and a move toward transcendent whiteness. In this racism the slavebody disappears but the blackbody remains and is morphed into a synonym for poor people, a synonym for criminalism and a flash point for public policy. For there is no discourse in economics, in education, in housing, in religion, in health care, in entertainment, in the criminal justice system, in welfare, in labor policy—in almost any of the national debates that continue to baffle us—in which the blackbody is not the elephant in the room; the ghost in the machine; the subject, if not the topic, of the negotiations.

This museum's projects have enormous powers. First is the power of memorializing. The impulse to memorialize certain events, people, and populations comes at certain times. When what has happened is finally understood or is a forthright assertion of civic or personal pride, tombs and palaces are built, flowers heaped, statues rise, archives, hospitals, parks, and museums are constructed. Time being such an important factor in this process, most of the participants in the events being remembered never see them. But the growth of this country in the sixteenth, seventeenth, and eighteenth centuries, resting heavily on the availability of free labor, is complicated and exceptional. Exceptional because of its length and its chattel nature; complex because of its intricate relationship to the cultural, economic, and intellectual development of the nation. That is what must be remembered. There is another power this project has: of making us aware of the ever flexible, always adaptable, persistently slippery forms of modern racism in which the slavebody is reconstructed and reenters the blackbody as an American form of ethnic cleansing in which a monstrously large number of black men and women are carefully swept into prisons, where they become once again free labor; once again corralled for profit. Make no mistake, the privatization of prisons is less about unburdening taxpayers than it is about providing bankrupt communities with sources of income and especially about providing corporations with a captured population available for unpaid labor.

The third power of the museum's project, perhaps its most important, certainly its most gratifying, is the gaze it has cast on the ameliorating, triumphant aspects of the history of the republic—in black and white. This is what I sense: in spite of all the commercial and political strategies to separate, divide, and distort us, young people seem to be truly tired of racism's control over their lives. The art community is exhausted by and rebellious toward its limitations. Low-income people who discover how entangled and held down they are in its divisive economic grasp loathe it. Scholars unintimidated by its cling are disassembling it. We are becoming more industrious in substituting accuracy, other perspectives, other narratives in place of phantom histories, polluted politics, and media manipulation.

I am pleased that my appearance coincides with the exhibition of African American artists whose eyes encountered at every level the stereotyping and visual debasement prevalent elsewhere. Through their art, their taste, their genius we see African American subjects as individuals, as cherished, as understood. Viewing this display of their force, their life-giving properties, their humanity, their joy, their will ought to be enough to forestall the reach of racism's tentacles. Ought to be enough to protect us from its uninformed, uneducated, relentlessly toxic touch. Just as the commitment of this community ought to be enough. Don't you think? Thank you.

Harlem on My Mind

Contesting Memory—Meditation on Museums, Culture, and Integration

TODAY'S DEBATE on the place, power, and purpose of museums as reservoirs of cultural memory and/or a source of community integration is vital. Such debates are endemic to museums. The history of the Louvre itself bears witness to radical attacks and passionate rescue, yet it survives as a revered model and indispensable example of the universal survey museum. As Neil Harris writes, "The size, wealth, internal arrangements, and architecture of museums, as well as the inherent decontextualization of museum exhibits, had attracted hostility in the nineteenth century and certainly in the early twentieth century. The gargantuan temples of the early twentieth century were labeled by some critics 'dignified disasters'; their organization of exhibits . . . a 'Minotaur's labyrinth,' . . . museum policies were condemned as socially aloof and indifferent. Some educators fumed about museum failures to acknowledge contemporary needs and interests, while others condemned large-scale collecting as the poisoned fruit of capitalism." Furthermore, he notes, "museums have been labeled racist, revisionist, hegemonic, elitist, politically correct, mercenary, greedy, and self-serving." Why, then, one wonders, are museums experiencing what can only be called a "boom," as larger constituencies are solicited, as revenues increase along with the sale of goods and services that "blockbuster" shows produce, as patrons and funding sources compete with one another for standing and generosity to museums? Transitions are taking place, not least of which is recognition that the "foreigner is already home." And the mission of today's museums takes into account their claims.

Curators, artists, directors, art critics, and historians recognize the urgency of these deliberations anew. Their articles fill journals; boards of traditional museums reconsider structure and content; recent arrivals in the landscape of museums shape their acquisitions to accommodate the demands of new or underrepresented audiences.

The provenance of one such demand for representation in the United States provides a map that dramatizes both the vulnerabilities and opportunities under discussion.

As the New York scene in the sixties roiled with fresh visions within the art world (abstract expressionism, pop art), the Metropolitan Museum in New York welcomed its new director, Thomas P. F. Hoving. A medieval scholar become city parks commissioner, he was excited about introducing new projects into an institution some believed had become moribund. One of his projects was an exhibit designed to reflect the culture of Harlem—an African American neighborhood in New York City famous for its writers, poets, painters, musicians, and nightclub life. The exhibition, announced in 1968 and called *Harlem on My Mind*, opened at the Metropolitan Museum in January 1969 as a fifteen-gallery portrayal of Harlem history, identity, and cultural tradition consisting of photographs, murals, slides, films, documentary recordings, music, and memorabilia. Encouraged and directed by Allon Schoener, the visual arts director of the New York State Council on the Arts, Hoving mounted what they both described as a "total ethnic environmental show" covering Harlem from 1900 to 1968. Using the then-radical exhibition techniques including photographs on the ceiling and as murals, soundscapes and television, the show paralleled an earlier one in which Schoener was involved: *The Lower East Side: Portal to American Life* at the Jewish Museum—a paean to immigration in America. Great as the enthusiasm for the Harlem show was in many quarters and funding sources, there were rumblings of discontent before the show opened: there were accusations of marginalizing the counsel and the advice of Harlemites; of blacks being used as "window dressing." But the denouement was louder with more virulent outrage not only from the black community, but from a wide range of groups including some of the directors of and donors to the Metropolitan. Conservative art critics such as Hilton Kramer held that such shows had no place in an art museum. "In mounting the *Harlem on My Mind* exhibition," he wrote, "Mr. Hoving has for the first time politicized the Metropolitan, and has thereby cast doubt on its future integrity as an institution consecrated above all to the task of preserving our artistic heritage from the fickle encroachments of history." Jewish, Irish, and Hispanic groups found Candice Van Ellison's introduction to the catalog patently racist vilification, since in it she wrote, as follows, "Psychologically, blacks may find that anti-Jewish sentiments place them, for once, within a majority. Thus, our contempt for the Jew makes us feel more completely American in sharing a national prejudice." Patently racist vilification. Hoving himself was reviled for his apparent condescension to his black servants (his "sunny maid," his black "dour" chauffeur) and his remark that peer relationships between the races were "ludicrous." Schoener, too, for his assertions that "Harlem is [black culture's] capital. White mores and values are not universal." From Hoving's populist intentions there arose strong class conflicts. Certainly the controversy was heightened by the turbulence of the sixties, yet the implications of what went wrong with Hoving's multimedia show are resonant today. From insult to cultural injury, artists, politicians, scholars, journalists identified quite serious objections to the intellectual and aesthetic premises of the exhibit. Among these complaints were: no African American representation on the selection committee; near total reliance on photography, principally the work of James VanDerZee, and deliberate exclusion of painters and sculptors; the museum's promise of a "separate" show never materialized; the theme was more entertainment than art—another example of white voyeurism with a camera set up in Harlem at 125th Street for a closed-circuit viewing, rather like a zoo, for patrons at the museum. The dismissal of such artists as Norman Lewis, Jacob Lawrence, Romare Bearden, Cliff Joseph, Elizabeth Catlett, Raymond Saunders, and many others, both established and emerging, prompted a protest group, forced Roy DeCarava to withdraw his work and Romare Bearden to leave the committee. Without the full participation of these artists, the focus misled viewers toward sentimentalized and caricatured representations of black life as criminal, impoverished, exclusively sensual. Further insult was perceived in the choice of an African American high school student, rather than a knowledgeable scholar or artist, to handle the catalog's introduction. Even the show's title, selected by Schoener, inflamed already raw sensibilities. Borrowed from Irving Berlin's song, it followed the same pattern Schoener followed: a white man writing knowingly, authoritatively about Harlem culture, the lyrics describing a black showgirl (and perhaps mistress) in Paris missing the "low-down"—that is, licentious—life among urban blacks. "I've a longing to be low-down / And my parlez-vous will not ring true / With Harlem on my mind." Minus local working artists, without board representation, without even an art scholar to introduce the catalog, with no reference to Harlem's prosperous civic life, what the community believed was the real importance, meaning, and variety of its cultural life was completely, arrogantly dismissed. It appeared to many that *Harlem on My Mind* was fundamentally an ethnographic exhibition presented in an art museum—one of the leading universal survey museums. Thus it angered those who thought ethnographic displays did not belong there and frustrated those who wanted work by African Americans to be there. The crux of these charges and frustrations seemed to be that the Metropolitan Museum had treated black culture as "foreign," as the work product of strangers whose home it first appropriated then selectively celebrated. A kind of petri dish for the curious.

The consequences, however, of the *Harlem on My Mind* show did create opportunity. Among disgruntled "minorities," the citizens of Harlem and African American artists were not alone. Their experience of being silenced by an exhibition ostensibly about them is duplicated in many places, and the hierarchy of cultures is being intently questioned and refuted. Communities are no longer content to remain passive recipients of museum activities. The Studio Museum in Harlem, with its concentration on African American art, is one of the success stories directly related to the fallout of the controversy. The proliferation of ethnic museums in New York and elsewhere is another. Furthermore, less than a year after the show closed, the black artists who formed the Black Emergency Cultural Coalition and protested against *Harlem* (Norman Lewis, Romare Bearden, Raymond Saunders, Vivian Browne, and Cliff Joseph, among others) met with officials at the Whitney Museum of American Art to begin negotiations over its policies of discrimination against black artists. In 1971 the coalition called for a boycott of the Whitney's exhibition *Contemporary Black Artists in America* because black participation in its organization was limited. Fifteen of the seventy-five artists chosen by curator Robert M. Doty scheduled to participate withdrew, and, true to form, critical response to those who remained in the exhibition centered on black political reaction, with little discussion of the art itself.

New York's Guggenheim Museum's 1996 survey *Abstraction in the 20th Century: Total Risk, Freedom, Discipline* included no artists of color. Nearly twenty-eight years after *Harlem on My Mind,* a major American art museum excluded African American painters and sculptors from a major exhibition, and in doing so once again raised questions of race, politics, and aesthetics. But the thrust of the criticism had shifted. The art museum was still being asked, What is the domain of black visual art—figuration, abstraction?, while the artists themselves and some critics were asking whether racially defined art was limiting and whether the question was a problem itself, especially when critical response to the exhibition of black visual artists centered on politics with little discussion of the art itself. What was the art museum's aesthetic evaluation of visual art created by blacks? Cliff Joseph hazarded an approach in an interview: "I would not say that there is black art per se. . . . There is, however, a black experience in art; I think every culture has its own experience which the artists of the culture brings to his work."

Many of today's young black artists agree with Mr. Joseph and see racially defined art as stifling if not condescending; as a problem itself. An increasing number of them insist their work be evaluated on the basis of aesthetics only, wondering if their art was not classified under the rubric of black culture would it read as African American? If the artists were not presented according to their race, would their work be mined for racial or political content? These questions and others have given rise to the term "postblack" among the newer artists—a term that both signals racial identity and refutes its established borders.

The narrative and consequences of the *Harlem on My Mind* show are at the heart of this current debate on the mission of museums as it relates to the foreigner's home. And much of the news is good. If the Guggenheim failed to recognize American abstract painters and sculptors of color, other opportunities have not been wasted. Kellie Jones's recent show at the Studio Museum in Harlem, *Energy/Experimentation: Black Artists and Abstraction, 1964–1980,* is a strong response to the Guggenheim's omission from its abstract survey show. Since *Harlem* closed in 1969, new generations of curators, scholars, art historians are deepening and broadening the idea of the visual art museum and the material and cultural museum. In 1968 the ethnographic replaced the artistic at the Metropolitan Museum's exhibition; ethnography and art were largely separate. But in the 1990s the development of these areas of study—art and ethnology—began to converge, and fields such as world art history seem to have gained increasing attention, as well as controversy. Fred Wilson's 1992 show, *Mining the Museum,* at the Contemporary museum in Baltimore included works from the Maryland Historical Society. Wilson plumbed these works for new information about black American life from the figuration and portraiture in the work of white artists in early American history and reframed the works to tell that story. It became increasingly apparent that museological decisions and curatorial ones are as much ideologically determined as they are aesthetically determined, and that such decisions are made in the context of power. Yves Le Fur argues intelligently, in my view, that the twenty-first-century art museum cannot remain a cultural site "where nonWestern art is judged according to the standards of modern art."

European "high art" and the foreigner's "material or craft work" is bridged by archaeology (the unearthing of both craft and art from dead cultures and ferried to museums in Europe) and is being reassembled, recontextualized among scholars who accept the position that exhibitions claiming to be authentic representations of peoples and their cultures—that attempt to define what is essentially African or European—are hegemonic practices that reproduce the values and privileges of the center.

Happily, the dialogue is ongoing: in the history of art production; on issues of culturally specific aesthetics; about the invisibility of the foreigner in established institutions and the curricula of art departments; the expansion of "homes" for the art of non-Western people; discrete collections of modern art in rural, less metropolitan sites.

Museums and galleries are an artist's home; his and her place in art history, in cultural history, where national identities are shaped and reimagined. Increasingly, the focus of these art places is on the relationship among what is outside the museum as well as what is inside. Increasingly the erstwhile "stranger" enriches all of our homes.

Women, Race, and Memory

I N 1 8 6 8 a forty-five-year-old woman asked the United States Senate for three years' back pay. She had been hired during the Civil War to do three kinds of work: as nurse, cook, and "commander of several men." It took thirty years for the men in the nation's Capitol to make up their minds on a matter in which money, sex, race, and class were so hopelessly entangled. One hundred and fifteen years have passed since this woman's original request, and the combination of explicit issues in her claim is still a witches' brew of confusion, anger, fear, ignorance, and malice. At the heart of her nineteenth-century battle for veteran's pay is the burning question of twentieth-century feminism: How can a woman be viewed and respected as a human being without becoming a male-like or male-dominated citizen?

For a variety of complex reasons, the final answer is not in yet, but it is impossible not to come to the dreary conclusion that chief among these reasons is our (women's) own conscious and unconscious complicity with the forces that have kept sexism the oldest class oppression in the world. This casual or deliberate treason is like a bone lodged in the throat of every woman who tries to articulate the present condition of women, and, until expelled, it is a bone that will continue to choke, and may soon silence, what could have been the first successful, bloodless revolution in America.

The self-sabotage rife among women is no secret, but what may be unclear is why we insist on chains. Because sexism is not confined to men, psychology, schooling, and theology are frequently scoured to explain this subversion—to locate its origin in the oppressor. But the most effective and reliable saboteur is she who needs no orders.

American women fall into one of three general categories: feminists, anti-feminists, and nonaligned humanists. Each of these admittedly ill-defined groups generates some hostility for at least one other, and each contains subgroups intent on evangelical work among the others.

Avowed feminists, their consciousnesses sufficiently raised to be active workers for women's rights, have been around for a long time. Feminism is as old as sexual repression. In this country, women's liberation flowered best in the soil prepared by black liberation. The mid-nineteenth-century abolitionist movement yielded suffragettes; the mid-twentieth-century Civil Rights movement yielded Woman's Liberation. Both movements were loudly championed by black men (no white men so distinguished themselves), but both abandoned black civil rights and regarded the shift away from the race problem as an inevitable and necessary development—an opportunity to concentrate on exclusively sexist issues. Each time that shift took place it marked the first stage of divisiveness and heralded a future of splinter groups and self-sabotage.

Among modern feminists this first split quickly gave way to a second from which two main groups emerged: socialist feminists, who blame capitalism for the virulence of sexual oppression, and radical feminists, who blame men. The outrage of both socialist and radical feminism is directed toward the cause of sexism, yet in pursuit of the enemy, much of the emotional violence spills over to the victims. Regardless of how they define the enemy (men or the "system") both camps recognize the need to neutralize the hostility of women toward one another—sisters, mothers, and daughters, women friends and employees. They see betrayal among women as a residue of minority self-contempt and the competitiveness of the marriage market. Nevertheless, the result of a raised consciousness in the company of a repressed one is frequently an explosive internecine conflict. There is stark terror in Andrea Dworkin's account of her attempts to talk to right-to-life women in Houston. There is real arsenic in Simone de Beauvoir's recollection of her rivalry with her mother. Even among advanced feminists sabotage is a serious threat. A nice little feminist collective bookstore in California (called Woman's Place) ended up in court when the separatists locked the integrationists out.

The anti-feminists, who have the greatest support of men, are presumed by feminists to be endlessly gestating and lactating; happy for any system, political, economic, or cultural, that manages men and keeps them if not responsible, then certainly at bay. Blaming feminists' communism, and atheism, anti-feminists are convinced that the male role as providers and fathers is the apex of civilized society. It does not trouble them that finding a role for men, other than fathers or husbands, is still a serious problem for anthropology. That while "nature" easily defines a woman's role, "society" must provide a definition of male roles. Trying to figure out what—other than fathering and providing for children—men are *for* leads the researcher into an investigation of "civilization" and male-dominated positions within it. Since fatherhood is not fulfilling enough for men, they see themselves as doers, leaders, and inventors, and it does not take a major intellect to see that women, free of home and child care, may be expected to do, lead, and invent as well. Contemplating such a radical change in expectations can range from uneasiness to terror. Anti-feminists are not categorically opposed to male-like activities for women, but they regard them as either secondary freedoms or not freedoms at all, but rather as heavy requirements that will deprive them of a hard-won protectionism. Thus their disgust with ERA, abortion on demand, and a host of other feminist goals.

The agnostics, or nonaligned humanists, are probably the largest of all three groups and, although courted by feminists and anti-feminists alike to swell their numbers, they have earned the contempt and mistrust of both. Feminists regard them as scabs and opportunists, benefiting from feminist work while contributing nothing to it—even scorning it. They are the women in academia who accept their tenured positions as part of the fruit of feminist labor, who identify themselves as representing womanpower, but who are quick to disassociate themselves from "merely" feminist scholarship ("I teach Milton"). Anti-feminists see them as cowards and profiteers benefiting from protectionism when it suits them but flagrantly chucking it when it does not. They are the dissatisfied wives making feminist claims about house and child care and sexual freedom without parallel claims of responsibility. All of their energy is channeled into the competitive ethos of physical beauty. They decorate and market themselves in precisely the manner of a 1950 pinup; mutter about the hopelessness of men, but regard themselves and other women as incomplete without a male liaison. Nonaligned women are embarrassed by the extravagant or aggressive behavior of radical feminists and dismiss them as unattractive, male-minded Amazons. Equally contemptible to them are the anti-feminists, whose oratory amuses them and whom they see as ignorant, religious fanatics, or simply slavish. The "reasonable" neutrality of the nonaligned humanist is viewed as quisling by the converts of the right or left.

Among these three groups, the field for battle is wide and loaded with weaponry. Sad as these divisions are, they exist because of genuine concerns—serious unresolved questions about biology and bigotry.

The biological bind, whether blessing or curse, is real. Whatever the disposition of women today (radical, anti-, or nonaligned) they are forced relentlessly into selling or trading on their vaginas or their wombs. As "involuntary" mothers, trading on the womb means demanding protection as a class for the product that organ can manufacture—children. For "voluntary" mothers, the womb becomes the nexus for demanding the right to terminate its activity. As mistresses, prostitutes, housebound wives, and pornographic "actresses," women are involved in the dollar value of their vaginas and must come to terms with accepting that value as the way the world is and ought to be, or the way it is but ought not to be. Because a woman's livelihood has always been connected to her sexuality, whether maiden, mistress, wife, or prostitute, fidelity is women's work—not men's. "Relating to men in bed and in marriage is the conventional passport to normal femininity." And it is incumbent upon the woman to advertise her faithfulness and maintain his. It is this burden of fidelity, coupled with the economics of sexuality, that puts heterosexual women in direct conflict with lesbians.

Homosexual, or women-identified women, struggling to eliminate males and their domination from their personal and sexual lives, are convinced that lesbianism is the only way to achieve the full potential of women. Many look forward to a world that they envision as completely genderless, although it is not immediately clear where future lesbians will come from without some contact with men or, at the least, their bottled sperm. For the moment their position requires sharing with male scientists the lively optimism that fuck-free childbirth methods have encouraged. Yet female homosexuals are not alone in these dreams of a peaceable genderless kingdom, as the growing number of women writing science fiction is proof of. So problematic is the gender barricade, many feminist writers have turned to science fiction in order to invent a transcendent universe—free of the limitations of biology.

The second concern that generates divisiveness among women is the tenacity of male bigotry and its grave effect on the lives of all women regardless of what camp they belong to. Men still determine the scientific, political, and labor goals of this society. Scientific manipulation in areas of reproduction has turned out to be a very mixed blessing. It was a woman, Margaret Sanger, who had the idea and raised the money for a man, Dr. Pincus, to develop a "simple, cheap, safe contraceptive to be used in poverty-stricken slums, jungles, and among the most ignorant people." The specificity of the assignment was important and decisive, proving that the suspicions of minority women about all birth control campaigns are well-founded. Notwithstanding the original intention, "the pill" has been identified as the principal liberating factor for women of all colors since 1960. Yet the dramatic decline in infant births and mortality from pregnancy is outweighed by the staggering increase in reproductive death due to birth-control devices. The contraceptive that stops birth also kills women, but because the class and race implications in birth-control campaigns are systemic, there is no guarantee that the danger will decrease even if women do finally control fertility among themselves and their sisters in the jungle. The picture of wave upon wave of nonwhite babies growing into vocal hungry adulthood is routinely evoked by feminists trying to persuade others to their point of view.

In spite of some progressive legislation and increasing numbers of women in politics, and in spite of the percentage of registered women voters, no one questions the fact that politics is by men and for men. No one even bothers to wonder why so many women in politics are conservative. The eagerness for political heroines is so keen that apologies for reactionary women leaders can be safely left to the left. But these apologies do not hide the fury between left-wing women and their right-wing sisters. Witness any issue-oriented platform, such as those involving school desegregation, abortion rights, prayer in schools, and so on.

The control men exert on the labor market is exacting—more so now because house-free women are clearly superfluous to laissez-faire or corporate capitalism. There is too little work and too much skill. Too little work and too many workers. Teens, minorities, women, recently retired people, farmers, factory workers, and the work-trained disabled are the reserve workforce available for constantly changing labor needs. And built into this supply-demand system is a violent job-career struggle that seethes in offices and factories everywhere. Because of their dependency, women are the most disposable of laborers.

Biology and bigotry are the historical enemies—the ones women have long understood as the target if sexism is to be uprooted. What is newer and perhaps more sinister is the growth of the female saboteur, who seems to be crippling the movement as a whole: the internecine conflicts, cul-de-sacs, and mini-causes that have shredded the movement, steered it away from the serious political revolution of its origins, and trivialized it almost beyond recognition. Why have right-to-life and abortion-on-demand issues made women their own antagonists? Why do prostitutes regard women fighting pornography as uselessly obstructionist? Why are black and other minority women so quick to freeze out white feminist leadership? Why are women, for all our public talk of solidarity, firing our assistants because and when they are pregnant, voting against the appointment of women deans and chairpersons, relating to maids as though they were property, turning over buses on other mothers' black children? While these skirmishes continue, the movement comes dangerously close to an implosion of women-hating-women at worst, or a defeated disarray of cul-de-sac and mini-causes at best—all demonstrating the basest of male expectations: that any organization of women would end in a hair-pulling contest, as entertaining and irrelevant as those lady mud wrestlers.

How can a dignified, responsible women's liberation revive itself and proceed without shaming itself into women's lamentation? Perhaps if we listen closely to the ferocity, the eloquence, the pleas devoted to the cause of women, we will hear another message—one that informs the lament: that masculinity or male likeness is, after all, a superior idea. That all the way from radical feminists who believe men are less suited for masculinity than anybody, to "total" women, who believe men are simply better, the concept of masculinity still connotes adventure, integrity, intellect, freedom, and, most of all, power. "Man is the measure of man" is an easily dismissed observation in a modern context, but masculinity is very much the measure of adulthood (personhood). Proof is everywhere. It shapes the wishes of women who believe they are born to please men as well as those who want to have what males claim for themselves. It ignites the drive of women who wish to be thought of as competent, brilliant, tough, thorough, just, and reasonable. Rigorous intellect, commonly thought of as a male preserve, has never been confined to men—but it has always been regarded as a masculine trait. Relinquishing reproductive control to God is, in fact, relinquishing it to men. Demanding reproductive control is to usurp male sovereignty and acquire what masculinity takes for granted—dominion.

Rather than limit the definition of feminine to one chromosome, rather than change the definition to elevate the other chromosome, why not expand the definition to absorb both? We have both. Not wanting or needing children should not mean we must abandon a predilection for nurturing. Why not employ it to give feminism a new meaning—one that distinguishes it from woman-worship and from man-awe? The truth is that males are not a superior gender; nor are females a superior gender. Masculinity, however, as a concept, is envied by both sexes. The problem, therefore, is this: the tacit agreement that masculinity is preferable is also a tacit acceptance of male supremacy, whether the "males" are men, male-minded women, or male-dominated women, and male supremacy cannot exist without its genitalia. Each sexist culture has its own socio-genital formation, and in the United States the formation is racism and the hierarchy of class. When both are severed, male supremacy collapses and the sea of contention among women will dry up.

Pretending that racist elements in male supremacy are secondary to sexism is to avoid, once again, the opportunity to eradicate sexism completely. Just as it was avoided by nineteenth-century abolitionists, so it has been ignored in twentieth-century feminism. The persistent refusal to confront it not only supports male supremacy, it creates battle lines with forty million women on one side and sixty million on the other.

Accepting male-defined, male-blessed class hierarchy is also to strangle the movement and keep us locked in a fruitless war in which each of us is a female saboteur.

Complicity in the subjugation of race and class accounts for much of the self-sabotage women are prey to, for it is straight out of that subjugation that certain female-destroying myths have come. One is the myth of the malevolent matriarch, a myth so prevalent that Daniel Patrick Moynihan's conclusions about matriarchy as a cause of pathology among blacks is echoed in the literature of black men and women as well as white. This, in spite of the fact that only 16 percent of all households report males as the sole providers (governments insist a household have a "head" and are alarmed when it is not a man). Nothing in black life supports the thesis of black men as "feminized" by their women and everything points to white male suppression as the emasculating force. Yet this distortion is thriving like health. Italians, Jews, Hispanics, WASPs—all have had their social problems explained in part by their success or failure in taming a threatening matriarch.

Another female-destroying myth is the classlessness of laissez-faire capitalism and socialism. In advanced capitalism women have no economic autonomy and are dependent on the "uncertain male-determined fortunes as wives, mothers, and housekeepers." In Marxist societies, where classes are identified according to their relation to production, the family unit with its internal stratification (man equals head) defies any attempt to describe adequately the production of the "unwaged"—that is, the housewife.

Class stratification sharpens and politicizes the fight for goods and status. Along with all the other conflicts it generates, class inequality exacerbates the differences between black and white women, poor and rich women, old and young women, single welfare mothers and single employed mothers. It pits women against one another in male-invented differences of opinion—differences that determine who shall work, who shall be well educated, who controls the womb and/or the vagina; who goes to jail; who lives where.

The willingness of innocent, ignorant, or self-regarding women to dismiss the implications of class prejudice, and to play roles that act in concert with the male-defined interests of the state, produces and perpetuates reactionary politics—a slow and subtle form of sororicide.

There is no one to save us from that—no one except ourselves. So in the debris of what once looked like a vital liberation movement, one searches for signs of life. Three beacons wink in the wasteland. The dogged and often thankless work being done by fewer and fewer feminists to change oppressive laws; the starving self-help centers and mutual-aid networks; and, healthiest of all, the dazzling accomplishment of women's art and scholarship. Nothing, it seems to me, is more exhilarating, and more dramatically to the point, than what is happening among the artists and scholars. The pejorative, limiting intention of the labels is still around (*women* playwrights, *women* photographers, etc., are obligatory annual roundups in various media) but not for long. It may be the first hint of a possible victory in being viewed and respected as human beings without being male-like or male dominated. Where self-sabotage is harder to maintain; where the worship of masculinity as a concept dies; where intelligent compassion for women unlike ourselves can surface; where racism and class inequity do not help the vision or the research; where, in fact, the work itself, the very process of doing it, makes sororicide as well as fratricide repulsive.

Thirty years after Miss Harriet Tubman—black, female, mother, daughter, nurse, cook, wife, and "commander of several men"—asked a roomful of sexist, bigoted, class-conscious white men for her back pay they granted it. I have not chosen to begin and end this piece with her plea because it makes a poignant anecdote, but because the key to feminine oppression is most clearly seen in the response to her stand—a response that gathered together the full force of the special brand of American racism and sexism.

And don't think she didn't know it. They gave her twenty dollars a month for life. She was seventy-five years old then, and they probably did not expect the pension to have to last very long. Stubborn as a woman, she lived thirteen more years.

Literature and Public Life

To return to the site of one's graduate school life, one is always in danger of repeating one's original status in the place where inquiry occurs, problems surface, and help is needed to sort out all the difficulties so a clear and persuasive argument can be advanced. I feel like that now, lo, these many years later: perhaps a committee is sitting somewhere ready to interrogate me following their listening to this paper. It is a useful bit of recollection because I want to use this occasion and this provocative site to examine (or float) a few thoughts I have had no chance to articulate, except in my fiction. And to identify how those thoughts are made manifest in my work.

The problem I want to address this evening is, as I see it, the loss of public life, which is exacerbated by the degradation of private life. And I am proposing literature as an amelioration to this crisis in ways even literature could not have imagined.

During the eighties and nineties, technology and the regime of the electronically visual world have altered perception of the public and our experience of one another. (The current Age of the Spectacle promised intimacy and universalization in a global village setting. But it has delivered frightful confusion about private and public existence.) Following the demise of the much maligned sixties and seventies, during which there was an actual, contested, fought over, fought for, and fought against public (and publicly expressed) life, it seems unlikely that there will ever be a decade like that: where issues of conscience, morality, law, and ethics were liberationist rather than oppressive. And it is interesting to note that it is a decade that, unlike any previous one, is embarrassed by itself. That kind of public life (the Civil Rights movement, etc.) is not experienced as media phenomena made possible by "the enormous weight of advertising and media fantasy [which suppresses] the realities of division and exploitation; [disguises] the disconnexion of private and public existence." The consequence may be apathy, disgust, resignation, or a kind of inner vacuum (numbness), "a dream world of artificial stimuli and televised experience," where, as F. Jameson observed, "never in any previous civilization have the great metaphysical preoccupations, the fundamental questions of being and the meaning of life, seemed so utterly remote and pointless." That was 1971 when those comments were made and they are inapplicable to some degree now, when product ethics and media ethics have greater force than social ethics or justice.

We live in the Age of Spectacle. Spectacle promises to engage us, to mediate between us and objective reality in nonjudgmental ways. Very like the promise of nuclear energy: to be safe, clean, and cheap, but turned out to be dangerous, dirty (contaminated), and expensive. The promise made by the spectacle has been forfeited. Not only are we not engaged, we are profoundly distanced—unable to discriminate, edit, or measure shock or empathy. The "regime of visual authority [is a] coercive organization of images according to a stopwatch" and passes its organization off to us as a simulacrum of the real.

The news promises to inform us. Yet "the promiscuity of the nightly news—the jostling together of tornadoes in Pennsylvania, gunmen in Bosnia, striking teachers in Manchester . . . infant heart surgery in California—is dictated by the time constraints of the medium." But the jumble of events is presented to the viewer as if it were a representation of the promiscuity of the external world, which we find, as a result, incoherent.

"Millions of people look to the screen for signs of their collective identity as a national society and as citizens of the world. The media now play the decisive role in constituting the 'imagined community' of nation and globe." In this fashion "the news is validated as a system of authority, as a national institution with a privileged role as purveyor of the nation's identity and taker of its pulse."

Recent events, however, suggest something has gone wrong. The formula, the authority, the paradigm, the goals of the spectacle may not be working. The erstwhile "church of modern authority," television once routinely presented news as sacred spectacle: the funeral of John F. Kennedy, the wedding of Prince Charles, presidential inaugurations, the death of Diana—all implying that what was on view was of grave national and international significance. But in the merging of news (which is not news unless pictorial) with spectacle at the service of profit-making entertainment, certain electronic narratives originally constructed as official or national stories revealed not the promised national identity but the fault lines within. War becomes a timed and shaped "story" where the electronic question becomes the political one: When will we get out? When will the troops come home? When will the despot be dead? In other national narratives—the Clarence Thomas hearing, the O.J. trial, the Whitewater investigation, the impeachment hearings—time and narrative shape as well as plot are all subject to televised programming needs. It is fascinating to recall that virtually all of these recent stories are highly inflected by race and/ or sex and the power wielded or withheld by either one.

These national spectacles did not hide divisions as they wished, but exacerbated them. We cannot count on the spectacle to heal and distract completely. It is more likely to damage, alter, or distort time, language, the moral imagination, concepts of liberty, access to knowledge, as our consciousnesses are being reduced to self-commodification. We become "ads" for ourselves under the pressure of the spectacle that flattens our experience of the public/private dichotomy. The question becomes how and where can we experience the public in time, in language, as affect, and in context in order to participate fully in our own personal, singular, even invented life in relation to the life of the various communities to which we claim or wish to belong.

What is the source of this flattened perception of private and public? Part of the confusion may simply be the reckless use of the terms: there is private life and there is the privatization of prisons, health care, and so-called public schools. The first use emanates from constitutional guarantees as well as a personal claim. The second is a corporate investment publicly traded.

The first (personal claim to privacy) can be abandoned (on a talk show, for instance) or lost in the courts (by celebrities and "public" figures), but in any case such connotations of privacy are under surveillance at all times. The second (the privatization of formally public institutions) can be thwarted in the courts also, but are presented to us and represented to us as for the "public" good (encouraging competition and so forth, which ought to lower prices and increase quality for consumers). Public interest is often redefined as "special" interests.

The slippage in these definitions so erases the boundaries between an individual and his imagined community, we are not surprised or agitated by the fact that public life is now rendered as visual phenomena of a chosen narrative that exploits and sensationalizes sex, race, and family threats for the national resonance and marketability they provide. This chaotic collapse of private and public—the constantly surveyed private life—and the public sphere over which we have no control encourages retreat into the narcissism of difference, a surrender to the shallow delights of entertainment. Or participation in a wholly illusory community shaped by fear and unquenchable desire.

It seems to me that given these already realized subversions and the possibility of more, literature offers a special kind of amelioration. The history of claims for the study of literature circles around three major benefits: (1) literature's character-building, moral-strengthening capacities, (2) its suitability for high-minded, politics-free leisure activity, (3) its role in "cultivating powers of imagination that are essential to citizenship." While being educated to citizenship is superior to being educated to consumership, citizenship as a goal has troublesome nationalistic associations. "The problem with nationalism is not the desire for self-determination . . . but the particular epistemological illusion that you can be at home, you can be understood, only among people like yourself. What is wrong with nationalism is not the desire to be master in your own house, but the conviction that only people like yourself deserve to be in the house." Whether the character-building properties of literature, its rigorous politics-free intellectualism, or its utility in producing good and caring citizens—whether any of those claims still resonate among readers (and I am not sure that the case for literature has changed much since Emerson's "American Scholar" or F. R. Leavis's pronouncements), there is nevertheless a level of urgency in the study and production of literature hitherto unimaginable that has manifested itself: fictional literature may be (and I believe it is) the last and only route to remembrance, the only staunch in the wasteful draining away of conscience and memory. Fictional literature can be an alternative language that can contradict and elude or analyze the regime, the authority of the electronically visual, the seduction of "virtual." The study of fiction may also be the mechanism of repair in the disconnect between public and private.

Literature has features that make it possible to experience the public without coercion and without submission. Literature refuses and disrupts passive or controlled consumption of the spectacle designed to nationalize identity in order to sell us products. Literature allows us—no, demands of us—the experience of ourselves as multidimensional persons. And in so doing is far more necessary than it has ever been. As art it deals with the human consequences of the other disciplines: history, law, science, economics, labor studies, medicine. As narrative its form is the principal method by which knowledge is appropriated and translated. As a simultaneous apprehension of human character in time, in context, in space, in metaphorical and expressive language, it organizes the disorienting influence of an excess of realities: heightened, virtual, mega, hyper, cyber, contingent, porous, and nostalgic. Finally, it can project an alleviated future.

These theoretical moves (about the novel's peculiar affinity for experiencing a receding public life) become explicit moves in the last three books I have written. *Beloved, Jazz, Paradise*—each has a structural anomaly in common. A postnarrative, extratext, outside-the-book coda that comments not on the plot or story, but on the experience of the plot; not on the meaning of the story, but on the experience of gathering meaning from the story. These coda play an advocacy role, insisting on the consequences of having read the book, intervening in the established intimacy between reader and page, and forcing, if successful, a meditation, debate, argument that needs others for its fullest exploration. In short, social acts complete the reading experience.

Beloved ends narratively with Sethe's question about her individuality. The extranarrative activity is the reestablishment of the haunting—larger now than what it was assumed to be and what it was limited to in the beginning: a frustrated child, a justifiably malevolent creature of will. Much larger than its own problem of annihilation, it, the figure of Beloved summoned in the book's "afterlife," is now the responsibility of those who have shared, participated in, witnessed the story. A private responsibility disguising public or community obligations: "This is not a story to pass on." "They can touch it if they like." "They forgot her." "Loneliness that can be rocked [individual]" "Loneliness that roams [public]."

In *Jazz* the beyond-the-book gestures are stronger: the characters themselves escape the prognosis of the book, are different from and more complicated than the book ever imagined. Thus the final paragraphs constitute not merely a plea for the compassionate understanding of a misleading, self-involved narrative, but for an exquisite, shared, highly eroticized private relationship between reader and page. These paragraphs also activate the complicity by calling attention strenuously, aggressively to the act of reading as having public consequences and even public responsibility. From "Look, look. Look where your hands are. Now," one can infer something is to be done, something is to be reimagined, altered, and that something is literally in the reader's hands.

In *Paradise,* again the novel ends (or closes) with activity almost irrelevant to the narrative. "Almost" because it does allow some speculation as to what in fact happened to the women in the Convent. But mostly to complete the play on gospel with the "visitations" and "sightings" of the New Testament and finally to refigure paradise's imaginary. And paradise is everything but a solitary existence—is, in every projection, a community with a shared public life.

The novel, I believe, allows, encourages ways to experience the public—in time, with affect, in a communal space, with other people (characters), and in language that insists on individual participation. It also tries to illuminate and recover the relationship between literature and public life.

The Nobel Lecture in Literature

O NCE UPON A TIME there was an old woman. Blind but wise."
       Or was it an old man? A guru, perhaps. Or a griot soothing
       restless children. I have heard this story, or one exactly like
it, in the lore of several cultures.

"Once upon a time there was an old woman. Blind. Wise."

In the version I know the woman is the daughter of slaves, black,
American, and lives alone in a small house outside of town. Her reputation for wisdom is without peer and without question. Among her
people she is both the law and its transgression. The honor she is paid
and the awe in which she is held reach beyond her neighborhood to
places far away; to the city where the intelligence of rural prophets is
the source of much amusement.

One day the woman is visited by some young people who seem
to be bent on disproving her clairvoyance and showing her up for the
fraud they believe she is. Their plan is simple: they enter her house and
ask the one question the answer to which rides solely on her difference from them, a difference they regard as a profound disability: her
blindness. They stand before her, and one of them says, "Old woman,
I hold in my hand a bird. Tell me whether it is living or dead."

She does not answer, and the question is repeated. "Is the bird I
am holding living or dead?"

Still she doesn't answer. She is blind and cannot see her visitors, let
alone what is in their hands. She does not know their color, gender,
or homeland. She only knows their motive.

The old woman's silence is so long, the young people have trouble holding their laughter.

Finally she speaks and her voice is soft but stern. "I don't know," she says. "I don't know whether the bird you are holding is dead or alive, but what I do know is that it is in your hands. It is in your hands."

Her answer can be taken to mean: If it is dead, you have either found it that way or you have killed it. If it is alive, you can still kill it. Whether it is to stay alive, it is your decision. Whatever the case, it is your responsibility.

For parading their power and her helplessness, the young visitors are reprimanded, told they are responsible not only for the act of mockery but also for the small bundle of life sacrificed to achieve its aims. The blind woman shifts attention away from assertions of power to the instrument through which that power is exercised.

Speculation on what (other than its own frail body) that bird in the hand might signify has always been attractive to me, but especially so now, thinking as I have been, about the work I do that has brought me to this company. So I choose to read the bird as language and the woman as a practiced writer. She is worried about how the language she dreams in, given to her at birth, is handled, put into service, even withheld from her for certain nefarious purposes. Being a writer she thinks of language partly as a system, partly as a living thing over which one has control, but mostly as agency—as an act with consequences. So the question the children put to her, "Is it living or dead?" is not unreal because she thinks of language as susceptible to death, erasure, certainly imperiled and salvageable only by an effort of the will. She believes that if the bird in the hands of her visitors is dead the custodians are responsible for the corpse. For her a dead language is not only one no longer spoken or written, it is unyielding language content to admire its own paralysis. Like statist language, censored and censoring. Ruthless in its policing duties, it has no desire or purpose other than maintaining the free range of its own narcotic narcissism, its own exclusivity and dominance. However, moribund, it is not without effect, for it actively thwarts the intellect, stalls conscience, suppresses human potential. Unreceptive to interrogation, it cannot form or tolerate new ideas, shape other thoughts, tell another story, fill baffling silences. Official language smitheried to sanction ignorance and preserve privilege is a suit of armor, polished to shocking glitter, a husk from which the knight departed long ago. Yet there it is: dumb, predatory, sentimental. Exciting reverence in schoolchildren, providing shelter for despots, summoning false memories of stability, harmony among the public.

She is convinced that when language dies, out of carelessness, disuse, and absence of esteem, indifference or killed by fiat, not only she herself, but all users and makers are accountable for its demise. In her country children have bitten their tongues off and use bullets instead to iterate the void of speechlessness, of disabled and disabling language, of language adults have abandoned altogether as a device for grappling with meaning, providing guidance, or expressing love. But she knows tongue-suicide is not only the choice of children. It is common among the infantile heads of state and power merchants whose evacuated language leaves them with no access to what is left of their human instincts for they speak only to those who obey, or in order to force obedience.

The systematic looting of language can be recognized by the tendency of its users to forgo its nuanced, complex, midwifery properties for menace and subjugation. Oppressive language does more than represent violence, it is violence; does more than represent the limits of knowledge, it limits knowledge. Whether it is obscuring state language or the faux-language of mindless media; whether it is the proud but calcified language of the academy or the commodity-driven language of science; whether it is the malign language of law without ethics, or language designed for the estrangement of minorities, hiding its racist plunder in its literary cheek—it must be rejected, altered, and exposed. It is the language that drinks blood, laps vulnerabilities, tucks its fascist boots under crinolines of respectability and patriotism as it moves relentlessly toward the bottom line and the bottomed-out mind. Sexist language, racist language, theistic language—all are typical of the policing languages of mastery and cannot, do not permit new knowledge or encourage the mutual exchange of ideas.

The old woman is keenly aware that no intellectual mercenary or insatiable dictator, no paid-for politician or demagogue, no counterfeit journalist would be persuaded by her thoughts. There is and will be rousing language to keep citizens armed and arming; slaughtered and slaughtering in the malls, courthouses, post offices, playgrounds, bedrooms, and boulevards; stirring, memorializing language to mask the pity and waste of needless death. There will be more diplomatic language to countenance rape, torture, assassination. There is and will be more seductive, mutant language designed to throttle women, to pack their throats like pâté-producing geese with their own unsayable, transgressive words; there will be more of the language of surveillance disguised as research; of politics and history calculated to render the suffering of millions mute; language glamorized to thrill the dissatisfied and bereft into assaulting their neighbors; arrogant pseudo-empirical language crafted to lock creative people into cages of inferiority and hopelessness.

Underneath the eloquence, the glamour, the scholarly associations, however stirring or seductive, the heart of such language is languishing, or perhaps not beating at all—if the bird is already dead.

She has thought about what could have been the intellectual history of any discipline if it had not insisted upon, or been forced into, the waste of time and life that rationalizations for and representations of dominance required—lethal discourses of exclusion blocking access to cognition for both the excluder and the excluded.

The conventional wisdom of the Tower of Babel story is that the collapse was a misfortune. That it was the distraction, or the weight of many languages that precipitated the tower's failed architecture. That one monolithic language would have expedited the building and heaven would have been reached. Whose heaven, she wonders? And what kind? Perhaps the achievement of paradise was premature, a little hasty if no one could take the time to understand other languages, other views, other narratives. Had they, the heaven they imagined might have been found at their feet. Complicated, demanding, yes, but a view of heaven as life; not heaven as postlife.

She would not want to leave her young visitors with the impression that language should be forced to stay alive merely to be. The vitality of language lies in its ability to limn the actual, imagined, and possible lives of its speakers, readers, writers. Although its poise is sometimes in displacing experience it is not a substitute for it. It arcs toward the place where meaning may lie. When a president of the United States thought about the graveyard his country had become and said, "The world will little note, nor long remember what we say here, but it can never forget what they did here." His simple words are exhilarating in their life-sustaining properties because they refused to encapsulate the reality of six hundred thousand dead men in a cataclysmic race war. Refusing to monumentalize, disdaining the "final word," the precise "summing up," acknowledging their "poor power to add or detract," his words signal deference to the uncapturability of the life it mourns. It is the deference that moves her, that recognition that language can never live up to life once and for all. Nor should it. Language can never "pin down" slavery, genocide, war. Nor should it yearn for the arrogance to be able to do so. Its force, its felicity is in its reach toward the ineffable.

Be it grand or slender, burrowing, blasting, or refusing to sanctify; whether it laughs out loud or is a cry without an alphabet, the choice word, the chosen silence, unmolested language surges toward knowledge, not its destruction. But who does not know of literature banned because it is interrogative; discredited because it is critical; erased because alternate? And how many are outraged by the thought of a self-ravaged tongue?

Word work is sublime, she thinks, because it is generative; it makes meaning that secures our difference, our human difference—the way in which we are like no other life.

We die. That may be the meaning of life. But we *do* language. That may be the measure of our lives.

"Once upon a time . . . ," visitors ask an old woman a question. Who are they, these children? What did they make of that encounter? What did they hear in those final words: "It is in your hands"? A sentence that gestures toward possibility or one that drops a latch?

Perhaps what the children heard was "It's not my problem. I am old, female, black, blind. What wisdom I have now is in knowing I cannot help you. The future of language is yours."

They stand there. Suppose nothing was in their hands? Suppose the visit was only a ruse, a trick to get to be spoken to, taken seriously as they have not been before? A chance to interrupt, to violate the adult world, its miasma of discourse about them, for them, but never to them? Urgent questions are at stake, including the one they have asked: "Is the bird I am holding living or dead?" Perhaps the question meant: "Could someone tell us what is life? What is death?" No trick at all; no silliness. A straightforward question worthy of the attention of a wise one. An old one. And if the old and wise who have lived life and faced death cannot describe either, who can? But she does not; she keeps her secret; her good opinion of herself; her gnomic pronouncements; her art without commitment. She keeps her distance, enforces it and retreats into the singularity of isolation, in sophisticated, privileged space.

Nothing, no word follows her declaration of transfer. That silence is deep, deeper than the meaning available in the words she has spoken. It shivers, this silence, and the children, annoyed, fill it with language invented on the spot.

"Is there no speech," they ask her, "no words you can give us that help us break through your dossier of failures? Through the education you have just given us that is no education at all because we are paying close attention to what you have done as well as to what you have said? To the barrier you have erected between generosity and wisdom?

"We have no bird in our hands, living or dead. We have only you and our important question. Is the nothing in our hands something you could not bear to contemplate, to even guess? Don't you remember being young, when language was magic without meaning? When what you could say could not mean? When the invisible was what imagination strove to see? When questions and demands for answers burned so brightly you trembled with fury at not knowing?

"Do we have to begin consciousness with a battle heroines and heroes like you have already fought and lost leaving us with nothing in our hands except what you have imagined is there? Your answer is artful, but its artiness embarrasses us and ought to embarrass you. Your answer is indecent in its self-congratulation. A made-for-television script that makes no sense if there is nothing in our hands.

"Why didn't you reach out, touch us with your soft fingers, delay the sound bite, the lesson, until you knew who we were? Did you so despise our trick, our modus operandi you could not see that we were baffled about how to get your attention? We are young. Unripe. We have heard all our short lives that we have to be responsible. What could that possibly mean in the catastrophe this world has become, where, as a poet said, 'nothing needs to be exposed since it is already barefaced.' Our inheritance is an affront. You want us to have your old, blank eyes and see only cruelty and mediocrity. Do you think we are stupid enough to perjure ourselves again and again with the fiction of nationhood? How dare you talk to us of duty when we stand waist deep in the toxin of your past?

"You trivialize us and trivialize the bird that is not in our hands. Is there no context for our lives? No song, no literature, no poem full of vitamins, no history connected to experience that you can pass along to help us start strong? You are an adult. The old one, the wise one. Stop thinking about saving your face. Think of our lives and tell us your particularized world. Make up a story. Narrative is radical, creating us at the very moment it is being created. We will not blame you if your reach exceeds your grasp, if love so ignites your words they go down in flames and nothing is left but their scald. Or if, with the reticence of a surgeon's hands, your words suture only the places where blood might flow. We know you can never do it properly—once and for all. Passion is never enough; neither is skill. But try. For our sake and yours forget your name in the street; tell us what the world has been to you in the dark places and in the light. Don't tell us what to believe, what to fear. Show us belief's wide skirt and the stitch that unravels fear's caul. You, old woman, blessed with blindness, can speak the language that tells us what only language can: how to see without pictures. Language alone protects us from the scariness of things with no names. Language alone is meditation.

"Tell us what it is to be a woman so that we may know what it is to be a man. What moves at the margin. What it is to have no home in this place. To be set adrift from the one you knew. What it is to live at the edge of towns that cannot bear your company.

"Tell us about ships turned away from shorelines at Easter, placenta in a field. Tell us about a wagonload of slaves, how they sang so softly their breath was indistinguishable from the falling snow. How they knew from the hunch of the nearest shoulder that the next stop would be their last. How, with hands prayered in their sex, they thought of heat, then suns. Lifting their faces, as though it was there for the taking. Turning as though there for the taking. They stop at an inn. The driver and his mate go in with the lamp leaving them humming in the dark. The horse's void steams into the snow beneath its hooves and its hiss and melt is the envy of the freezing slaves.

"The inn door opens: a girl and a boy step away from its light. They climb into the wagon bed. The boy will have a gun in three years, but now he carries a lamp and a jug of warm cider. They pass it from mouth to mouth. The girl offers bread, pieces of meat, and something more: a glance into the eyes of the one she serves. One helping for each man, two for each woman. And a look. They look back. The next stop will be their last. But not this one. This one is warmed."

It's quiet again when the children finish speaking, until the woman breaks into the silence.

"Finally," she says. "I trust you now. I trust you with the bird that is not in your hands because you have truly caught it. Look. How lovely it is, this thing we have done—together."

Cinderella's Stepsisters

L ET ME BEGIN by taking you back a little. Back before the days at college. To nursery school, probably, to a once-upon-a-time when you first heard, or read, or, I suspect, even saw "Cinderella." Because it is Cinderella that I want to *talk* about; because it is Cinderella who causes me a feeling of urgency. What is unsettling about that fairy tale is that it is essentially the story of a household—a world, if you please—of women gathered together and held together in order to abuse another woman. There is, of course, a rather vague absent father and a nick-of time prince with a foot fetish. But neither has much personality. And there are the surrogate "mothers," of course (god- and step-), who contribute both to Cinderella's grief and to her release and happiness. But it is the stepsisters who interest me. How crippling it must have been for those young girls to grow up with a mother, to watch and imitate that mother, enslaving another girl.

I am curious about their fortunes after the story ends. For contrary to recent adaptations, the stepsisters were not ugly, clumsy, stupid girls with outsize feet. The Grimm collection describes them as "beautiful and fair in appearance." When we are introduced to them they are beautiful, elegant women of status, and clearly women of power. Having watched and participated in the violent domination of another woman, will they be any less cruel when it comes their turn to enslave other children, or even when they are required to take care of their own mother?

It is not a wholly medieval problem. It is quite a contemporary one: feminine power when directed at other women has historically been wielded in what has been described as a "masculine" manner. Soon you will be in a position to do the very same thing. Whatever your background (rich or poor) whatever the history of education in your family (five generations or one) you have taken advantage of what has been available to you at Barnard and you will therefore have both the economic and social status of the stepsisters and you will have their power.

I want not to ask you but to *tell* you not to participate in the oppression of your sisters. Mothers who abuse their children are women, and another woman, not an agency, has to be willing to stay their hands. Mothers who set fire to school buses are women, and another woman, not an agency, has to tell them to stay their hands. Women who stop the promotion of other women in careers are women, and another woman must come to the victims' aid. Social and welfare workers who humiliate their clients may be women, and other women colleagues have to deflect their anger.

I am alarmed by the violence that women do to one another: professional violence, competitive violence, emotional violence. I am alarmed by the willingness of women to enslave other women. I am alarmed by a growing absence of decency on the killing floor of professional women's worlds. You are the women who will take your place in the world where *you* can decide who shall flourish and who shall wither; you will make distinctions between the deserving poor and the undeserving poor; where you can yourself determine which life is expendable and which is indispensable. Since you will have the power to do it, you may also be persuaded that you have the right to do it. As educated women the distinction between the two is first-order business.

I am suggesting that we pay as much attention to our nurturing sensibilities as to our ambition. You are moving in the direction of freedom, and the function of freedom is to free somebody else. You are moving toward self-fulfillment, and the consequences of that fulfillment should be to discover that there is something just as important as you are and that just-as-important thing may be Cinderella—or your stepsister.

In your rainbow journey toward the realization of personal goals, don't make choices based only on your security and your safety. Nothing is safe. That is not to say that anything ever was, or that anything worth achieving ever should be. Things of value seldom are. It is not safe to have a child. It is not safe to challenge the status quo. It is not safe to choose work that has not been done before. Or to do old work in a new way. There will always be someone there to stop you.

But in pursuing your highest ambitions, don't let your personal safety diminish the safety of your stepsister. In wielding the power that is deservedly yours, don't permit it to enslave your stepsisters. Let your might and your power emanate from that place in you that is nurturing and caring.

Women's rights is not only an abstraction, a cause; it is also a personal affair. It is not only about "us"; it is also about me and you. Just the two of us.

The Future of Time

Literature and Diminished Expectations

TIME, IT SEEMS, has no future. That is, time no longer seems to be an endless stream through which the human species moves with confidence in its own increasing consequence and value. It certainly seems not to have a future that equals the length or breadth or sweep or even the fascination of its past. Apparently, infinity is now, the domain of the past. In spite of frenzied anticipation of imminent entry into the next millennium, the quality of human habitation within its full span occupies very little space in public exchange. Twenty or forty years into the twenty-first century appears to be all there is of the "real time" available to our imagination. Time is, of course, a human concept, yet in the late twentieth century (unlike in earlier ones) it seems to have no future that can accommodate the species that organizes, employs, and meditates on it. The course of time seems to be narrowing to a vanishing point beyond which humanity neither exists nor wants to. It is singular, this diminished, already withered desire for a future. Although random outbreaks of armageddonism and a persistent trace of apocalyptic yearnings have disrupted a history that was believed to be a trajectory, it is the past that has been getting longer and longer. From an earth thought in the seventeenth century to have begun around 4000 BC; to an eighteenth-century notion of an earth 168,000 years old; to a "limitless" earthly past by the nineteenth century; to Charles Darwin's speculation that one area of land was 300 million years old, we see no reason not to accept Henri Bergson's image of a "past which gnaws into the future and which swells as it advances."

Oddly enough it is in the modern West—where advance, progress, and change have been signatory features—where confidence in an enduring future is at its slightest.

Pharaohs packed their tombs for time without end. The faithful were once content to spend a century perfecting a cathedral. But now, at least since 1945, the comfortable assurance of a "world without end" is subject to debate and, as we approach the year 2000, there is clearly no year 4000 or 5000 or 20,000 that hovers in or near our consciousness.

What is infinite, it appears, what is always imaginable, always subject to analysis, adventure, and creation is past time. Even our definitions of the period we are living in have prefixes pointing backward: postmodern, poststructuralist, postcolonial, post–Cold War. Our contemporary prophecies look back, behind themselves, post, after, what has gone on before. It is true, of course, that all knowledge requires a grasp of its precedents. Still it is remarkable how often imaginative forays into the far and distant future have been solely and simply opportunities to reimagine or alter the present as past. And this looking back, though enabled by technology's future, offers no solace whatsoever for humanity's future. Surrounding the platform from which the backward glance is cast is a dire, repulsive landscape.

Perhaps it is the disruptive intervention of telecommunication technology, which so alters our sense of time, that encourages a longing for days gone by when the tempo was less discontinuous, closer to our own heartbeat. When time was anything but money. Perhaps centuries of imperialist appropriations of the future of other countries and continents have exhausted faith in our own. Perhaps the visions of the future that H. G. Wells saw—a stagnant body of never rippled water—have overwhelmed us and precipitated a flight into an eternity that has already taken place.

There are good reasons for this rush into the past and the happiness its exploration, its revision, its deconstruction affords. One reason has to do with the secularization of culture. Where there will be no Messiah, where afterlife is understood to be medically absurd, where the concept of an "indestructible soul" is not only unbelievable but increasingly unintelligible in intellectual and literate realms, where passionate, deeply held religious belief is associated with ignorance at best, violent intolerance at its worst, in times as suspicious of eternal life as these are, when "life in history supplants life in eternity," the eye, in the absence of resurrected or reincarnated life, becomes trained on the biological span of a single human being. Without "eternal life," which casts humans in all time to come—forever—the future becomes discoverable space, outer space, which is, in fact, the discovery of more past time. The discovery of billions of years gone by. Billions of years—ago. And it is ago that unravels before us like a skein, the origins of which remain unfathomable.

Another reason for this preference for an unlimited past is certainly fifty years of life in the nuclear age in which the end of time (that is human habitation within it) was and may still be a very real prospect. There seemed no point in imagining the future of a species there was little reason to believe would survive. Thus an obsession for time already spent became more than attractive; it became psychologically necessary. And the terrible futurelessness that accompanied the Cold War has not altered so much (in the wake of various disarmaments and freezes and nonproliferation treaties) as gone underground. We are tentative about articulating a long earthly future; we are cautioned against the luxury of its meditation as a harmful deferral and displacement of contemporary issues. Fearful, perhaps, of being likened to missionaries who were accused of diverting their converts' attention from poverty during life to rewards following death, we accept a severely diminished future.

I don't want to give the impression that all current discourse is unrelievedly oriented to the past and indifferent to the future. The social and natural sciences are full of promises and warnings that will affect us over very long stretches of future time. Scientific applications are poised to erase hunger, annihilate pain, extend individual life spans by producing illness-resistant people and disease-resistant plants. Communication technology is already making sure that virtually everyone on earth can "interact" with one another and be entertained, maybe even educated, while doing so. We are warned about global changes in terrain and weather that can alter radically human environments; we are warned of the consequences of maldistributed resources on human survival and warned of the impact of overdistributed humans on natural resources. We invest heavily in these promises and sometimes act intelligently and compassionately on the warnings. But the promises trouble us with ethical dilemmas and a horror of playing God blindly, while the warnings have left us less and less sure of how and which and why. The prophecies that win our attention are those with bank accounts large enough or photo ops sensational enough to force the debates and outline corrective action, so we can decide which war or political debacle or environmental crisis is intolerable enough; which disease, which natural disaster, which institution, which plant, which mammal, bird, or fish needs our attention most. These are obviously serious concerns. What is noteworthy among the promises and warnings is that other than products and a little bit more personal time in the form of improved health, and more resources in the form of leisure and money to consume these products and services, the future has nothing to recommend itself.

What will we think during these longer, healthier lives? How efficient were we in deciding whose genes were chosen to benefit from these "advances" and whose were deemed unworthy? No wonder the next twenty or forty years is all anyone wants to contemplate. To weigh the future of future thoughts requires some powerfully visionary thinking about how the life of the mind can operate in a moral context increasingly dangerous to its health. It will require thinking about the generations to come as life forms at least as important as cathedral-like forests and glistening seals. It will require thinking about generations to come as more than a century or so of one's own family line, group stability, gender, sex, race, religion. Thinking about how we might respond if certain that our own line would last two thousand, twelve thousand more earthly years. It will require thinking about the quality of human life, not just its length. The quality of intelligent life, not just its strategizing abilities. The obligations of moral life, not just its ad hoc capacity for pity.

It is abundantly clear that in the political realm the future is already catastrophe. Political discourse enunciates the future it references as something we can leave to or assure "our" children or—in a giant leap of faith—"our" grandchildren. It is the pronoun, I suggest, that ought to trouble us. We are not being asked to rally for *the* children, but for *ours*. "Our children" stretches our concern for two or five generations. "The children" gestures toward time to come of greater, broader, brighter possibilities—precisely what politics veils from view. Instead, political language is dominated by glorifications of some past decade, summoning strength from the pasted-on glamour of the twenties—a decade rife with war and the mutilation of third-world countries; from attaching simplicity and rural calm to the thirties—a decade of economic depression, worldwide strikes, and want so universal it hardly bears coherent thought; from the righteous forties when the "good war" was won and millions upon millions of innocents died wondering, perhaps what that word, "good," could possibly mean. The fifties, a favorite, has acquired a gloss of voluntary orderliness, of ethnic harmony, although it was a decade of outrageous political and ethnic persecution. And here one realizes that the dexterity of political language is stunning, stunning and shameless. It enshrines the fifties as a model decade peopled by model patriots while at the same time abandoning the patriots who lived through them to reduced, inferior, or expensive health care; to gutted pensions; to choosing suicide or homelessness.

What will we think during these longer, healthier lives? How successful we were in convincing our children that it doesn't matter that their comfort was wrested and withheld from other children? How adept we were in getting the elderly to agree to indignity and poverty as their reward for good citizenship?

In the realm of cultural analyses, not only is there no notion of an extended future, history itself is over. Modern versions of Oswald Spengler's *Decline of the West* are erupting all over the land. Minus, however, his conviction that the modern world contained an unsurpassable "will to the Future." The "landslide" began in 1973 according to Eric Hobsbawm. And that postsixties date is more or less the agreed-upon marker for the beginning of the end. Killing the sixties, turning that decade into an aberration, an exotic malady ripe with excess, drugs, and disobedience, is designed to bury its central features—emancipation, generosity, acute political awareness, and a sense of a shared and mutually responsible society. We are being persuaded that all current problems are the fault of the sixties. Thus contemporary American culture is marketed as being in such disrepair it needs all our energy to maintain its feeble life-support system.

Seen through the selectively sifted grains of past time, the future thins out, is dumbed down, limited to the duration of a thirty-year Treasury bond. So we turn inward, clutching at a primer-book dream of family—strong, ideal, protective. Small but blessed by law, and shored up by nineteenth-century "great expectations." We turn to sorcery: summoning up a brew of aliens, pseudo-enemies, demons, false "causes" that deflect and soothe anxieties about gates through which barbarians saunter; anxieties about language falling into the mouths of others. About authority shifting into the hands of strangers. Civilization in neutral, then grinding to a pitiful, impotent halt. The loudest voices are urging those already living in dread of the future to speak of culture in military terms—as a cause for and expression of war. We are being asked to reduce the creativity and complexity of our ordinary lives to cultural slaughter; we are being bullied into understanding the vital exchange of passionately held views as a collapse of intelligence and civility; we are being asked to regard public education with hysteria and dismantle rather than protect it; we are being seduced into accepting truncated, short-term, CEO versions of our wholly human future. Our everyday lives may be laced with tragedy, glazed with frustration and want, but they are also capable of fierce resistance to the dehumanization and trivialization that politico-cultural punditry and profit-driven media depend upon.

We are worried, for example, into catalepsy or mania by violence—our own and our neighbors' disposition toward it. Whether that worry is exacerbated by violent images designed to entertain, or by scapegoating analyses of its presence, or by the fatal smile of a tele-genic preacher, or by weapons manufacturers disguised as occupants of innocent duck blinds or bucolic hunting lodges, we are nevertheless becoming as imprisoned as the felons who feed the booming prison industry by the proliferation of a perfect product: guns. I say perfect because from the point of view of the weapons industry the market-ing is for protection, virility, but the product's real value, whether it is a single bullet, a thousand tons of dynamite, or a fleet of missiles, is that it annihilates itself immediately and creates, thereby, the instant need for more. That it also annihilates life is actually a by-product.

What will we think during these longer, more comfortable lives? How we allowed resignation and testosteronic rationales to purloin the future and sentence us to the dead end that endorsed, glamorized, legitimated, commodified violence leads to? How we took our cue to solving social inequities from computer games, winning points or votes for how many of the vulnerable and unlucky we eliminated? Winning seats in government riding on the blood lust of capital pun-ishment? Winning funding and attention by revamping 1910 sociol-ogy to credit "innate" violence and so make imprisonment possible at birth? No wonder our imagination stumbles beyond 2030—when we may be regarded as monsters to the generations that follow us.

If scientific language is about a longer individual life in exchange for an ethical one; if political agenda is the xenophobic protection of a few families against the catastrophic others; if religious language is discredited as contempt for the nonreligious; if secular language bridles in fear of the sacred; if market language is merely an excuse for inciting greed; if the future of knowledge is simply "upgrade," where else might we look for hope in time's own future?

I am not interested here in signs of progress, an idea whose time has come and gone—gone with the blasted future of the monolithic communist state; gone also with the fallen mask of capitalism as free, unlimited, and progressive; gone with the deliberate pauperization of peoples that capitalism requires; gone also with the credibility of phallocentric "nationalisms." But gone already by the time Germany fired its first death chamber. Already gone by the time South Africa

legalized apartheid and gunned down its children in dust too thin to
absorb their blood. Gone, gone in the histories of so many nations
mapping their geography with lines drawn through their neighbors'
mass graves; fertilizing their lawns and meadows with the nutrients
of their citizens' skeletons; supporting their architecture on the spines
of women and children. No, it isn't progress that interests me. I am
interested in the future of time.

Because art is temporal and because of my own interests, my glance
turns easily to literature in general and narrative fiction in particular. I
know that literature no longer holds a key place among valued systems
of knowledge; that it has been shoved to the edge of social debate; is of
minimal or purely cosmetic use in scientific, economic discourse. But
it is precisely there, at the heart of that form, where the serious ethical
debates and probings are being conducted. What does narrative tell
us about this crisis in diminished expectations?

I could look for an Edith Wharton shouting "Take your life"—that
is, Take on your life! For a Henry James appalled (in *The Sense of the
Past*) by an ancient castle that encloses and devours its owner. For a
William Faulkner envisioning a postnuclear human voice, however
puny. For a Ralph Ellison posing a question in the present tense signaling a sly and smiling promise of a newly sighted (visible) future.
For a James Baldwin's intense honesty coupled with an abiding faith
that the price of the ticket had been paid in full and the ride begun.
Those voices have been followed, perhaps supplanted, by another kind
of response to our human condition. Modern searches into the past
have produced extraordinary conceptual and structural innovations.

The excitement of anticipating a future, once a fairly consistent preoccupation of nineteenth- and early-twentieth-century literature, has
recently been reproduced in an amazing book by Umberto Eco—*The
Island of the Day Before*. And its title makes my point. The genius of
the novel's narrative structure is having the protagonist located in the
seventeenth century in order to mesmerize us with future possibilities.
We are made to take desperate pleasure in learning what we already
know to have taken place long ago. And this extraordinary novel is,
as the author tells us, "a palimpsest of a rediscovered manuscript."

Through its construction and its reading we move forward into an already documented history. When the power and brilliance of many late-twentieth-century writers focus on our condition, they often find a rehearsal of the past to yield the most insightful examination of the present, and the images they leave with us are instructive.

Peter Høeg, whose first novel nailed us relentlessly in the present, turns, in *The History of Danish Dreams,* to a kind of time travel (associated with though not similar to Eco's) in which regression becomes progression.

"If I persist," Høeg writes at the end of this novel, "in writing the history of my family, then it is out of necessity. Those laws and regulations and systems and patterns that my family and every other family in Denmark have violated and conformed to and nudged and writhed under for two hundred years are now in fact in a state of foaming dissolution. . . . Ahead lies the future, which I refuse to view as Carl Laurids did: down a gun barrel; or as Anna did: through a magnifying glass. I want to meet it face-to-face, and yet I am certain that if nothing is done, then there will be no future to face up to, since although most things in life are uncertain, the impending disaster and decline look like a safe bet. Which is why I feel like calling for help . . . and so I have called out to the past. . . .

"Now and again the thought strikes me that perhaps I have never really *seen* other people's expectations, that I have only ever seen my own, and the loneliest thought in the world is the thought that what we have glimpsed is nothing other than ourselves. But now it is too late to think like that and something must be done, and before we can do anything we will have to form a picture of the twentieth century."

Forming a picture of the twentieth century then—not the twenty-first—is, in this novel, the future's project.

William Gass, in a masterful work, *The Tunnel,* sustains a brilliant meditation on the recent past forever marked by Nazi Germany. In it his narrator/protagonist, having completed a "safe" morally ambivalent history of German fascism, a work titled *Guilt and Innocence in Hitler's Germany,* finds himself unable to write the book's preface. The paralysis is so long and so inflexible, he turns to the exploration of his own past life and its complicitous relationship to the historical subject of his scholarship—"a fascism of the heart." Gass ends the novel in heartbreaking images of loss. "Suppose," he writes,

> that instead of bringing forth flowers the bulb retreated to some former time just before it burgeoned, that pollen blew back into the breeze which bore it toward its pistil; suppose the tables were turned on death, it was bullied to begin things, and bear its children backward, so that the first breath didn't swell the lung but stepped on it instead, as with a heavy foot upon a pedal; that there was . . . a rebellion in the ranks, and life picked the past to be in rather than another round of empty clicks called present time. . . . I made . . . a try. I abandoned Poetry for History in my Youth.
>
> What a journey, though, to crawl in earth first, then in filth swim; to pass through your own plumbing, meet the worms within. And realize it. That you were. Under all the world. When I was a kid I lied like a sewer system. I told my sometime chums I went there. To the realm of shades. And said I saw vast halls, the many chambers of endless caves, magic pools guarded by Merlins dressed in mole fur and cobweb, chests overflowing with doubtless dime-store-jewelry, rooms of doubloons, and, suddenly, through an opening jagged as a rip in rotten cloth, a new sun shining, meadows filled with healthy flowers, crayon-colored streams, oh, the acres of Edens inside ourselves. . . .
>
> Meanwhile carry on without complaining. No arm with armband raised on high. No more booming bands, no searchlit skies. Or shall I, like the rivers, rise? Ah. Well. Is rising wise? Revolver like the Führer near an ear. Or lay my mind down by sorrow's side.

This is no predictable apocalyptic reflex, surfacing out of the century's mist like a Loch Ness hallucination. This is a mourning, a requiem, a folding away of time's own future.

What becomes most compelling, therefore, are the places and voices where the journey into the cellar of time is a rescue of sorts, an excavation for the purposes of building, discovering, envisioning a future. I am not, of course, encouraging and anointing happy endings—forced or truly felt—or anointing bleak ones intended as correctives or warnings. I mean to call attention to whether the hand that holds the book's metaphors is an open palm or a fist.

In *The Salt Eaters,* Toni Cade Bambara opens this brilliant novel with a startling question: "Are you sure, sweetheart, that you want to be well?" Are you sure you want to be well? What flows from that very serious inquiry is a healing that requires a frightened modern-day Demeter to fathom and sound every minute of her and her community's depths, to rethink and relive the past—simply to answer that question. The success of her excavation is described in these terms:

"What had driven Velma into the oven . . . was nothing compared to what awaited her, was to come. . . . Of course she would fight it, Velma was a fighter. Of course she would reject what could not be explained in terms of words, notes, numbers or those other systems whose roots had been driven far underground. . . . Velma's next trial might lead to an act far more devastating than striking out at the body or swallowing gas. . . .

"The patient turning smoothly on the stool, head thrown back about to shout, to laugh, to sing. No need of Minnie's hands now. That is clear. Velma's glow aglow and two yards wide of clear and unstreaked white and yellow. Her eyes scanning the air surrounding Minnie, then examining her own hands, fingers stretched and radiant. No need of Minnie's hands now so the healer withdraws them, drops them in her lap just as Velma, rising on steady legs, throws off the shawl that drops down on the stool a burst cocoon."

The title of Salman Rushdie's latest novel, *The Moor's Last Sigh,* suggests the narrative will end on a deathbed or in a graveyard. In fact it does. The storyteller/protagonist, Moraes Zogoiby, leads us on an exhilarating journey in order to nail his papers on the wall. Papers that are the result of his "daily, silent singing for [his daily] life." Telling, writing, recording four generations of family and national history. A history of devastating loves, transcendent hatreds; of ambition without limit and sloth without redemption; loyalties beyond understanding and deceptions beyond imagination. When every step, every pause of this imaginary is finally surrendered to our view, this is the close:

The rough grass in the graveyard has grown high and spiky and as I sit upon this tombstone I seem to be resting upon the grass's yellow points, weightless, floating free of burdens, borne aloft by a thick brush of miraculously unbending blades. I do not have long. My breaths are numbered, like the years of the ancient world, in reverse, and the countdown to zero is well advanced. I have used the last of my strength to make this pilgrimage. . . .

At the head of this tombstone are three eroded letters; my fingertip reads them for me. R I P. Very well: I will rest, and hope for peace. The world is full of sleepers waiting for their moment of return. . . . Somewhere, in a tangle of thorns, a beauty in a glass coffin awaits a prince's kiss. See: here is my flask. I'll drink some wine; and then, like a latter-day Van Winkle, I'll lay me down upon this graven stone, lay my head beneath these letters R I P, and close my eyes, according to our family's old practice of falling asleep in times of trouble, and hope to awaken, renewed and joyful, into a better time.

The rest, the peace is twice enunciated, but so is the hope. For renewal, joy, and, most importantly, "a better time."

In 1991 Ben Okri ended his novel *The Famished Road* with a dream so deeply felt it is prioritized over the entire narrative:

The air in the room was calm. There were no turbulences. His [father's] presence protected our nightspace. There were no forms invading our air, pressing down on our roof, walking through the objects. The air was clear and wide. In my sleep I found open spaces where I floated without fear. . . . The sweetness dissolved my fears. I was not afraid of Time.

And then it was another morning. . . .

A dream can be the highest point of a life.

In 1993, continuing the story of this sighted child, Okri concludes *Songs of Enchantment* with a more pronounced gesture toward the future: "Maybe one day we will see the mountains ahead of us. . . .

Maybe one day we will see the seven mountains of our mysterious destiny. Maybe one day we will see that beyond our chaos there could always be a new sunlight, and serenity."

The symbolisms of the mountains he is referring to make up the opening of the book:

> We didn't see the seven mountains ahead of us. We didn't see how they are always ahead. Always calling us, always reminding us that there are more things to be done, dreams to be realized, joys to be rediscovered, promises made before birth to be fulfilled, beauty to be incarnated, and love embodied.
>
> We didn't notice how they hinted that nothing is ever finished, that struggles are never truly concluded, that sometimes we have to redream our lives, and that life can always be used to create more light.

The expectation in these lines is palpable, insistent on the possibility of "one great action lived out all the way to the sea, chang[ing] the history of the world."

Leslie Marmon Silko in *Almanac of the Dead* flails and slashes through thousands of years of New World history, from centuries before the conquistadors made their appearances on these shores to the current day. The novel rests on a timelessness that is not only past, but a future timelessness as well—time truly without end. The final image of this narrative is the snake spirit "pointing toward the South in the direction from which the people will come." The future tense of the verb is attached to a direction that is, unlike the directions of most of the comings we approve of, the south. And it is impossible to ignore the fact that it is precisely "the south" where walls, fences, armed guards, and foaming hysteria are, at this very moment, gathering.

Cocoons from which healed women burst, dreams that take the terror from time, tombstone hopes for a better time, a time beyond chaos where the seven mountains of destiny lie, snake gods anticipating the people who will come from the south—these closing images following treks into the past lead one to hazard the conclusion that some writers disagree with prevailing notions of futurelessness. That they very much indeed not only have but insist on a future. That for them, for us, history is beginning again.

I am not ferreting out signs of tentative hope, obstinate optimism in contemporary fiction; I believe I am detecting an informed vision based on harrowing experience that nevertheless gestures toward a redemptive future. And I notice the milieu from which this vision rises. It is race inflected, gendered, colonialized, displaced, hunted.

There is an interesting trace here of divergent imaginaries, between the sadness of no more time, of the poignancy of inverted time—time that has only a past—of time itself living on "borrowed time," between that imaginary and the other one that has growing expectations of time with a relentless future. One looks to history for the feel of time or its purgative effects; one looks through art for its signs of renewal.

Literature, sensitive as a tuning fork, is an unblinking witness to the light and shade of the world we live in.

Beyond the world of literature, however, is another world; the world of commentary that has a quite other view of things. A Janus head that has masked its forward face and is at pains to assure us that the future is hardly worth the time. Perhaps it is the reality of a future as durable and far-reaching as the past, a future that will be shaped by those who have been pressed to the margins, by those who have been dismissed as irrelevant surplus, by those who have been cloaked with the demon's cape; perhaps it is the contemplation of that future that has occasioned the tremble of latter-day prophets afraid that the current disequilibria is a stirring, not an erasure. That not only is history not dead, but that it is about to take its first unfettered breath. Not soon, perhaps not in thirty years or fifty, because such a breath, such a massive intake, will take time. But it will be there. If that is so, then we should heed the meditations of literature. William Gass is correct. There are "acres of Edens inside ourselves." Time does have a future. Longer than its past and infinitely more hospitable—to the human race.

Black Matter(s)

Tribute to Martin Luther King Jr.

Pursuing the recollections of several people for projects he is engaged in, Martin Luther King III recently asked me for my thoughts on his father. And one of his questions was predictable, designed to elicit some subjective response. He said, "If you were having a conversation with my father, what would you like to ask him?" And for some wholly unaccountable reason, my heart skipped and I fairly keened into the telephone. "Oh, I hope he is not disappointed. Do you think he's disappointed? There must be something here to please him." Well, I calmed my voice to disguise what was becoming obvious to me, that what I really meant was, "I hope he is not disappointed in me."

I went on to frame a question that I would like to put to him, and I set aside my thoughts about the current state of affairs for the dispossessed: some wins, but some big-time losses; some vaulting leaps, but much slow sinking into muddy despair.

But all the while, I was wondering, Would he be disappointed in me? And it was odd, because I never met Reverend King. My memory of him is print-bound, electronic, through the narratives of other people. Yet I felt this personal responsibility to him. He did that to people. I realized later that I was responding to something other, and more durable, than the complex personhood of King.

Not to the preacher he was or the scholar he was or the vulnerable human being, not to the political strategist, the orator, the brilliant, risk-taking activist. But I was responding to his mission. His, as he coined it, audacious faith. His expectation of transforming, appending, cosmic elegy into a psalm of brotherhood.

His confidence that we were finer than we thought, that there were moral grounds we would not abandon, lines of civil behavior we simply would not cross. That there were things we would gladly give up for the public good, that a comfortable life, resting on the shoulders of other people's misery, was an abomination this country, especially, among all nations, found offensive.

I know the world is better, finer, because he lived in it. My anxiety was personal. Was I any better? Finer? Because I have lived in a world that is imaginary. Would he be disappointed in me? The answer isn't important. But the question really is, and that is the legacy of Martin Luther King Jr. He made the act of assuming personal responsibility for alleviating social harm ordinary, habitual, and irresistible. My tribute to him is the profound gratitude I feel for the gift that his life truly was.

Race Matters

ARLY ON in my life as a writer, I looked for but never actually found a sovereignty, an authority like that available to me in fiction writing, but at no other site. In that activity alone did I feel completely coherent and totally unfettered. There, in the process of writing, was the illusion, the deception of control, of nestling up ever closer to meaning. There was (and still is) the delight of redemption, the seduction of origineity. But I have known for a good portion of the past twenty-nine years that those delights, those seductions are rather more than less deliberate inventions necessary both to do the work and to legislate its mystery. But it became increasingly clear how language was both liberating and imprisoning. Whatever the forays of my imagination, the keeper, whose keys tinkled always in earshot, was race.

I have never lived, nor have any of you, in a world in which race did not matter. Such a world, a world free of racial hierarchy, is frequently imagined or described as dreamscape, Edenesque, utopian so remote are the possibilities of its achievement. From Martin Luther King Jr.'s hopeful language, to Doris Lessing's four-gated city, from Saint Augustine to Jean Toomer's "American," the race-free world has been posited as ideal, millennial, a condition possible only if accompanied by the Messiah or situated in a protected preserve, rather like a wilderness park.

But, for the purposes of this talk and because of certain projects

I am engaged in, I prefer to think of a world in which race does *not* matter—not as a theme park, or a failed and always failing dream, nor as the father's house of many rooms. I am thinking of it as home. For three reasons.

First, making a radical distinction between the metaphor of house and the metaphor of home helps me clarify my thinking on racial construction. Second, it moves the concept of unmattering race away from yearning and desire; away from an impossible future or an irretrievable and probably nonexistent past to a manageable, doable human activity. Third because eliminating the potency of racial constructs in language is the work I can do. I can't wait for the ultimate liberation theory to imagine its practice and do its work. Also matters of race and matters of home are priorities in my work and both have in one way or another initiated my search for sovereignty as well as my abandonment of that search once I recognized its disguise.

As an already and always raced writer, I knew at once, from the very beginning, that I could not, would not reproduce the master's voice and its assumptions of the all-knowing law of the white father. Nor would I substitute his voice with that of his fawning mistress or his worthy opponent, for both of those positions (mistress or opponent) seemed to confine me to his terrain, in his arena, accepting the house rules in the dominance game. If I have to live in a racial house, it was important at the least to rebuild it so that it was not a windowless prison into which I was forced, a thick-walled, impenetrable container from which no sound could be heard, but rather an open house, grounded, yet generous in its supply of windows and doors. Or at the most, it became imperative for me to transform this house completely. I was tempted to convert it into a palace where racism didn't hurt so much; to crouch in one of its many rooms where coexistence offered the delusion of agency. At some point I tried to use the race house as a scaffolding from which to launch a movable feast that could operate, be celebrated on any number of chosen sites. That was the authority, the glossy comfort, the redemptive quality, the freedom writing at first seemed to promise. Yet in that freedom, as in all freedoms (especially stolen ones), lay danger. Could I redecorate, redesign, even reconceive the racial house without forfeiting a home of my own? Would this forged, willed freedom demand an equally forged homelessness? Would it condemn me to eternal bouts of nostalgia for the home I have never had and would never know? Or would it require intolerable circumspection, a self-censoring bond to the original locus of racial architecture? In short, wasn't I (wouldn't I always be) tethered to a death-dealing ideology even (and especially) when I honed all my intelligence toward subverting it?

These questions, which have engaged so many, have troubled all of my work. How to be both free and situated; how to convert a racist house into a race-specific yet nonracist home? How to enunciate race while depriving it of its lethal cling? They are questions of concept, of language, of trajectory, of habitation, of occupation, and, although my engagement with them has been fierce, fitful, and constantly (I think) evolving, they remain in my thoughts as aesthetically and politically unresolved. Frankly, I look to readers for literary and extraliterary analyses for much of what can be better understood. I believe, however, that my literary excursions, and my use of a house/home antagonism, are related to the matters under discussion during the course of the next two days, because so much of what seems to lie about in discourses about race concerns legitimacy, authenticity, community, belonging—is, in fact, about home. An intellectual home; a spiritual home; family and community as home; forced and displaced labor in the destruction of home; the dislocation of and alienation within the ancestral home; the creative responses to exile, the devastations, pleasures, and imperatives of homelessness as it is manifested in discussions on globalism, diaspora, migrations, hybridity, contingency, interventions, assimilations, exclusions. The estranged body, the legislated body, the body as home. In virtually all of these formations, whatever the terrain, race magnifies the matter that matters.

There was a moment of some significance to me that followed the publication of *Beloved* and was a part of my reflection on the process of doing it. It is a moment that telescopes part of the territory to be mapped during this conference. This moment concerns the complexity inherent in creating narrative language both racially referential and figuratively logical.

Someone saw the last sentence of *Beloved* as it was originally written. In fact it was the penultimate sentence if one thinks of the last word—the resurrection of the title, the character, and the epigraph—as the very last sentence. In any case the phrase "Certainly no clamor for a kiss," which appears in the printed book, is not the one with which I had originally closed the book, and this friend was startled by the change. I told him that my editor had suggested an alteration at that point, although he in no way offered a description of what the change might be. The friend railed at my editor for the audacity of suggesting a change, and at me, too, for considering, let alone admitting one. I then went to some pains to explain to him why I made the change but became entangled in what the original phrase had meant, or, rather, what the original last word of the phrase had meant to me. How long it took to arrive at it, how I thought it was the perfect final word; that it connected everything together from the epigraph and the difficult plot to the struggles of the characters through the process of re-membering the body and its parts, re-membering the family, the neighborhood . . . and our national history. And that this last word reflected this re-membering, revealed its necessity, and provided the bridge I wanted from the beginning of the book to its end, as well as to the beginning of the book that was to follow. As I went on with the importance of this original last word, my friend became angrier and angrier. Nevertheless, I said, I thought there was something to be considered in the editor's objection—which was simply that, not a command. He wondered if a better word could be found to end the book because the one I had chosen was too dramatic, too theatrical. At first I disagreed with the editor about that. It was a very simple common word, but in the context of the previous sentences he believed it stood out like a sore thumb. That may even have been his phrase.

So I resisted it for a long time. A long time considering that we were in galley. Or rather late stages of manuscript, I guess. At any rate, I went away and thought about it. Thought about it every day in terms of whether to leave it the way I had originally written it or whether to change it. I decided, finally, to let the decision rest on whether I could indeed find a better word. One that produced the same meaning.

I didn't find any satisfactory replacement for weeks. And I was eager to find something because the point that gripped me was that even if the word I had chosen originally was the absolute right one, something was wrong if it stood out that way and did not complete the meaning of the text, but dislodged it. So it wasn't a question of simply substituting one word for another that meant the same thing—a synonym—or of trying to decide whether my original word was apt. I might have to rewrite a good deal in order to assure myself that my original last word worked.

I decided that it didn't. I decided that there was another word that could do the same thing with less mystification. That word was "kiss."

Well, the discussion with my friend made me realize that I'm still unhappy about it, because "kiss" works at a level a bit too shallow. "Kiss" works at a level that searches for and locates a quality or element of the novel that was not, and is not, its primary feature. The primary feature is not love, or the fulfillment of physical desire. The feature was necessity, something that precedes love, follows love, informs love, shapes love, and to which love is subservient. In this case the necessity was for a kind of connection, an acknowledgment, a paying out of homage still due.

I was inclined to believe that there were poorly lit passages leading up to that original word if indeed it was so very misunderstood and so strongly and wrongly unsettling. I have been reading some analyses of revisions of texts out of copyright and thinking about the ways in which books get not only reread but also rewritten not only in one's own language with the ambivalence of the writer and the back-and-forth between editor and writer, but also what happens in translation. The liberties taken that enhance; the liberties taken that diminish. And for me the alarm. There is always the threat of not being taken seriously, of having the work reduced to a primer, of having the politics of language, the politics of another language imposed on the writer's own politics.

My effort to manipulate American English was not to take standard English and use vernacular to decorate or to paint over it, but to carve away its accretions of deceit, blindness, ignorance, paralysis, and sheer malevolence so that certain kinds of perceptions were not only available but were inevitable. That is what I thought my original last word accomplished, then I became convinced that it did not, and now am sorry I made the change. The trouble it takes to find just one word and know that it is that note and no other that would do is an extraordinary battle. To have found it and lost it is in retrospect infuriating. On the one hand, what could it matter? Can a book really fall apart because of one word, even if it's in a critical position? Probably not. On the other hand, maybe so, if the writing of it tries for racial specificity and figurative coherence. In this instance, I settled for the latter. I gave up a word that was racially resonant and figuratively logical for one that was only the latter, because my original last word was so clearly disjunctive, a sore thumb, a jarring note combining as it did two functions linguistically incompatible except when signaling racial exoticism.

Actually I think my editor was right. The original word was the "wrong" word. But I also know that my friend was right: the "wrong" word, in this case, was the only word. As you can see, my assertion of agency outside the raced house turned into a genuflection in its familiar (more comfortable) yard.

That experience of regret highlights for me the need to rethink the subtle yet pervasive attachments we may all have to the architecture of race. The need to think about what it means and what it takes to live in a redesigned racial house and to defiantly, if erroneously, call it diversity or multiculturalism—to call it home. To think about how invested some of the best theoretical work may be in clinging to its simulacra. To think about what new dangers present themselves when escape or chosen exile from that house is achieved.

I risk charges here of escapism and of encouraging futile efforts to transcend race or pernicious ones to trivialize it, and it would worry me a great deal if my remarks and the project I am working on were to be so completely misunderstood. What I am determined to do is to take what is articulated as the elusive future and domesticate it; to concretize what is, outside of science fiction, rendered in political language and thought as permanently unrealizable dream. My confrontation is piecemeal and very slow, of course, because unlike the successful advancement of an argument, narration requires the complicity of a reader in discovery. And there are no pictures to ease the difficulty.

In various novels the adventure for me has been explorations of seemingly impenetrable, race-inflected, race-clotted topics. From the first book, where I was interested in racism as a cause, consequence, and manifestation of individual and social psychosis; to the next one, in which I was preoccupied with the culture of gender, the invention of identity, both of which acquired astonishing meaning when placed in a racial context. On to *Song of Solomon* and *Tar Baby,* where I was interested in the impact of race on the romance of community and individuality; in *Beloved* the revelatory possibilities of historical narration when the body-mind, subject-object, past-present oppositions, viewed through the lens of race, collapse and become seamless. In *Jazz* I tried to locate modernity as a response to the race house, in an effort to blow up its all-encompassing shelter, its all-knowingness, and its assumptions of control. And currently to first enunciate and then destabilize the racial gaze altogether in *Paradise.*

In *Jazz* the dynamite fuse was lit under narrative voice. The voice that could begin with claims of knowledge, inside knowledge, and indisputable authority—"I know that woman . . ."—and end with the blissful epiphany of its humanity and its own needs.

In my current project I want to see whether or not race-specific, race-free language is both possible and meaningful in narration. And I want to inhabit, walk around, a site clear of racist detritus; a place where race both matters and is rendered impotent; a place "already made for me, both snug and wide open. With a doorway never needing to be closed, a view slanted for light and bright autumn leaves but not rain. Where moonlight can be counted on if the sky is clear and stars no matter what. And below, just yonder, a river called Treason to rely on." I want to imagine not the threat of freedom, or its tentative, gasping fragility, but the concrete thrill of borderlessness—a kind of out-of-doors safety where "a sleepless woman could always rise from her bed, wrap a shawl around her shoulders and sit on the steps in the moonlight. And if she felt like it she could walk out the yard and on down the road. No lamp and no fear. A hiss-crackle from the side of the road would never scare her because whatever it was that made the sound, it wasn't something creeping up on her. Nothing for ninety miles around thought she was prey. She could stroll as slowly as she liked, think of food preparations, war, of family things, or lift her eyes to stars and think of nothing at all. Lampless and without fear she could make her way. And if a light shone from a house up a ways and the cry of a colicky baby caught her attention, she might step over to the house and call out softly to the woman inside trying to soothe the baby. The two of them might take turns massaging the infant stomach, rocking, or trying to get a little soda water down. When the baby quieted they could sit together for a spell, gossiping, chuckling low so as not to wake anybody else.

"The woman could decide to go back to her own house then, refreshed and ready to sleep, or she might keep her direction and walk further down the road. . . . On out, beyond the limits of town, because nothing at the edge thought she was prey."

The overweening event of the modern world is not its technology; it is the mass movement of populations. Beginning with the largest forcible transfer of people in the history of the world: slavery. The consequences of which transfer have determined all the wars following it as well as the current ones being waged on every continent. The contemporary world's work has become policing, forming policy regarding, and trying to administrate the perpetual movement of people. Nationhood—the very definition of citizenship—is marked by exile, refugees, guest arbiter, immigrants, migrations, the displaced, the fleeing, and the under siege. Hunger for home is entombed among the central metaphors in the discourse on globalism, transnationalism, nationalism, the breakup of nations, and the fictions of sovereignty. Yet these dreams of home are frequently as raced themselves as the originating racial house that has defined them. When they are not raced, they are, as I suggested earlier, landscape, never inscape; utopia, never home.

I applaud and am indebted to scholars here and elsewhere who are clearing (theoretical) space where racial constructs are being forced to reveal their struts and bolts; their technology and their carapace, so that political action, intellectual thought, and cultural production can be generated.

The defenders of Western hegemony sense the encroachment and have already described, defined, and named the possibility of imagining race without dominance, without hierarchy as "barbarism"; as destroying the four-gated city; as the end of history—all of which can be read as garbage, rubbish, an already damaged experience, a valueless future. If, once again, the political consequence of theoretical work is already named catastrophe, it is more urgent than ever to develop nonmessianic language to refigure the raced community, to decipher the deracing of the world. More urgent than ever to develop an epistemology that is neither intellectual slumming nor self-serving reification. You are marking out space for critical work that neither bleeds the race house for the gains it provides in authenticity and insiderism nor abandons it to its signifying gestureism. If the world-as-home that we are working for is already described in the race house as waste, the work this scholarship draws our attention to is not just interesting—it may save our lives.

These campuses where we mostly work and frequently assemble will not remain alien terrain within whose fixed borders we travel from one kind of race-inflected community to another as interpreters, native guides; or campuses resigned to the status of segregated castles from whose balustrades we view—even invite—the homeless; or markets where we permit ourselves to be auctioned, bought, silenced, and vastly compromised depending on the whim of the master and the going rate.

The distrust that race studies receive from the authenticating off-campus community is legitimate only when the scholars themselves have not imaged their own homes; have not unapologetically realized and recognized that the valuable work they do can be done in no other place; have not envisioned academic life as neither straddling opposing worlds nor as a flight from any. W. E. B. Du Bois's observation is a strategy, not a prophecy or a cure. Beyond the outside/inside double consciousness, this new space postulates the inwardness of the outside; imagines safety without walls where we can conceive of a third, if you will pardon the expression, world, "already made for me, both snug and wide open, with a doorway never needing to be closed."

Home.

Black Matter(s)

I HAVE BEEN thinking for some time now about the validity or vulnerability of a certain set of assumptions conventionally accepted among literary historians and critics and circulated as "knowledge." This "knowledge" holds that traditional, canonical American literature is free of, unformed by, and unshaped by the four-hundred-year-old presence of first Africans and then African Americans in the United States. It assumes that this presence—which shaped the body politic, the Constitution, and the entire history of the culture—has had no significant place or consequence in the origin and development of that culture's literature. Moreover, it assumes that the characteristics of our national literature emanate from a particular "Americanness" that is separate from and unaccountable to this presence. There seems to be a more or less tacit agreement among literary scholars that because American literature has been clearly the preserve of white male views, genius, and power, those views, genius, and power are removed from and without relationship to the presence of black people in the United States—a population that antedated every American writer of renown and was perhaps the most furtively radical, impinging force on the country's literature.

The contemplation of this black presence is central to any understanding of our national literature and should not be relegated to the margins of the literary imagination. It may be that American literature distinguishes itself as a coherent entity because of and in reference to this unsettled and unsettling population. I have begun to wonder whether the major, much celebrated themes of American literature—individualism, masculinity, the conflict between social engagement and historical isolation—are not acute and ambiguous moral problematics, but in fact responses to a dark, abiding, signing Africanistic presence. The coded language and purposeful restriction by which the newly formed nation dealt with the racial disingenuousness and moral frailty at its heart are maintained in its literature, even through the twentieth century. A real or fabricated Africanistic presence has been crucial to writers' sense of their Americanness. And it shows: through significant and underscored omissions, startling contradictions, heavily nuanced conflicts, and the way their work is peopled with the signs and bodies of this presence.

My curiosity has developed into a still-informal study of what I am calling American Africanism. It is an investigation into the ways in which a nonwhite, Africanistic presence was constructed in the United States, and the imaginative uses this fabricated presence served. I am using "Africanism" as a term for the denotative and connotative blackness African peoples have come to signify, as well as the entire range of views, assumptions, readings, and misreadings that characterize these peoples in Eurocentric eyes. It is important to recognize the lack of restraint attached to the uses of this trope. As a disabling virus within literary discourse, Africanism has become, in the Eurocentric tradition favored by American education, both a way of talking about and a way of policing matters of class, sexual license, and repression, the formation and the exercise of power, and ethics and accountability. Through the simple expedient of demonizing and reifying the range of color on a palette, American Africanism makes it possible to say and not say, to inscribe and erase, to escape and engage, to act out and act on, to historicize and render timeless. It provides a way of contemplating chaos and civilization, desire and fear, and a mechanism for testing the problems and blessings of freedom.

What Africanism became and how it functioned in the literary imagination are of paramount interest because it may be possible to discover, through a close look at literary "blackness," the nature and even the source of literary "whiteness." What is it *for*? What parts do the invention and development of "whiteness" play in the construction of what is described as an "American"? If this inquiry of mine ever comes to maturity, it may provide me access to a coherent reading of American literature, a reading that is not completely available to me now—not least, I suspect, because of the studied indifference of literary criticism to these matters.

One likely reason for the paucity of critical material on this large and compelling subject is that in matters of race, silence and evasion have historically ruled literary discourse. Evasion has fostered another, substitute language in which the issues are encoded and made unavailable for open debate. The situation is aggravated by the anxiety that breaks into discourse on race. It is further complicated by the fact that ignoring race is understood to be a graceful, liberal, even generous habit. To notice is to recognize an already discredited difference; to maintain its invisibility through silence is to allow the black body a shadowless participation in the dominant cultural body. Following this logic, every well-bred instinct argues against noticing and forecloses adult discourse. It is just this concept of literary and scholarly *moeurs* (which functions smoothly in literary criticism, but neither makes nor receives credible claims in other disciplines) that has terminated the shelf life of some once extremely well-regarded American authors and blocked access to the remarkable insights some of their works contain.

Another reason for this ornamental vacuum in literary discourse is the pattern of thinking about racialism asymmetrically, in terms of its consequences on its victims alone. A good deal of time and intelligence have been invested in exposing racialism and its horrific effects on its objects. The result has been constant, if erratic, efforts to legislate preventive regulations. There have also been powerful and persuasive attempts to analyze the origin of racialism itself, contesting the assumption that it is an inevitable and permanent part of all social landscapes. I do not wish to disparage these inquiries in any way. It is precisely because of them that any progress has been accomplished in matters of racial discourse. But I do want to see that well-established study joined by another, equally important: the effect of racialism on those who perpetuate it. It seems to me both poignant and striking how the effect of racialism on the subject has been avoided and unanalyzed. The scholarship that looks into the mind, the imagination, and the behavior of slaves is valuable; equally so is a serious intellectual examination of what racial ideology did and does to the mind, the imagination, and the behavior of the master.

National literatures, like writers, get along as best they can and with what they can. Yet they do seem to end up describing and inscribing what is really on the national mind. For the most part, literature of the United States has taken as its concern the architecture of a *new white man*. If I am disenchanted with the indifference of literary criticism toward examining the nature of that concern, I do have a last resort: the writers themselves.

Writers are among the most sensitive, most intellectually anarchic, most representative, most probing of artists. The writer's ability to imagine what is not the self, to familiarize the strange, and to mystify the familiar—all this is the test of her or his power. The languages she or he uses (imagistic, structural, narrative) and the social and historical context in which these languages signify are indirect and direct revelations of that power and its limitations. So it is to them, the creators of American literature, that I look for some clarification about the invention and effect of Africanism in the United States.

How does literary utterance arrange itself when it tries to imagine an Africanistic Other? What are the signs, the codes, the literary strategies designed to accommodate this encounter? In short, what happens? What does the inclusion of Africans and African Americans do to and for the text? As a reader, I had always assumed that nothing "happens." That Africans and their descendants are *there* in no sense that matters; that when they are *there,* they are decorative, displays of the facile writer's technical expertise. I assumed that since the author was not Africanistic, the appearance of Africanistic characters, narrative, or idiom in his or her work could never be about anything other than the "normal," unracialized, illusory white world that provides the backdrop for the work. Certainly no American text of the sort I am discussing was ever written *for* black people, any more than *Uncle Tom's Cabin* was written for Uncle Tom to read or be persuaded by. As a writer reading, I realized the obvious: that the subject of the dream is the dreamer. The fabrication of an Africanistic persona was reflexive; it was an extraordinary meditation on the self, a powerful exploration of the fears and desires that reside in the writerly consciousness (as well as in others), an astonishing revelation of longing, of terror, of perplexity, of shame, of magnanimity.

Reading these texts as a writer allowed me deeper access to them. It was as though I had been looking at a fishbowl, seeing the glide and flick of the golden scales, the green tip, the bolt of white careening back from the gills, the castles at the bottom, surrounded by pebbles and tiny, intricate fronds of green, the barely disturbed water, the flecks of waste and food, the tranquil bubbles traveling to the surface—and suddenly I saw the bowl itself, the structure transparently, invisibly, permitting the ordered life it contained to exist in the larger world. In other words, I began to rely on my knowledge of how books get written, how language arrives, on my sense of how and why writers abandon or take on certain aspects of their project. I began to rely on my understanding of what the linguistic struggle requires of writers and what they make of the surprise that is the inevitable, necessary concomitant of the act of creation. What became transparent were the self-evident ways Americans chose to talk about themselves through and within a sometimes allegorical, sometimes metaphorical, but always choked representation of an Africanistic presence.

Young America distinguished itself by pressing with full awareness toward a future, a freedom, a kind of human dignity believed to be unprecedented in the world. A whole tradition of "universal" yearnings collapsed into that well-fondled phrase "the American Dream." While the immigrants' dream deserves the exhaustive scrutiny it has received in the scholarly disciplines and the arts, it is just as important to know what these people were rushing from as it is to know what they were hastening to. If the New World fed dreams, what was the

Old World reality that whetted the appetite for them? And how might that reality caress and grip the shaping of a new one?

The flight from the Old World to the New is generally understood to be a flight from oppression and limitation to freedom and possibility. In fact, for some the escape was a flight from license—from a society perceived to be unacceptably permissive, ungodly, and undisciplined. For those fleeing for reasons other than religious ones, however, constraint and limitation impelled the journey. The Old World offered these emigrants only poverty, prison, social ostracism, and not infrequently death. There was, of course, another group of immigrants who came for the adventures possible in founding a colony for rather than against one or another mother country or fatherland. And of course there were the merchants, who came for the cash.

To all these people, the attraction was of the "clean slate" variety, a once-in-a-lifetime opportunity not only to be born again, but to be born again in new clothes, as it were: the new setting would provide new raiments of self. The New World offered the vision of a limitless future that gleamed more brightly against the constraint, dissatisfaction, and turmoil being left behind. A promise genuinely promising. With luck and endurance one could discover freedom, find a way to make God's law manifest in Man, or end up rich as a prince. The desire for freedom is preceded by oppression; a yearning for God's law is born of the detestation of man's license and corruption; the glamour of riches is in thrall to poverty, hunger, and debt.

There was much more to make the trip worth the risk. The habit of genuflection would be replaced by the thrill of command. Power—control of one's own destiny—would replace the powerlessness felt before the gates of class, caste, and cunning persecution. One could move from discipline and punishment to disciplining and punishing; from being socially ostracized to becoming an arbiter of social rank. One could be released from a useless, binding, repulsive past into a kind of historylessness—a blank page waiting to be inscribed. Much was to be written there: noble impulses were made into law and appropriated for a national tradition, but so were base ones, learned and elaborated in the rejected and rejecting homeland.

The body of literature produced by the young nation is one place it inscribed these fears, forces, and hopes. It is difficult to read the literature of young America without being struck by how antithetical it is to our modern conception of "the American Dream," how pronounced is the absence of that term's elusive mixture of hope, realism, materialism, and promise. Coming from a people who made much of their "newness"—their potential, their freedom, their innocence—it is striking how dour, how troubled, how frightened, and how haunted the early, founding literature truly is.

We have words and labels for this haunting—"gothic," "romantic," "sermonic," "Puritan"—whose sources are, of course, to be found in the literature of the world from which they fled. But the strong affinity between the nineteenth-century American psyche and gothic romance has, rightly, been much remarked upon. It is not surprising that a young country, repelled by Europe's moral and social disorder and swooning in a fit of desire and rejection, would devote its talents to reproducing in its own literature the typology of diabolism from which its citizens and their fathers had fled. After all, one way to benefit from the lessons of earlier mistakes and past misfortunes was to record them—an inoculation against their repetition, as it were.

Romance was the form in which this uniquely American prophylaxis was played out. Long after it had faded in Europe, romance remained the cherished expression of young America. What was there in American romanticism that made it so attractive to Americans as a battle plain upon which to fight, to engage, to imagine their demons?

It has been suggested that romance is an evasion of history, and thus perhaps attractive to a people trying to evade the recent past. But I am more persuaded by arguments that find in it the head-on encounter with very real, very pressing historical forces and the contradictions inherent in them, as these come to be experienced by writers. Romance, an exploration of anxiety imported from the shadows of European culture, made possible the embrace—sometimes safe, other times risky—of some quite specific, understandably human, American fears: the fear of being outcast, of failing, of powerlessness; of boundarylessness, of Nature unbridled and crouched for attack; of the absence of so-called civilization; of loneliness, of aggression both external and internal. In short, the terror of human freedom—the thing they coveted most of all. Romance offered writers not less but more; not a narrow historical canvas but a wide one; not escape but enlargement. It offered platforms for moralizing and fabulation, and for the imaginative entertainment of violence, sublime incredibility, and terror—whose most significant, overweening ingredient was darkness, with all the connotative value it contained.

There is no romance free of what Melville called "the power of black-ness," especially not in a country in which there was a resident popula-tion, already black, upon which the imagination could articulate the fears, the dilemmas, the divisions that obsessed it historically, morally, metaphysically, and socially. This slave population seemed to volun-teer as objects for meditation on the lure and elusiveness of human freedom, on the outcast's terror and his dread of failure, of powerless-ness, Nature without limits, inborn loneliness, internal aggression, evil, sin, greed . . . ; in other words, on human freedom in all terms except those of human potential and the rights of man.

And yet the rights of man, an organizing principle upon which the nation was founded, was inevitably, and especially, yoked to Afri-canism. Its history and origin are permanently allied with another seductive concept—the hierarchy of race. As Orlando Patterson has noted, we should not be surprised that the Enlightenment could accommodate slavery; we should be surprised if it could not. The concept of freedom did not emerge in a vacuum. Nothing highlighted freedom—if it did not in fact create it—like slavery.

In that construction of blackness and enslavement could be found not only the not-free but also the projection of the not-me. The result was a playground for the imagination. And what rose up out of collec-tive needs to allay internal fears and rationalize external exploitation was an Africanism—a fabricated brew of darkness, otherness, alarm, and desire—that is uniquely American. (There also exists a European Africanism with its counterpart in its own colonial literature.)

What I wish to examine is how the image of reigned-in, bound, suppressed, and repressed darkness became objectified in American literature as an Africanistic persona. I want to show how the duties of that persona—duties of mirroring and embodying and exorcism—are demanded and displayed throughout much of the national literature and help provide its distinguishing characteristics.

Earlier I said that cultural identities are formed and informed by a nation's literature, and that what seemed to be on the "mind" of the literature of the United States was the self conscious but highly problematic construction of the American as a new white man. Emerson's call for that new man, "The American Scholar," indicates the deliberateness of the construction, the conscious necessity for establishing difference. But the writers who responded to this call, accepting or rejecting it, did not look solely to Europe to establish a reference for difference. There was a very theatrical difference underfoot. Writers were able to celebrate or deplore an identity—already existing or rapidly taking form—that was elaborated through racial difference. That difference provided a huge trove of signs, symbols, and agencies for organizing, separating, and consolidating identity along valuable lines of interest.

Bernard Bailyn has provided us with an extraordinary investigation of European settlers in the act of becoming Americans. Particularly relevant is a description in his *Voyagers to the West*. I want to quote a rather long passage from that book because it helps to clarify and underscore the salient aspects of this American character that I have been describing:

> William Dunbar, seen through his letters and diary, appears to be more fictional than real. . . . He . . . was a man in his early twenties who appeared suddenly in the Mississippi wilderness to stake out a claim to a large parcel of land, then disappeared to the Caribbean, to return leading a battalion of "wild" slaves with whose labor alone he built an estate where before there had been nothing but trees and uncultivated soil. . . . He was . . . complex . . . and . . . part of a violent biracial world whose ten-

sions could lead in strange directions. For this wilderness planter was a scientist, who would later correspond with Jefferson on science and exploration, a Mississippi planter whose contributions to the American Philosophical Society . . . included linguistics, archaeology, hydrostatics, astronomy, and climatology, and whose geographical explorations were reported in widely known publications. . . . An exotic figure in the plantation world of early Mississippi . . . he . . . imported into that raw, half-savage world the niceties of European culture: not chandeliers and costly rugs, but books, surveyor's equipment of the finest kind, and the latest instruments of science.

Dunbar . . . was educated first by tutors at home, then at the university in Aberdeen, where his interest in mathematics, astronomy, and belles-lettres took mature shape. What happened to him after his return home and later in London, where he circulated with young intellectuals, what propelled, or led, him out of the metropolis on the first leg of his long voyage west is not known. But whatever his motivation may have been, in April 1771, aged only twenty-two, Dunbar appeared in Philadelphia. . . .

Ever eager for gentility, this well-educated product of the Scottish enlightenment and of London's sophistication—this bookish young *littérateur* and scientist who, only five years earlier, had been corresponding about scientific problems—about "Dean Swifts beatitudes," about the "virtuous and happy life," and about the Lord's commandment that mankind should "love one another"—was strangely insensitive to the suffering of those who served him. In July 1776 he recorded not the independence of the American colonies from Britain, but the suppression of an alleged conspiracy for freedom by slaves on his own plantation. . . .

Dunbar, the young *erudit,* the Scottish scientist and man of letters, was no sadist. His plantation regime was, by the standards of the time, mild; he clothed and fed his slaves decently, and frequently relented in his more severe punishments. But 4,000 miles from the sources of culture, alone on the far periphery of British civilization where physical survival was a daily struggle, where ruthless exploitation was a way of life, and where disorder, violence, and human degradation were commonplace, he had triumphed by successful adaptation. Endlessly enterprising and resourceful, his finer sensibilities dulled by the abrasions of frontier life, and feeling within himself a sense of authority and autonomy he had not known before, a force that flowed from his absolute control over the lives of others, he emerged a distinctive new man, a borderland gentleman, a man of property in a raw, half-savage world.

May I call your attention to some elements of this portrait, some pairings and interdependencies that are marked in this narrative of William Dunbar? First, the historical connection between the Enlightenment and the institution of slavery—the rights of man and his enslavement. Second, the relationship of Dunbar's education and his New World enterprise. His education was exceptionally cultivated and included the latest thoughts on theology and science—in an effort perhaps to make them mutually accountable, to make each support the other. He is a product not only of "the Scottish enlightenment" but also of "London's sophistication." He read Swift, discussed the Christian commandment to "love one another," and is described as "strangely" insensitive to the suffering of his slaves. On July 12, 1776, he records with astonishment and hurt the slave rebellion on his plantation: "Judge my surprise. Of what avail is kindness & good usage when rewarded by such ingratitude." "Constantly bewildered," Bailyn goes on, "by his slaves' behavior . . . [Dunbar] recovered two runaways and 'condemned them to receive 500 lashes each at five dif[feren]t times, and to carry a chain & log fixt to the ancle.'" I take this to be a succinct portrait of the process by which the American as new, white, and male was constituted. It is a formation that has at least four desirable consequences, all of which are referred to in Bailyn's summation of Dunbar's character and located in how Dunbar feels "within himself." Let me repeat: "feeling . . . a sense of authority and autonomy he had not known before, a force that flowed from his absolute control over the lives of others, he emerged a distinctive new man, a borderland gentleman, a man of property in a raw, half-savage world." A power, a sense of freedom he had not known before. But what had he "known before"? Fine education, London sophistication, theological and scientific thought. None of these, one gathers, could provide him with the authority and autonomy Mississippi planter life did. His "sense" is a "force" that "flows": not a willed domination, a thought-out, calculated choice, but rather a kind of natural resource, already present, a Niagara Falls waiting to spill over as soon as he is in a position to possess "absolute control over the lives of others." And once he has moved into that position, he is resurrected as a new man, a distinctive man, a different man. Whatever his social status in London, in the New World he is a gentleman. More gentle; more man. Because the site of his transformation is within rawness. He is backgrounded by savagery.

Autonomy, newness, difference, authority, absolute power: these are the major themes and concerns of American literature, and each one is made possible, shaped, and activated by a complex awareness and use of a constituted Africanism that, deployed as rawness and savagery, provided the staging ground and arena for the elaboration of that quintessential American identity.

Autonomy—freedom—translates into the much championed and revered "individualism"; newness translates into "innocence"; distinctiveness becomes difference and strategies for maintaining it; authority becomes a romantic, conquering "heroism" and "virility" and raises the problematics of wielding absolute power over the lives of others. These four are made possible, finally, by the fifth: absolute power called forth and acted out against, upon, and within a natural and mental landscape conceived of as a "raw, half-savage world."

Why "raw and half-savage"? Because it is peopled by a nonwhite indigenous population? Perhaps. But certainly because there is readily at hand a bound and unfree, rebellious but serviceable black population by which Dunbar and all white men are enabled to measure these privileging and privileged differences.

Eventually individualism will lead to a prototype of Americans as solitary, alienated malcontents. What, one wants to ask, are Americans alienated from? What are Americans always so insistently innocent of?

Different from? And over whom is absolute power held, from whom withheld, to whom distributed?

Answers to these questions lie in the potent and ego-reinforcing presence of an Africanistic population. The new white male can now persuade himself that savagery is "out there": that the lashes ordered (five hundred, applied five times: twenty-five hundred in total) are not one's own savagery; that repeated and dangerous breaks for freedom are "puzzling" confirmations of black irrationality; that the combination of Dean Swift's beatitudes and a life of regularized violence is civilized; that, if sensibilities are dulled enough, the rawness remains external.

These contradictions cut and slash their way through the pages of American literature. How could they not have? As Dominick LaCapra reminds us, " 'Classic' novels, are not only worked over . . . by common contextual forces (such as ideologies) but also rework and at least partially work through those forces in critical and at times potentially transformative fashion."

The imaginative and historical terrain upon which early American writers journey is in very large measure shaped and determined by the presence of the racial Other. Statements to the contrary insisting upon the meaninglessness of race to American identity are themselves full of meaning. The world does not become raceless or will not become unracialized by assertion. The act of enforcing racelessness in literary discourse is itself a racial act. Pouring rhetorical acid on the fingers of a black hand may indeed destroy the prints, but not the hand. Besides, what happens, in that violent, self-serving act of erasure, to the hands, the fingers, the fingerprints of the one who does the pouring? Do they remain acid-free? The literature itself suggests otherwise.

Explicit or implicit, the Africanistic presence informs in significant, compelling, and inescapable ways the texture and shape of American literature. It is a dark and abiding presence that serves the literary imagination as both a visible and an invisible meditating force. So that even, and especially, when American texts are not "about" Africanistic presences, or characters, or narrative, or idiom, their shadows hover there, implied, signified, as boundaries. It is no accident and no mistake that immigrant populations (and much immigrant literature) understood their "Americanness" as an opposition to the resident population. Race, in fact, now functions as a metaphor so necessary to the construction of "Americanness" that it rivals the old pseudoscientific and class-informed racialisms whose dynamics we are more used to deciphering.

As a means of transacting the whole process of Americanization while burying its particular racial ingredients, this Africanistic presence may be something the United States cannot do without. For in this part of the twentieth century, the word "American" contains its association with race deep within. This is not true of "Canadian" or "English." To identify someone as South African is to say very little; we need the adjective "white" or "black" or "colored" to make our meaning clear. In the United States it is quite the reverse. "American" means "white," and Africanistic people struggle to make the terms applicable to themselves with ethnicity and hyphens. Americans did not have an immanent nobility from which to wrest and against which to define an identity of national virtue while continuing to covet aristocratic license and luxury. The American nation negotiated both its disdain and its envy in the same way Dunbar did: through a self-reflexive contemplation of fabricated, mythological Africanism. For Dunbar, and for American writers generally, this Africanistic Other became the means of thinking about the body, mind, chaos, kindness, and love; became the occasion for exercises in the absence of restraint, the presence of restraint, the contemplation of freedom, of aggression; for the exploration of ethics and morality, for meeting the obligations of the social contract, for bearing the cross of religion and following out the ramifications of power.

Reading and charting the emergence of an Africanistic persona in the development of a national literature is both a fascinating project and an urgent one, if the history and criticism of our literature are to become coherent. Emerson's plea for intellectual independence was like the offer of an empty plate that writers could fill with nourishment from an indigenous kitchen. The language was, of course, to be English, but the content of the language, its subject, was to be deliberately, insistently un-English and anti-European, insofar as it rhetorically repudiated an adoration of the Old World and defined the past as corrupt and indefensible.

In the scholarship on the formation of an American character and the production of a national literature, a number of items have been cataloged. A major item to be added to the list must be an Africanistic presence—decidedly not-American, decidedly Other.

The necessity for establishing difference stemmed not only from the Old World but from a difference within the New. What was distinctive in the New was, first of all, its claim to freedom and, second, the presence of the unfree at the heart of the democratic experiment—the critical absence of democracy, its echo, its shadow, its silence, and its silent force in the political and intellectual activity of some not-Americans. The distinguishing features of the not-Americans were their slave status, their social status—and their color. It is conceivable that the first would have self-destructed in a variety of ways had it not been for the last. These slaves, unlike many others in the world's history, were visible to a fault. And they had inherited, among other things, a long history of the "meaning" of color. It was not simply that this slave population had a distinctive color; it was that this color "meant" something. This "meaning" had been named and deployed by scholars from at least the moment, in the eighteenth century, when other and sometimes the same scholars investigated both the natural history and the inalienable rights of man—that is to say, human freedom.

One supposes that if Africans all had three eyes, or one ear, the significance of that difference from the small but conquering European invaders would also have been found to have "meaning." In any case, the subjective nature of ascribing value and meaning to color cannot be questioned this late in the twentieth century. The point for this discussion is the alliance of "visually rendered ideas with linguistic utterances." And this leads into the social and political nature of received knowledge as it is revealed in American literature.

Knowledge, however mundane and utilitarian, creates linguistic images and cultural practices. Responding to culture—clarifying, explicating, valorizing, translating, transforming, critiquing—is what artists everywhere do, and this is especially true of writers involved in the development of a literature at the founding of a new nation. Whatever their personal and formally "political" responses to the "problem" inherent in the contradiction of a free republic deeply committed to a slave population, nineteenth-century writers were mindful of the presence of these blacks. More importantly, they addressed, in more or less passionate ways, their views on that difficult presence.

Awareness of this slave population did not confine itself to the personal encounters writers may have had. The publication of slave narratives was a nineteenth-century publication boom. The discussion of slavery and freedom filled the press, as well as the campaigns and policies of political parties and elected government. One would have to have been isolated indeed to be unaware of the most explosive issue in the nation. How could one speak of profit, economy, labor, progress, suffragism, Christianity, the frontier, the formation of new states, the acquisition of new lands, education, transportation (freight and passengers), neighborhoods, quarters, the military—practically anything a country concerns itself with—without having as a referent, at the heart of the discourse, at the heart of definition, the presence of Africans and their descendants?

It was not possible. And it did not happen. What did happen, frequently, was an effort to talk about these things with a vocabulary designed to disguise the subject. This did not always succeed, and in the work of many writers disguise was never intended. But the consequence was a master narrative that spoke *for* the African and his descendants, or of him. The legislator's narrative could not coexist with a response from the Africanistic persona.

Whatever popularity the slave narratives had—and they inspired abolitionists and converted anti-abolitionists—the slaves' own narrative, while freeing the narrator in many ways, did not destroy the master narrative. That latter narrative could accommodate many shifts, could make any number of adjustments to keep itself intact. Silence from and about the subject was the order of the day. Some of the silences were broken and some maintained by authors who lived with and within the policing narrative. I am interested in the strategies for maintaining the silence and for breaking it. How did the founding writers of young America engage, imagine, employ, and create an Africanistic presence and persona? In what ways do these strategies explicate American literature? How does excavating these pathways lead to fresher and more profound analyses of what they contain and how they contain it?

Let me take one example: a major American novel that is both an example and a critique of romance as a genre. If we supplement our reading of *Huckleberry Finn,* expand it, move beyond its clutch of sentimental nostrums about lighting out to the territory, river gods, and the fundamental innocence of Americanness; if we incorporate into our reading the novel's combative critique of antebellum America, thus shedding much light on the problems created by traditional readings too shy to linger over the implications of the Africanistic presence at its center, it seems to be another, somehow fuller novel. We understand that at a certain level, the critique of class and race is there, although disguised or enhanced through a combination of humor, adventure, and the naïve.

Twain's readers are free to dismiss the novel's combative, contestatory qualities and focus on its celebration of savvy innocence, while voicing polite embarrassment at the symptomatic racial attitude it espouses. Early criticism, those reappraisals in the fifties that led to the canonization of *Huckleberry Finn* as a great novel, missed or dismissed the social quarrel because the work appears to have fully assimilated the ideological assumptions of its society and culture; because it is narrated in the voice and controlled by the gaze of a child without status (an outsider, marginal, and already "othered" by the middle-class society he loathes and seems never to envy); and because the novel masks itself in the comic, the parody, and exaggeration of the tall tale.

In this young but street-smart innocent, Huck, who is virginally uncorrupted by bourgeois yearnings, fury, and helplessness, Mark Twain inscribes the critique of slavery and the pretensions of the would-be middle class, the resistance to the loss of Eden, and the difficulty of becoming that oxymoron, "a social individual." The agency for Huck's struggle, however, is the nigger Jim, and it is absolutely necessary that the term "nigger" be inextricable from Huck's deliberations about who and what he himself is. Or, more precisely, is not. The major controversies about the greatness or near-greatness of *Huckleberry Finn* as an American (or even "world") novel exist as controversies because they forgo a close examination of the interdependence of slavery and freedom, of Huck's growth and Jim's serviceability within it, and even of Twain's inability to continue, to explore the journey into free territory.

The critical controversy focuses on the collapse of the so-called fatal ending of the novel. It has been suggested that the ending is a brilliant finesse that returns Tom Sawyer to center stage where he should be. That it is a brilliant play on the dangers and limitations of romance. That the ending is a valuable learning experience for Jim and for Huck for which we and they should be grateful. That it is a sad and confused ending to a book that the author, after a long blocked period, did not know what to do with and so changed back to a child's story out of disgust. What is not stressed is that there is no way, given the confines of the novel, for Huck to mature into a moral human being in America without Jim, and therefore that to let Jim go free, to let him not miss the mouth of the Ohio River and passage into free territory, would be to abandon the whole premise of the book.

Neither Huck nor Twain can tolerate in imaginative terms Jim freed. To do so would blast the predilection from its mooring. Thus the "fatal" ending becomes an elaborate deferment of a necessary and necessarily unfree Africanistic character's escape, because freedom has no meaning to Huck or the text without the specter of enslavement, the anodyne to individualism, the yardstick of absolute power over the life of another: the signed, marked, informing, and mutating presence of a black slave. The novel addresses at every point in its structural edifice, and lingers over it in every fissure, the slave's body and personality: the way it spoke, what passion, legal or illicit, it was prey to, what pain it could endure, what limits, if any, there were to its suffering, what possibilities there were for forgiveness, for compassion, for love.

Two things strike us in this novel: the apparently limitless store of love and compassion the black man has for his white masters, and his assumptions that the whites are indeed what they say they are—superior and adult. This representation of Jim as the visible Other can be read as white yearning for forgiveness and love, but the yearning is made possible only when it is understood that the black man has recognized his inferiority (not as a slave but as a black) and despised it; that, as Jim is made to, he has permitted his persecutors to torment and humiliate him, and responds to the torment and humiliation with boundless love. The humiliation Huck and Tom subject Jim to is baroque, endless, foolish, mind-softening—and it comes *after* we have experienced Jim as an adult, a caring father, and a sensitive man. If Jim had been a white ex-convict befriended by Huck, the ending could not have been imagined or written because it would not have been possible for two children to play so painfully with the life of a white man (regardless of his class, education, or fugitiveness) once he had been revealed to us as a moral adult. Jim's slave status makes the "play and deferment" possible, and also actualizes, in its style and mode of narration, the significance of slavery to the achievement (in actual terms) of freedom. Jim seems unassertive, loving, irrational, passionate, dependent, inarticulate (except for the "talks" he and Huck have, long sweet talks we are not privy to. What did you talk about, Huck?). What should solicit our attention is not what Jim *seems,* but what Twain, Huck, and especially Tom need from him. *Huckleberry Finn* may indeed be "great," because in its structure, in what hell it puts its readers through at the end, the frontal debate it forces, it simulates and describes the parasitical nature of white freedom.

My suggestion that Africanism has come to have a metaphysical necessity should in no way be understood to imply that it has lost its ideological one. There is still much ill-gotten gain to reap from rationalizing power grabs and clutches with inferences of inferiority and the ranking of differences. There is still much national solace in continuing dreams of democratic egalitarianism to be gained by hiding class conflict, rage, and impotence in figurations of race. And there is quite a lot of juice to be extracted from plummy reminiscences of "individualism" and "freedom" if the tree upon which such fruit hangs is a black population forced to serve as freedom's polar opposite. "Individualism" is foregrounded and believed in when its background is stereotyped, enforced dependency. "Freedom" (to move, to earn, to learn, to be allied with a powerful center, to narrate the world) can be relished more deeply cheek by jowl with the bound and the unfree, the economically oppressed, the marginalized, the silenced. The ideological dependence on racialism is intact.

Surely, it will be said, white Americans have considered questions of morality and ethics, the supremacy of mind and the vulnerability of body, the blessings and liabilities of progress and modernity, without reference to the situation of its black population. Where, it will be asked, does one find the record that such a referent was part of these deliberations?

My answer to this question is another one: In what public discourse can the reference to black people be said not to exist? It is there in every moment of the nation's mightiest struggles. The presence of black people not only lies behind the framing of the Constitution, it is also in the battle over enfranchising unpropertied citizens, women, and the illiterate. In the construction of a free and public school system, in the balancing of representation in legislative bodies, in jurisprudence and the legal definitions of justice. In theological discourse, in the memoranda of banking houses, in the concept of manifest destiny and the narrative that accompanies the initiation of every immigrant into the community of American citizenship.

The literature of the United States, like its history, illustrates and represents the transformations of biological, ideological, and metaphysical concepts of racial differences. But literature has an additional concern and subject matter: the private imagination interacting with the external world it inhabits. Literature redistributes and mutates in figurative language the social conventions of Africanism. In minstrelsy, a layer of blackness applied to a white face released it from law. Just as entertainers, through blackface, could render permissible topics that would otherwise have been taboo, so American writers have been able to employ an imagined Africanistic persona to articulate and imaginatively act out the forbidden in American culture.

Encoded or implicit, indirect or overt, the linguistic responses to an Africanistic presence complicate the texts, sometimes contradicting them entirely. They can serve as allegorical fodder for the contemplation of Eden, expulsion, and the availability of grace. They provide paradox, ambiguity; they reveal omissions, repetitions, disruptions, polarities, reifications, violence. In other words, they give the texts a deeper, richer, more complex life than the sanitized one commonly presented to us. It would be a pity if criticism of this literature continued to shellac these texts, immobilizing their complexities and power beneath its tight, reflecting surface. It would be a pity if the criticism remained too polite or too fearful to notice a disrupting darkness before its eyes.

Unspeakable Things Unspoken

The Afro-American Presence in American Literature

I

I planned to call this paper "Canon Fodder," because the terms put me in mind of a kind of trained muscular response that appears to be on display in some areas of the recent canon debate. Also I liked the clash and swirl of those two words. At first they reminded me of that host of young men—black or "ethnics" or poor or working class—who left high school for the war in Vietnam and were perceived by war resisters as "fodder." Indeed many of those who went, as well as those who returned, were treated as one of that word's definitions: "coarse food for livestock," or, in the context of my thoughts about the subject of this paper, a more applicable definition: "people considered as readily available and of little value." Rude feed to feed the war machine. There was also the play of *cannon* and *canon*. The etymology of the first includes *tube, cane*, or *cane-like, reed*. Of the second, sources include *rod* becoming *body of law, body of rules, measuring rod*. When the two words faced each other, the image became the shape of the cannon wielded on (or by) the body of law. The boom of power announcing an "officially recognized set of texts." Cannon defending canon, you might say. And without any etymological connection I heard *father* in *fodder*, and sensed *father* in both cannon and canon, ending up with "father food." And what does this father eat? Readily available people/texts of little value. But I changed my mind (so many have used the phrase) and hope to make clear the appropriateness of the title I settled on.

My purpose here is to observe the panoply of this most recent and most anxious series of questions concerning what should or does constitute a literary canon in order to suggest ways of addressing the Afro-American presence in American literature that require neither slaughter nor reification—views that may spring the whole literature of an entire nation from the solitude into which it has been locked. There is something called American literature that, according to conventional wisdom, is certainly not Chicano literature, or Afro-American literature, or Asian American, or Native American, or . . . It is somehow separate from them and they from it, and in spite of the efforts of recent literary histories, restructured curricula and anthologies, this separate confinement, be it breached or endorsed, is the subject of a large part of these debates. Although the terms used, like the vocabulary of earlier canon debates, refer to literary and/or humanistic value, aesthetic criteria, value-free or socially anchored readings, the contemporary battle plain is most often understood to be the claims of others against the white male origins and definitions of those values; whether those definitions reflect an eternal, universal, and transcending paradigm or whether they constitute a disguise for a temporal, political, and culturally specific program.

Part of the history of this particular debate is located in the successful assault that the feminist scholarship of men and women (black and white) made and continues to make on traditional literary discourse. The male part of the white male equation is already deeply engaged, and no one believes the body of literature and its criticism will ever again be what it was in 1965: the protected preserve of the thoughts and works and analytical strategies of white men.

It is, however, the "white" part of the question that this paper focuses on, and it is to my great relief that such terms as "white" and "race" can enter serious discussion of literature. Although still a swift and swiftly obeyed call to arms, their use is no longer forbidden.[1] It may appear churlish to doubt the sincerity, or question the proclaimed well-intentioned selflessness of a nine-hundred-year-old academy struggling through decades of chaos to "maintain standards." Yet of what use is it to go on about "quality" being the only criterion for greatness knowing that the definition of quality is itself the subject of much rage and is seldom universally agreed upon by everyone at all times? Is it to appropriate the term for reasons of state; to be in the position to distribute greatness or withhold it? Or to actively pursue the ways and places in which quality surfaces and stuns us into silence or into language worthy enough to describe it? What is possible is to try to recognize, identify, and applaud the fight for and triumph of quality when it is revealed to us and to let go the notion that only the dominant culture or gender can make those judgments, identify that quality, or produce it.

Those who claim the superiority of Western culture are entitled to that claim only when Western civilization is measured thoroughly against other civilizations and not found wanting, and when Western civilization owns up to its own sources in the cultures that preceded it.

A large part of the satisfaction I have always received from reading Greek tragedy, for example, is in its similarity to Afro-American communal structures (the function of song and chorus, the heroic struggle between the claims of community and individual hubris) and African religion and philosophy. In other words, that is part of the reason it has quality for me—I feel intellectually at home there. But that could hardly be so for those unfamiliar with my "home," and hardly a requisite for the pleasure they take. The point is, the form (Greek tragedy) makes available these varieties of provocative love because *it* is masterly—not because the civilization that is its referent was flawless or superior to all others.

One has the feeling that nights are becoming sleepless in some quarters, and it seems to me obvious that the recoil of traditional "humanists" and some postmodern theorists to this particular aspect of the debate, the "race" aspect, is as severe as it is because the claims for attention come from that segment of scholarly and artistic labor in which the mention of "race" is either inevitable or elaborately, painstakingly masked, and if all of the ramifications that the term demands are taken seriously, the bases of Western civilization will

require rethinking. Thus, in spite of its implicit and explicit acknowledgment, "race" is still a virtually unspeakable thing, as can be seen
in the apologies, notes of "special use," and circumscribed definitions
that accompany it[2]—not least of which is my own deference in surrounding it with quotation marks. Suddenly (for our purposes, suddenly) "race" does not exist. For three hundred years black Americans
insisted that "race" was no usefully distinguishing factor in human
relationships. During those same three centuries every academic discipline, including theology, history, and natural science, insisted "race"
was *the* determining factor in human development. When blacks discovered they had shaped or become a culturally formed race, and that
it had specific and revered difference, suddenly they were told there is
no such thing as "race," biological or cultural, that matters and that
genuinely intellectual exchange cannot accommodate it.[3] In trying to
understand the relationship between "race" and culture, I am tempted
to throw my hands up. It always seemed to me that the people who
invented the hierarchy of "race" when it was convenient for them
ought not to be the ones to explain it away, now that it does not suit
their purposes for it to exist. But there *is* culture, and both gender and
"race" inform and are informed by it. Afro-American culture exists,
and though it is clear (and becoming clearer) how it has responded
to Western culture, the instances where and means by which it has
shaped Western culture are poorly recognized or understood.

I want to address ways in which the presence of Afro-American
literature and the awareness of its culture both resuscitate the study
of literature in the United States and raise that study's standards. In
pursuit of that goal, it will suit my purposes to contextualize the route
canon debates have taken in Western literary criticism.

I do not believe this current anxiety can be attributed solely to the
routine, even cyclical arguments within literary communities reflecting unpredictable yet inevitable shifts in taste, relevance, or perception. Shifts in which an enthusiasm for and official endorsement of
William Dean Howells, for example, withered; or in which the legal-
ization of Mark Twain in critical court rose and fell like the fathoming of a sounding line (for which he may or may not have named

himself); or even the slow, delayed, but steady swell of attention and devotion on which Emily Dickinson soared to what is now, surely, a permanent crest of respect. No. Those were discoveries, reappraisals of individual artists. Serious but not destabilizing. Such accommodations were simple because the questions they posed were simple: Are there one hundred sterling examples of high literary art in American literature and no more? One hundred and six? If one or two fall into disrepute, is there space, then, for one or two others in the vestibule, waiting like girls for bells chimed by future husbands who alone can promise them security, legitimacy—and in whose hands alone rests the gift of critical longevity? Interesting questions, but, as I say, not endangering.

Nor is this detectable academic sleeplessness the consequence of a much more radical shift, such as the mid-nineteenth-century one heralding the authenticity of American literature itself. Or an even earlier upheaval—receding now into the distant past—in which theology and thereby Latin was displaced for the equally rigorous study of the classics and Greek to be followed by what was considered a strangely arrogant and upstart proposal: that English literature was a suitable course of study for an aristocratic education and not simply morally instructive fodder designed for the working classes. (The Chaucer Society was founded in 1848, four hundred years after Chaucer died.) No. This exchange seems unusual somehow, keener. It has a more strenuously argued (and felt) defense and a more vigorously insistent attack. And both defenses and attacks have spilled out of the academy into the popular press. Why? Resistance to displacement within or expansion of a canon is not, after all, surprising or unwarranted. That's what canonization is for. (And the question of whether there should be a canon or not seems disingenuous to me—there always is one whether there should be or not—for it is in the interests of the professional critical community to have one.) Certainly a sharp alertness as to *why* a work is or is not worthy of study is the legitimate occupation of the critic, the pedagogue, and the artist. What is astonishing in the contemporary debate is not the resistance to displacement of works or to the expansion of genre within it, but the virulent passion that accompanies this resistance and, more importantly, the quality of its defense weaponry. The guns are very big; the trigger fingers quick. But I am convinced the mechanism of the defenders of the flame is faulty. Not only may the hands of the gunslinging cowboy-scholars be blown off, not only may the target be missed, but the subject of the conflagration (the sacred texts) is sacrificed, disfigured in the battle. This canon fodder may kill the canon. And I, at least, do not intend to live without Aeschylus or William Shakespeare, or James or Twain or Hawthorne, or Melville, etc., etc., etc. There must be some way to enhance canon readings without enshrining them.

When Milan Kundera, in *The Art of the Novel*, identified the historical territory of the novel by saying, "The novel is Europe's creation" and that "the only context for grasping a novel's worth is the history of the European novel," the *New Yorker* reviewer stiffened. Kundera's "personal 'idea of the novel,'" he wrote, "is so profoundly Eurocentric that it's likely to seem exotic, even perverse, to American readers. . . . 'The Art of the Novel' gives off the occasional (but pungent) whiff of cultural arrogance, and we may feel that Kundera's discourse . . . reveals an aspect of his character that we'd rather not have known about. . . . In order to become the artist he now is, the Czech novelist had to discover himself a second time, as a European. But what if that second, grander possibility hadn't been there to be discovered? What if Broch, Kafka, Musil—all that reading—had never been a part of his education, or had entered it only as exotic, alien presences? Kundera's polemical fervor in 'The Art of the Novel' annoys us, as American readers, because we feel defensive, excluded from the transcendent 'idea of the novel' that for him seems simply to have been there for the taking. (If only he had cited, in his redeeming version of the novel's history, a few more heroes from the New World's culture.) Our novelists don't discover cultural values within themselves; they invent them."[4]

Kundera's views, obliterating American writers (with the exception of William Faulkner) from his own canon, are relegated to a "smugness" that Terrence Rafferty disassociates from Kundera's imaginative work and applies to the "sublime confidence" of his critical prose. The confidence of an exile who has the sentimental education of, and the choice to become, a European.

I was refreshed by Rafferty's comments. With the substitution of certain phrases, his observations and the justifiable umbrage he takes can be appropriated entirely by Afro-American writers regarding their own exclusion from the "transcendent 'idea of the novel.'" For the present turbulence seems not to be about the flexibility of a canon, its range among and between Western countries, but about its miscegenation. The word is informative here and I do mean its use. A powerful ingredient in this debate concerns the incursion of third-world or so-called minority literature into a Eurocentric stronghold. When the topic of third-world culture is raised, unlike the topic of Scandinavian culture, for example, a possible threat to and implicit criticism of the reigning equilibrium is seen to be raised as well. From the seventeenth century to the twentieth, the arguments resisting that incursion have marched in predictable sequence: (1) there is no Afro-American (or third-world) art, (2) it exists but is inferior, (3) it exists and is superior when it measures up to the "universal" criteria of Western art, (4) it is not so much "art" as ore—rich ore—that requires a Western or Eurocentric smith to refine it from its "natural" state into an aesthetically complex form.

A few comments on a larger, older, but no less telling academic struggle—an extremely successful one—may be helpful here. It is telling because it sheds light on certain aspects of this current debate and may locate its sources. I made reference above to the radical upheaval in canon building that took place at the inauguration of classical studies and Greek. This canonical rerouting from scholasticism to humanism was not merely radical, it must have been (may I say it?) savage. And it took some seventy years to accomplish. Seventy years to eliminate Egypt as the cradle of civilization *and* its model and replace it with Greece. The triumph of that process was that Greece lost its own origins and became itself original. A number of scholars in various disciplines (history, anthropology, ethnobotany, etc.) have put forward their research into cross-cultural and intercultural transmissions with varying degrees of success in the reception of their work. I am reminded of the curious publishing history of Ivan Van Sertima's work *They Came Before Columbus*, which researches the African presence in ancient America. I am reminded of Edward Said's *Orientalism*, and especially the work of Martin Bernal, a linguist trained in Chinese history, who has defined himself as an interloper in the field of classical civilization but who has offered, in *Black Athena*, a stunning investigation of the field. According to Bernal, there are two "models" of Greek history: one views Greece as Aryan or European (the Aryan Model); the other sees it as Levantine—absorbed by Egyptian and Semitic culture (the Ancient Model). "If I am right," writes Professor Bernal, "in urging the overthrow of the Aryan Model and its replacement by the Revised Ancient one, it will be necessary not only to rethink the fundamental bases of 'Western Civilization' but also to recognize the penetration of racism and 'continental chauvinism' into all our historiography, or philosophy of writing history. The Ancient Model had no major 'internal' deficiencies or weaknesses in explanatory power. It was overthrown for external reasons. For eighteenth- and nineteenth-century Romantics and racists it was simply intolerable for Greece, which was seen not merely as the epitome of Europe but also as its pure childhood, to have been the result of the mixture of native Europeans and *colonizing* Africans and Semites. Therefore the Ancient Model had to be overthrown and replaced by something more acceptable."[5]

It is difficult not to be persuaded by the weight of documentation Martin Bernal brings to his task and his rather dazzling analytical insights. What struck me in his analysis were the *process* of the fabrication of Ancient Greece and the *motives* for the fabrication. The latter (motive) involved the concept of purity, of progress. The former (process) required misreading, predetermined selectivity of authentic sources, and—silence. From the Christian theological appropriation of Israel (the Levant), to the early nineteenth-century work of the prodigious Karl Müller, work that effectively dismissed the Greeks' own record of their influences and origins as their "Egyptomania," their tendency to be "wonderstruck" by Egyptian culture, a tendency "manifested in the 'delusion' that Egyptians and other non-European 'barbarians' had possessed superior cultures, from which the Greeks had borrowed massively,"[6] on through the Romantic response to the Enlightenment, and the decline into disfavor of the Phoenicians, "the essential force behind the rejection of the tradition of massive Phoenician influence on early Greece was the rise of racial—as opposed to religious—anti-Semitism. This was because the Phoenicians were correctly perceived to have been culturally very close to the Jews."[7]

I have quoted at perhaps too great a length from Bernal's text because *motive*, so seldom an element brought to bear on the history of history, is located, delineated, and confronted in Bernal's research and has helped my own thinking about the process and motives of scholarly attention to and an appraisal of Afro-American presence in the literature of the United States.

Canon building is empire building. Canon defense is national defense. Canon debate, whatever the terrain, nature, and range (of criticism, of history, of the history of knowledge, of the definition of language, the universality of aesthetic principles, the sociology of art, the humanistic imagination), is the clash of cultures. And *all* of the interests are vested.

In such a melee as this one—a provocative, healthy, explosive melee—extraordinarily profound work is being done. Some of the controversy, however, has degenerated into ad hominem and unwarranted speculation on the personal habits of artists, specious and silly arguments about politics (the destabilizing forces are dismissed as merely political; the status quo sees itself as not—as though the term "*apolitical*" were only its prefix and not the most obviously political stance imaginable since one of the functions of political ideology is to pass itself off as immutable, natural, and "innocent"), and covert expressions of critical inquiry designed to neutralize and disguise the political interests of the discourse. Yet much of the research and analysis has rendered speakable what was formerly unspoken and has made humanistic studies, once again, the place where one has to go to find out what's going on. Cultures, whether silenced or monologistic, whether repressed or repressing, seek meaning in the language and images available to them.

Silences are being broken, lost things have been found, and at least two generations of scholars are disentangling received knowledge from the apparatus of control, most notably those who are engaged in investigations of French and British colonialist literature, American slave narratives, and the delineation of the Afro-American literary tradition.

Now that Afro-American artistic presence has been "discovered" actually to exist, now that serious scholarship has moved from silencing the witnesses and erasing their meaningful place in and contribution to American culture, it is no longer acceptable merely to imagine us and imagine for us. We have always been imagining ourselves. We are not Isak Dinesen's "aspects of nature," nor Conrad's unspeaking. We are the subjects of our own narrative, witnesses to and participants in our own experience, and, in no way coincidentally, in the experience of those with whom we have come in contact. We are not, in fact, "Other." We are choices. And to read imaginative literature by and about us is to choose to examine centers of the self and to have the opportunity to compare these centers with the "raceless" one with which we are, all of us, most familiar.

II

Recent approaches to the reading of Afro-American literature have come some distance; have addressed those arguments, mentioned earlier (which are not arguments, but attitudes), that have, since the seventeenth century, effectively silenced the autonomy of that literature. As for the charge that "there is no Afro-American art," contemporary critical analysis of the literature and the recent surge of reprints and rediscoveries have buried it, and are pressing on to expand the traditional canon to include classic Afro-American works where generically and chronologically appropriate, and to devise strategies for reading and thinking about these texts.

As to the second silencing charge, "Afro-American art exists, but is inferior," again, close readings and careful research into the culture out of which the art is born have addressed and still address the labels that once passed for stringent analysis but can no more: that it is imitative, excessive, sensational, mimetic (merely), and unintellectual, though very often "moving," "passionate," "naturalistic," "realistic," or sociologically "revealing." These labels may be construed as compliments or pejoratives and if valid, and shown as such, so much the better. More often than not, however, they are the lazy, easy, brand-name applications when the hard work of analysis is deemed too hard, or when the critic does not have access to the scope the work demands. Strategies designed to counter this lazy labeling include the application of recent literary theories to Afro-American literature so that noncanonical texts can be incorporated into existing and forming critical discourse.

The third charge, that "Afro-American art exists, but is superior only when it measures up to the 'universal' criteria of Western art," produces the most seductive form of analysis, for both writer and critic, because comparisons are a major form of knowledge and flattery. The risks, nevertheless, are twofold: (1) the gathering of a culture's difference into the skirts of the queen is a neutralization designed and constituted to elevate and maintain hegemony, (2) circumscribing and limiting the literature to a mere reaction to or denial of the queen, judging the work solely in terms of its referents to Eurocentric criteria, or its sociological accuracy, political correctness, or its pretense of having no politics at all, cripple the literature and infantilize the serious work of imaginative writing. This response-oriented concept of Afro-American literature contains the seeds of the next (fourth) charge: that when Afro-American art is worthy, it is because it is "raw" and "rich," like ore, and like ore needs refining by Western intelligences. Finding or imposing Western influences in/on Afro-American literature has value, but when its sole purpose is to *place* value only where that influence is located it is pernicious.

My unease stems from the possible, probable consequences these approaches may have upon the work itself. They can lead to an incipient orphanization of the work in order to issue its adoption papers. They can confine the discourse to the advocacy of diversification within the canon and/or a kind of benign coexistence near or within reach of the already sacred texts. Either of these two positions can quickly become another kind of silencing if permitted to ignore the indigenous created qualities of the writing. So many questions surface and irritate. What have these critiques made of the work's own canvas? Its paint, its frame, its framelessness, its spaces? Another list of approved subjects? Of approved treatments? More self-censoring, more exclusion of the specificity of the culture, the gender, the language? Is there perhaps an alternative utility in these studies? To advance power or locate its fissures? To oppose elitist interests in order to enthrone egalitarian effacement? Or is it merely to rank and grade the readable product as distinct from the writeable production? Can this criticism reveal ways in which the author combats and confronts received prejudices and even creates *other terms* in which to rethink one's attachment to or intolerance of the material of these works? What is important in all of this is that the critic not be engaged in laying claim on behalf of the text to his or her own dominance and power. Nor to exchange his or her professional anxieties for the imagined turbulence of the text. As has been said before, "the text should become a problem of passion, not a pretext for it."

There are at least three focuses that seem to me to be neither reactionary nor simple pluralism, nor the even simpler methods by which the study of Afro-American literature remains the helpful doorman into the halls of sociology. Each of them, however, requires wakefulness.

One is the development of a theory of literature that truly accommodates Afro-American literature: one that is based on its culture, its history, and the artistic strategies the works employ to negotiate the world it inhabits.

Another is the examination and reinterpretation of the American canon, the founding nineteenth-century works, for the "unspeakable things unspoken"; for the ways in which the presence of Afro-Americans has shaped the choices, the language, the structure—the meaning of so much American literature. A search, in other words, for the ghost in the machine.

A third is the examination of contemporary and/or noncanonical literature for this presence, regardless of its category as mainstream, minority, or what you will. I am always amazed by the resonances, the structural gear-shifts, and the uses to which Afro-American narratives, persona, and idiom are put in contemporary "white" literature. And in Afro-American literature itself the question of difference, of essence, is critical. What makes a work "black"? The most valuable point of entry into the question of cultural (or racial) distinction, the one most fraught, is its language—its unpoliced, seditious, confrontational, manipulative, inventive, disruptive, masked, and unmasking language. Such a penetration will entail the most careful study, one in which the impact of Afro-American presence on modernity becomes clear and is no longer a well-kept secret.

I would like to touch, for just a moment, on focuses two and three. We can agree, I think, that invisible things are not necessarily "not-there"; that a void may be empty, but is not a vacuum. In addition, certain absences are so stressed, so ornate, so planned, they call attention to themselves, arrest us with intentionality and purpose, like neighborhoods that are defined by the population held away from them. Looking at the scope of American literature, I can't help thinking that the question should never have been "Why am I, an Afro-American, absent from it?" It is not a particularly interesting query anyway. The spectacularly interesting question is "What intellectual feats had to be performed by the author or his critic to erase me from a society seething with my presence, and what effect has that performance had on the work?" What are the strategies of escape from knowledge? Of willful oblivion? I am not recommending an inquiry into the obvious impulse that overtakes a soldier sitting in a World War I trench to think of salmon fishing. That kind of pointed "turning from," deliberate escapism, or transcendence may be lifesaving in a circumstance of immediate duress. The exploration I am suggesting is, how does one sit in the audience observing, watching the performance of *Young America*, in 1915 say, and reconstruct the play, its director, its plot, and its cast in such a manner that its very point never surfaces? Not why. How? Ten years after Tocqueville's prediction in 1840 that " 'finding no stuff for the ideal in what is real and true, poets' would flee to imaginary regions,"[8] in 1850 at the height of slavery and burgeoning abolitionism, American writers chose romance.

Where, I wonder, in these romances is the shadow of the presence from which the text has fled? Where does it heighten, where does it dislocate, where does it necessitate novelistic invention; what does it release; what does it hobble?

The device (or arsenal) that serves the purpose of flight can be Romanticism versus verisimilitude; New Criticism versus shabbily disguised and questionably sanctioned "moral uplift"; the "complex series of evasions" that is sometimes believed to be the essence of modernism; the perception of the "evolution of art"; the cultivation of irony, parody; the nostalgia for "literary language"; the rhetorically unconstrained textuality versus socially anchored textuality, and the undoing of textuality altogether. These critical strategies can (but need not) be put into service to reconstruct the historical world to suit specific cultural and political purposes. Many of these strategies have produced powerfully creative work. Whatever uses to which romanticism is put, however suspicious its origins, it has produced an incontestably wonderful body of work. In other instances these strategies have succeeded in paralyzing both the work and its criticism. In still others they have led to a virtual infantilization of the writer's intellect, his sensibility, his craft. They have reduced the meditations on theory into a "power struggle among sects" reading unauthored and unauthorable material, rather than reading *with* the author the text that both construct.

In other words, the critical process has made wonderful work of some wonderful work, and recently the means of access to the old debates have altered. The problem now is putting the question. Is the nineteenth-century flight from blackness, for example, successful in mainstream American literature? Beautiful? Artistically problematic? Is the text sabotaged by its own proclamations of "universality"? Are there ghosts in the machine? Active but unsummoned presences that can distort the workings of the machine and can also *make* it work? These kinds of questions have been consistently put by critics of colonial literature vis-à-vis Africa and India and other third-world countries. American literature would benefit from similar critiques. I am made melancholy when I consider that the act of defending the

Eurocentric Western posture in literature as not only "universal" but also "race-free" may have resulted in lobotomizing that literature, and in diminishing both the art and the artist. Like the surgical removal of legs so that the body can remain enthroned, immobile, static—under house arrest, so to speak. It may be, of course, that contemporary writers deliberately exclude from their conscious writerly world the subjective appraisal of groups perceived as "Other," and white male writers frequently abjure and deny the excitement of framing or locating their literature in the political world. Nineteenth-century writers, however, would never have given it a thought. Mainstream writers in young America understood their competition to be national, cultural, but only in relationship to the Old World, certainly not vis-à-vis an ancient race (whether Native American or African) that was stripped of articulateness and intellectual thought, rendered, in D. H. Lawrence's term, "uncreate." For these early American writers, how could there be competition with nations or peoples who were presumed unable to handle or uninterested in handling the written word? One could write about them, but there was never the danger of their "writing back." Just as one could speak to them without fear of their "talking back." One could even observe them, hold them in prolonged gaze, without encountering the risk of being observed, viewed, or judged in return. And if, on occasion, they were themselves viewed and judged, it was out of a political necessity and, for the purposes of art, could not matter. Or so thought young America. It could never have occurred to Edgar Allan Poe in 1848 that I, for example, might read "The Gold-Bug" and watch his efforts to render my grandfather's speech to something as close to braying as possible, an effort so intense you can see the perspiration—and the stupidity—when Jupiter says, "I knows," and Mr. Poe spells the verb "nose."*

Yet in spite or because of this monologism there is a great, ornamental, prescribed absence in early American literature and, I submit,

---

* Author's note: Older America is not always distinguishable from its infancy. We may pardon Edgar Allan Poe in 1843 but it should have occurred to Kenneth Lynn in 1986 that some young Native American might read his Hemingway biography and see herself described as a "squaw" by this respected scholar, and that some young men might shudder reading the words "buck" and "half-breed" so casually included in his scholarly speculations.

it is instructive. It only seems that the canon of American literature is "naturally" or "inevitably" "white." In fact it is studiously so. In fact these absences of vital presences in young American literature may be the insistent fruit of the scholarship rather than the text. Perhaps some of these writers, although under current house arrest, have much more to say than has been realized. Perhaps some were not so much transcending politics, or escaping blackness, as they were transforming it into intelligible, accessible, yet artistic modes of discourse. To ignore this possibility by never questioning the strategies of transformation is to disenfranchise the writer, diminish the text, and render the bulk of the literature aesthetically and historically incoherent—an exorbitant price for cultural (white male) purity, and, I believe, a spendthrift one. The reexamination of founding literature of the United States for the unspeakable unspoken may reveal those texts to have deeper and other meanings, deeper and other power, deeper and other significances.

One such writer, in particular, it has been almost impossible to keep under lock and key is Herman Melville.

Among several astute scholars, Michael Rogin has done one of the most exhaustive studies of how deeply Melville's social thought is woven into his writing. He calls our attention to the connection Melville made between American slavery and American freedom, how heightened the one rendered the other. And he has provided evidence of the impact on the work of Melville's family, milieu, and, most importantly, the raging, all-encompassing conflict of the time: slavery. He has reminded us that it was Melville's father-in-law, Judge Shaw, who had, as judge, decided the case that made the Fugitive Slave Law law, and that "other evidence in *Moby-Dick* also suggests the impact of Shaw's ruling on the climax of Melville's tale. Melville conceived the final confrontation between Ahab and the white whale sometime in the first half of 1851. He may well have written his last chapters only after returning from a trip to New York in June. (Judge Shaw's decision was handed down in April 1851.) When New York antislavery leaders William Seward and John van Buren wrote public letters protesting the *Sims* ruling, the New York *Herald* responded. Its attack on 'The Anti-Slavery Agitators' began, 'Did you ever see a whale? Did you ever see a mighty whale struggling?' "[9]

Rogin also traces the chronology of the whale from its "birth in a state of nature" to its final end as commodity.[10] Central to his argument is that Melville in *Moby-Dick* was being allegorically and insistently political in his choice of the whale. But within his chronology, one singular whale transcends all others, goes beyond nature, adventure, politics, and commodity to an abstraction. What is this abstraction? This "wicked idea"? Interpretation has been varied. It has been viewed as an allegory of the state in which Ahab is Calhoun, or Daniel Webster; an allegory of capitalism and corruption, God and man, the individual and fate, and most commonly, the single allegorical meaning of the white whale is understood to be brute, indifferent Nature, and Ahab the madman who challenges that Nature.

But let us consider, again, the principal actor, Ahab, created by an author who calls himself Typee, signed himself Tawney, identified himself as Ishmael, and who had written several books before *Moby-Dick* criticizing missionary forays into various paradises.

Ahab loses sight of the commercial value of his ship's voyage, its point, and pursues an idea in order to destroy it. His intention, revenge, "an audacious, immitigable and supernatural revenge," develops stature—maturity—when we realize that he is not a man mourning his lost leg or a scar on his face. However intense and dislocating his fever and recovery had been after his encounter with the white whale, however satisfactorily "male" this vengeance is read, the vanity of it is almost adolescent. But if the whale is more than blind, indifferent Nature unsubduable by masculine aggression, if it is as much its adjective as it is its noun, we can consider the possibility that Melville's "truth" was his recognition of the moment in America when whiteness became ideology. And if the white whale is the ideology of race, what Ahab has lost to it is personal dismemberment and family and society and his own place as a human in the world. The trauma of racism is, for the racist and the victim, the severe fragmentation of the self, and has always seemed to me a cause (not a symptom) of psychosis—strangely of no interest to psychiatry. Ahab, then, is navigating between an idea of civilization that he renounces and an idea of savagery he must annihilate, because the two cannot coexist. The former is based on the latter. What is terrible in its complexity is that the idea of savagery is not the missionary one: it is white racial ideology that is savage and if, indeed, a white, nineteenth-century American male took on not abolition, not the amelioration of racist institutions or their laws, but the very concept of whiteness as an inhuman idea, he would be very alone, very desperate, and very doomed. Madness would be the only appropriate description of such audacity, and "he heaves me," the most succinct and appropriate description of that obsession.

I would not like to be understood to argue that Melville was engaged in some simple and simpleminded black/white didacticism, or that he was satanizing white people. Nothing like that. What I am suggesting is that he was overwhelmed by the philosophical and metaphysical inconsistencies of an extraordinary and unprecedented idea that had its fullest manifestation in his own time in his own country, and that that idea was the successful assertion of whiteness as ideology.

On the *Pequod* the multiracial, mainly foreign, proletariat is at work to produce a commodity, but it is diverted and converted from that labor to Ahab's more significant intellectual quest. We leave whale as commerce and confront whale as metaphor. With that interpretation in place, two of the most famous chapters of the book become luminous in a completely new way. One is chapter 9, "The Sermon." In Father Mapple's thrilling rendition of Jonah's trials, emphasis is given to the purpose of Jonah's salvation. He is saved from the fish's belly for one single purpose, "To preach the Truth to the face of Falsehood! That was it!" Only then the reward—"Delight"—which strongly calls to mind Ahab's lonely necessity.

> Delight is to him . . . who against the proud gods and commodores of this earth, ever stand forth his own inexorable self. . . . Delight is to him whose strong arms yet support him, when the ship of this base treacherous world has gone down beneath him. Delight is to him, who gives no quarter in the truth, and kills, burns, and destroys all *sin* though he pluck it out from under the robes of Senators and Judges. Delight—top-gallant delight is to him, who acknowledges no law or lord, but the Lord his God, and is only a *patriot to heaven* (italics mine).

No one, I think, has denied that the sermon is designed to be prophetic, but it seems unremarked what the nature of the sin is—the sin that must be destroyed, regardless. Nature? A sin? The terms do not apply. Capitalism? Perhaps. Capitalism fed greed lent itself inexorably to corruption, but probably was not in and of itself sinful to Melville. Sin suggests a moral outrage within the bounds of New World man to repair. The concept of racial superiority would fit seamlessly. It is difficult to read those words ("destroys all sin," "patriot to heaven") and not hear in them the description of a different Ahab. Not an adolescent male in adult clothing, a maniacal egocentric, or the "exotic plant" that V. L. Parrington thought Melville was. Not even a morally fine liberal voice adjusting, balancing, compromising with racial institutions. But another Ahab: the only white male American heroic enough to try to slay the monster that was devouring the world as he knew it.

Another chapter that seems freshly lit by this reading is chapter 42, "The Whiteness of the Whale." Melville points to the do-or-die significance of his effort to say something unsayable in this chapter. "I almost despair," he writes, "of putting it in a comprehensive form. It was the whiteness of the whale that above all things appalled me. But how can I hope to explain myself here; and yet, in some dim, random way, explain myself I must, *else all these chapters might be naught*" (italics mine). The language of this chapter ranges between benevolent, beautiful images of whiteness and whiteness as sinister and shocking. After dissecting the ineffable, he concludes: "Therefore . . . symbolize whatever grand or gracious thing he will by whiteness, no man can deny that in its profoundest *idealized significance* it calls up a peculiar apparition to the soul." I stress "idealized significance" to emphasize and make clear (if such clarity needs stating) that Melville is not exploring white *people*, but whiteness idealized. Then, after informing the reader of his "hope to light upon some chance clue to conduct us to the hidden cause we seek," he tries to nail it. To provide the key to the "hidden cause." His struggle to do so is gigantic. He cannot. Nor can we. But in nonfigurative language, he identifies the imaginative tools needed to solve the problem: "Subtlety appeals to subtlety, and without imagination no man can follow another into these halls." And his final observation reverberates with personal trauma. "This visible [colored] world seems formed in love, the invisible [white] spheres were formed in fright." The necessity for whiteness as privileged "natural" state, the invention of it, was indeed formed in fright.

"Slavery," writes Rogin, "confirmed Melville's isolation, decisively established in *Moby-Dick*, from the dominant consciousness of his time." I differ on this point and submit that Melville's hostility to and repugnance for slavery would have found company. There were many white Americans of his acquaintance who felt repelled by slavery, wrote journalism about it, spoke about it, legislated on it, and were active in abolishing it. His attitude to slavery alone would not have condemned him to the almost autistic separation visited upon him. And if he felt convinced that blacks were worthy of being treated like whites, or that capitalism was dangerous—he had company or could have found it. But to question the very notion of white progress, the very idea of racial superiority, of whiteness as privileged place in the evolutionary ladder of humankind, and to meditate on the fraudulent, self-destroying philosophy of that superiority, to "pluck it out from under the robes of Senators and Judges," to drag the "judge himself to the bar"—that was dangerous, solitary, radical work. Especially then. Especially now. To be "only a patriot to heaven" is no mean aspiration in young America for a writer—or the captain of a whaling ship.

A complex, heaving, disorderly, profound text is *Moby-Dick*, and among its several meanings it seems to me this "unspeakable" one has remained the "hidden cause," the "Truth to the face of Falsehood." To this day no novelist has so wrestled with his subject. To this day literary analyses of canonical texts have shied away from that perspective: the informing and determining Afro-American presence in traditional American literature. The chapters I have made reference to are only a fraction of the instances where the text surrenders such insights, and points a helpful finger toward the ways in which the ghost drives the machine.

Melville is not the only author whose works double their fascination and their power when scoured for this presence and the writerly strategies taken to address or deny it. Edgar Allan Poe will sustain such a reading. So will Nathaniel Hawthorne and Mark Twain, and in the twentieth century, Willa Cather, Ernest Hemingway, F. Scott Fitzgerald, T. S. Eliot, Flannery O'Connor, and William Faulkner, to name a few. Canonical American literature is begging for such attention.

It seems to me a more than fruitful project to produce some cogent analysis showing instances where early American literature identifies itself, risks itself, to assert its antithesis to blackness. How its linguistic gestures prove the intimate relationship to what is being nulled by implying a full descriptive apparatus (identity) to a presence-that-is-assumed-not-to-exist. Afro-American critical inquiry can do this work.

I mentioned earlier that finding or imposing Western influences in/on Afro-American literature had value provided the valued process does not become self-anointing. There is an adjacent project to be undertaken—the third focus in my list: the examination of contemporary literature (both the sacred and the profane) for the impact Afro-American presence has had on the structure of the work, the linguistic practice, and fictional enterprise in which it is engaged. Like focus two, this critical process must also eschew the pernicious goal of equating the fact of that presence with the achievement of the work. A work does not get better because it is responsive to another culture, nor does it become automatically flawed because of that responsiveness. The point is to clarify, not to enlist. And it does not "go without saying" that a work written by an Afro-American is automatically subsumed by an enforcing Afro-American presence. There is a clear flight from blackness in a great deal of Afro-American literature. In others there is the duel with blackness, and in some cases, as they say, "You'd never know."

III

It is on this area, the impact of Afro-American culture on contemporary American literature, that I now wish to comment. I have already said that works by Afro-Americans can respond to this presence (just as nonblack works do) in a number of ways. The question of what constitutes the art of a black writer, for whom that modifier is more search than fact, has some urgency. In other words, other than melanin and subject matter, what, in fact, may make me a black writer? Other than my own ethnicity—what is going on in my work that makes me believe it is demonstrably inseparable from a cultural specificity that is Afro-American?

Please forgive the use of my own work in these observations. I use it not because it provides the best example, but because I know it best, know what I did and why, and know how central these queries are to me. Writing is, *after* all, an act of language, its practice. But *first* of all it is an effort of the will to discover.

Let me suggest some of the ways in which I activate language and ways in which that language activates me. I will limit this perusal by calling attention only to the first sentences of the books I've written, and hope that in exploring the choices I made, prior points are illuminated.

The Bluest Eye begins, "Quiet as it's kept, there were no marigolds in the fall of 1941." That sentence, like the ones that open each succeeding book, is simple, uncomplicated. Of all the sentences that begin all the books, only two of them have dependent clauses; the other three are simple sentences and two are stripped down to virtually subject, verb, modifier. Nothing fancy here. No words need looking up; they are ordinary, everyday words. Yet I hoped the simplicity was not simpleminded, but devious, even loaded. And that the process of selecting each word, for itself and its relationship to the others in the sentence, along with the rejection of others for their echoes, for what is determined and what is not determined, what is almost there and what must be gleaned, would not theatricalize itself, would not erect a proscenium—at least not a noticeable one. So important to me was this unstaging, that in this first novel I summarized the whole of the book on the first page. (In the first edition, it was printed in its entirety on the jacket.)

The opening phrase of this sentence, "Quiet as it's kept," had several attractions for me. First, it was a familiar phrase, familiar to me as a child listening to adults; to black women conversing with one another; telling a story, an anecdote, gossip about someone or some event within the circle, the family, the neighborhood. The words are conspiratorial. "Shh, don't tell anyone else" and "No one is allowed to know this." It is a secret between us and a secret that is being kept from us. The conspiracy is both held and withheld, exposed and sustained. In some sense it was precisely what the act of writing the book was: the public exposure of a private confidence. In order fully to comprehend the duality of that position, one needs to think of the immediate political climate in which the writing took place, 1965–1969, during great social upheaval in the life of black people. The publication (as opposed to the writing) involved the exposure; the writing was the disclosure of secrets, secrets "we" shared and those withheld from us by ourselves and by the world outside the community.

"Quiet as it's kept" is also a figure of speech that is written, in this instance, but clearly chosen for how speakerly it is, how it speaks and bespeaks a particular world and its ambience. Further, in addition to its "back fence" connotation, its suggestion of illicit gossip, of thrilling revelation, there is also, in the "whisper," the assumption (on the part of the reader) that the teller is on the inside, knows something others do not, and is going to be generous with this privileged information. The intimacy I was aiming for, the intimacy between the reader and the page, could start up immediately because the secret is being shared, at best, and eavesdropped upon, at the least. Sudden familiarity or instant intimacy seemed crucial to me then, writing my first novel. I did not want the reader to have time to wonder, "What do I have to do, to give up, in order to read this? What defense do I need, what distance maintain?" Because I know (and the reader does not—he or she has to wait for the second sentence) that this is a terrible story about things one would rather not know anything about.

What, then, is the Big Secret about to be shared? The thing we (reader and I) are "in" on? A botanical aberration. Pollution, perhaps. A skip, perhaps, in the natural order of things: a September, an autumn, a fall without marigolds. Bright common, strong and sturdy marigolds. When? In 1941, and since that is a momentous year (the beginning of World War II for the United States), the "fall" of 1941, just before the declaration of war, has a "closet" innuendo. In the temperate zone where there is a season known as "fall" during which one expects marigolds to be at their peak, in the months before the beginning of U.S. participation in World War II, something grim is about to be divulged. The next sentence will make it clear that the sayer, the one who knows, is a child speaking, mimicking the adult black women on the porch or in the backyard. The opening phrase is an effort to be grown-up about this shocking information. The point of view of a child alters the priority an adult would assign the information. "We thought . . . it was because Pecola was having her father's baby that the marigolds did not grow" foregrounds the flowers, backgrounds illicit, traumatic, incomprehensible sex coming to its dreaded fruition. This foregrounding of "trivial" information and backgrounding of shocking knowledge secures the point of view but gives the reader pause about whether the voice of children can be trusted at all or is more trustworthy than an adult's. The reader is thereby protected from a confrontation too soon with the painful details, while simultaneously provoked into a desire to know them. The novelty, I thought, would be in having this story of female violation revealed from the vantage point of the victims or could-be victims of rape—the persons no one inquired of (certainly not in 1965): the girls themselves. And since the victim does not have the vocabulary to understand the violence or its context, gullible, vulnerable girlfriends, looking back as the knowing adults they pretended to be in the beginning, would have to do that for her, and would have to fill those silences with their own reflective lives. Thus, the opening provides the stroke that announces something more than a secret shared, but a silence broken, a void filled, an unspeakable thing spoken at last. And they draw the connection between a minor destabilization in seasonal flora with the insignificant destruction of a black girl. Of course "minor" and "insignificant" represent the outside world's view—for the girls both phenomena are earthshaking depositories of information they spend that whole year of childhood (and afterwards) trying to fathom, and cannot. If they have any success, it will be in transferring the problem of fathoming to the presumably adult reader, to the inner circle of listeners. At the least they have distributed the weight of these problematical questions to a larger constituency, and justified the public exposure of a privacy. If the conspiracy that the opening words announce is entered into by the reader, then the book can be seen to open with its close: a speculation on the disruption of "nature," as being a social disruption with tragic individual consequences in which the reader, as part of the population of the text, is implicated.

However, a problem, unsolved, lies in the central chamber of the novel. The shattered world I built (to complement what is happening to Pecola), its pieces held together by seasons in childtime and commenting at every turn on the incompatible and barren white-family primer, does not in its present form handle effectively the silence at its center. The void that is Pecola's "unbeing." It should have had a shape—like the emptiness left by a boom or a cry. It required a sophistication unavailable to me, and some deft manipulation of the voices around her. She is not *seen* by herself until she hallucinates a self. And the fact of her hallucination becomes a point of outside-the-book conversation, but does not work in the reading process.

Also, although I was pressing for a female expressiveness (a challenge that resurfaced in *Sula*), it eluded me for the most part, and I had to content myself with female personae because I was not able to secure throughout the work the feminine subtext that is present in the opening sentence (the women gossiping, eager and aghast in "Quiet as it's kept"). The shambles this struggle became is most evident in the section on Pauline Breedlove where I resorted to two voices, hers and the urging narrator's, both of which are extremely unsatisfactory to me. It is interesting to me now that where I thought I would have the most difficulty subverting the language to a feminine mode, I had the least: connecting Cholly's "rape" by the white men to his own of his daughter. This most masculine act of aggression becomes feminized in my language, "passive," and, I think, more accurately repellent when deprived of the male "glamor of shame" rape is (or once was) routinely given.

The points I have tried to illustrate are that my choices of language (speakerly, aural, colloquial), my reliance for full comprehension on codes embedded in black culture, my effort to effect immediate coconspiracy and intimacy (without any distancing, explanatory fabric), as well as my (failed) attempt to shape a silence while breaking it are attempts (many unsatisfactory) to transfigure the complexity and wealth of Afro-American culture into a language worthy of the culture.

In *Sula*, it's necessary to concentrate on *two* first sentences because what survives in print is not the one I had intended to be the first. Originally the book opened with "Except for World War II nothing ever interfered with National Suicide Day." With some encouragement, I recognized that it was a false beginning. "In medias res" with a vengeance, because there was no res to be in the middle of—no implied world in which to locate the specificity and the resonances in the sentence. More to the point, I knew I was writing a second novel, and that it too would be about people in a black community not just foregrounded but totally dominant, and that it was about black women—also foregrounded and dominant. In 1988, certainly, I would not need (or feel the need for) the sentence—the short section—that now opens *Sula*. The threshold between the reader and the black-topic text need not be the safe, welcoming lobby I persuaded myself it needed at that time. My preference was the demolition of the lobby altogether. As can be seen from *The Bluest Eye,* and in every other book I have written, only *Sula* has this "entrance." The others refuse the "presentation"; refuse the seductive safe harbor, the line of demarcation between the sacred and the obscene, public and private, them and us. Refuse, in effect, to cater to the diminished expectations of the reader, or his or her alarm heightened by the emotional luggage one carries into the black-topic text. (I should remind you that *Sula* was begun in 1969, while my first book was in proof, in a period of extraordinary political activity.)

Since I had become convinced that the effectiveness of the original beginning was only in my head, the job at hand became how to construct an alternate beginning that would not force the work to genuflect and would complement the outlaw quality in it. The problem presented itself this way: to fashion a door. Instead of having the text open wide the moment the cover is opened (or, as in *The Bluest Eye,* to have the book stand exposed before the cover is even touched, much less opened, by placing the complete "plot" on the first page—and finally on the jacket of the first edition), here I was to posit a door, turn its knob, and beckon for some four or five pages. I had determined not to mention any characters in those pages, there would be no people in the lobby—but I did, rather heavy-handedly in my view, end the welcome aboard with the mention of Shadrack and Sula. It was a craven (to me, still) surrender to a worn-out technique of novel writing: the overt announcement to the reader whom to pay attention to. Yet the bulk of the opening I finally wrote is about the community, a view of it, and the view is not from within (this is a door, after all) but from the point of view of a stranger—the "valley man" who might happen to be there on some errand, but who obviously does not live there and to and for whom all this is mightily strange, even exotic. You can see why I despise much of this beginning. Yet I tried to place in the opening sentence the signature terms of loss: "There used to be a neighborhood here; not anymore." That may not be the world's worst sentence, but it doesn't "play," as they say in the theater.

My new first sentence became "In that place, where they tore the nightshade and blackberry patches from their roots to make room for the Medallion City Golf Course, there was once a neighborhood." Instead of my original plan, here I am introducing an outside-the-circle reader into the circle. I am translating the anonymous into the specific, a "place" into a "neighborhood," and letting a stranger in through whose eyes it can be viewed. In between "place" and "neighborhood" I now have to squeeze the specificity and the *difference*; the nostalgia, the history, and the nostalgia for the history; the violence done to it and the consequences of that violence. (It took three months, those four pages, a whole summer of nights.) The nostalgia is sounded by "once"; the history and a longing for it is implied in the connotation of "neighborhood." The violence lurks in having something torn out by its roots—it will not, cannot grow again. Its consequences are that what has been destroyed is considered weeds, refuse necessarily removed in urban "development" by the unspecified but no less known "they" who do not, cannot, afford to differentiate what is displaced, and would not care that this is "refuse" of a certain kind. Both plants have darkness in them: "black" and "night." One is unusual (nightshade) and has two darkness words: "night" and "shade." The other (blackberry) is common. A familiar plant and an exotic one. A harmless one and a dangerous one. One produces a nourishing berry; one delivers toxic ones. But they both thrived there together, *in that place when it was a neighborhood.* Both are gone now, and the description that follows is of the other specific things, in this black community, destroyed in the wake of the golf course. "Golf course" conveys what it is not, in this context: not houses, or factories, or even a public park, and certainly not residents. It is a manicured place where the likelihood of the former residents showing up is almost nil.

I want to get back to those berries for a moment (to explain, perhaps, the length of time it took for the language of that section to arrive). I always thought of Sula as quintessentially black, metaphysically black, if you will, which is not melanin and certainly not unquestioning fidelity to the tribe. She is New World black and New World woman extracting choice from choicelessness, responding inventively to found things. Improvisational. Daring, disruptive, imaginative, modern, out-of-the-house, outlawed, unpolicing, uncontained, and uncontainable. And dangerously female. In her final conversation with Nel she refers to herself as a special kind of black person woman, one with choices. Like a redwood, she says. (With all due respect to the dream landscape of Freud, trees have always seemed feminine to me.) In any case, my perception of Sula's double-dose of *chosen* blackness and *biological* blackness is in the presence of those two words of darkness in "nightshade" as well as in the uncommon quality of the vine itself. One variety is called "enchanter," and the other "bittersweet" because the berries taste bitter at first and then sweet. Also nightshade was thought to counteract witchcraft. All of this seemed a wonderful constellation of signs for Sula. And "blackberry patches" seemed equally appropriate for Nel: nourishing, never needing to be tended or cultivated, once rooted and bearing. Reliably sweet but thorn-bound. Her process of becoming, heralded by the explosive dissolving of her fragilely-held-together ball of string and fur (when the thorns of her self-protection are removed by Eva), puts her back in touch with the complex, contradictory, evasive, independent, liquid modernity Sula insisted upon. A modernity that overturns prewar definitions, ushers in the Jazz Age (an age *defined* by Afro-American art and culture), and requires new kinds of intelligences to define oneself.

The stage-setting of the first four pages is embarrassing to me now, but the pains I have taken to explain it may be helpful in identifying the strategies one can be forced to resort to in trying to accommodate the mere fact of writing about, for, and out of black culture while accommodating and responding to mainstream "white" culture. The "valley man's" guidance into the territory was my compromise. Perhaps it "worked," but it was not the work I wanted to do.

Had I begun with Shadrack, I would have ignored the smiling welcome and put the reader into immediate confrontation with his wound and his scar. The difference my preferred (original) beginning would have made would be calling greater attention to the traumatic displacement this most wasteful capitalist war had on black people in particular, and throwing into relief the creative, if outlawed, determination to survive it whole. Sula as (feminine) solubility and Shadrack's (male) fixative are two extreme ways of dealing with displacement—a prevalent theme in the narrative of black people. In the final opening I replicated the demiurge of discriminatory, prosecutorial racial oppression in the loss to commercial "progress" of the village, but the references to the community's stability and creativeness (music, dancing, craft, religion, irony, wit all referred to in the "valley man's" presence) refract and subsume their pain while they are in the thick of it. It is a softer embrace than Shadrack's organized, public madness—his disruptive remembering presence, which helps (for a while) to cement the community, until Sula challenges them.

"The North Carolina Mutual Life Insurance agent promised to fly from Mercy to the other side of Lake Superior at three o'clock."

This declarative sentence is designed to mock a journalistic style; with a minor alteration it could be the opening of an item in a small-town newspaper. It has the tone of an everyday event of minimal local interest, yet I wanted it to contain (as does the scene that takes place when the agent fulfills his promise) the information that *Song of Solomon* both centers on and radiates from.

The name of the insurance company is real, a well-known black-owned company dependent on black clients, and in its corporate name are "life" and "mutual," "agent" being the necessary ingredient of what enables the relationship between them. The sentence also moves from North Carolina to Lake Superior—geographical locations, but with a sly implication that the move from North Carolina (the South) to Lake Superior (the North) might not actually involve progress to some "superior state"—which, of course, it does not. The two other significant words are "fly," upon which the novel centers, and "Mercy," the name of the place from which he is to fly. Both constitute the heartbeat of the narrative. Where is the insurance man flying to? The other side of Lake Superior is Canada, of course, the historic terminus of the escape route for black people looking for asylum. "Mercy," the other significant term, is the grace note; the earnest though, with one exception, unspoken wish of the narrative's population. Some grant it; some never find it; one, at least, makes it the text and cry of her extemporaneous sermon upon the death of her granddaughter. It touches, turns, and returns to Guitar at the end of the book—he who is least deserving of it—and moves him to make it his own final gift. It is what one wishes for Hagar; what is unavailable to and unsought by Macon Dead, senior; what his wife learns to demand from him, and what can never come from the white world as is signified by the inversion of the name of the hospital from Mercy to "No Mercy." It is only available from within. The center of the narrative is flight; the springboard is mercy.

But the sentence turns, as all sentences do, on the verb: promised. The insurance agent does not declare, announce, or threaten his act. He promises, as though a contract is being executed—faithfully—between himself and others. Promises broken, or kept; the difficulty of ferreting out loyalties and ties that bind or bruise wend their way throughout the action and the shifting relationships. So the agent's flight, like that of the Solomon in the title, although toward asylum (Canada, or freedom, or home, or the company of the welcoming dead), and although it carries the possibility of failure and the certainty of danger, is toward change, an alternative way, a cessation of things-as-they-are. It should not be understood as a simple desperate act, the end of a fruitless life, a life without gesture, without examination, but as obedience to a deeper contract with his people. It is his commitment to them, regardless of whether, in all its details, they understand it. There is, however, in their response to his action, a tenderness, some contrition, and mounting respect ("They didn't know he had it in him") and an awareness that the gesture enclosed rather than repudiated themselves. The note he leaves asks for forgiveness. It is tacked on his door as a mild invitation to whomever might pass by, but it is not an advertisement. It is an almost Christian declaration of love as well as humility of one who was not able to do more.

There are several other flights in the work and they are motivationally different. Solomon's the most magical, the most theatrical, and, for Milkman, the most satisfying. It is also the most problematic—to those he left behind. Milkman's flight binds these two elements of loyalty (Mr. Smith's) and abandon and self-interest (Solomon's) into a third thing: a merging of fealty and risk that suggests the "agency" for "mutual" "life," which he offers at the end and which is echoed in the hills behind him, and is the marriage of surrender and domination, acceptance and rule, commitment to a group *through* ultimate isolation. Guitar recognizes this marriage and recalls enough of how lost he himself is to put his weapon down.

The journalistic style at the beginning, its rhythm of a familiar, hand-me-down dignity is pulled along by an accretion of detail displayed in a meandering unremarkableness. Simple words, uncomplex sentence structures, persistent understatement, highly aural syntax—but the ordinariness of the language, its colloquial, vernacular, humorous, and, upon occasion, parabolic quality sabotage expectations and masks judgments when it can no longer defer them. The composition of red, white, and blue in the opening scene provides the national canvas/flag upon which the narrative works and against which the lives of these black people must be seen, but which must not overwhelm the enterprise the novel is engaged in. It is a composition of color that heralds Milkman's birth, protects his youth, hides its purpose and through which he must burst (through blue Buicks, red tulips in his waking dream, and his sisters' white stockings, ribbons, and gloves) before discovering that the gold of his search is really Pilate's yellow orange and the glittering metal of the box in her ear.

These spaces, which I am filling in, and can fill in because they were planned, can conceivably be filled in with other significances. That is planned as well. The point is that into these spaces should fall the ruminations of the reader and his or her invented or recollected or misunderstood knowingness. The reader as narrator asks the questions the community asks, and both reader and "voice" stand among the crowd, within it, with privileged intimacy and contact, but without any more privileged information than the crowd has. That egalitarianism that places us all (reader, the novel's population, the narrator's voice) on the same footing reflected for me the force of flight and mercy, and the precious, imaginative, yet realistic gaze of black people who (at one time, anyway) did not anoint what or whom it mythologized. The "song" itself contains this unblinking evaluation of the miraculous and heroic flight of the legendary Solomon, an unblinking gaze that is lurking in the tender but amused choral-community response to the agent's flight. Sotto (but not completely) is my own giggle (in Afro-American terms) of the proto-myth of the journey to manhood. Whenever characters are cloaked in Western fable, they are in deep trouble, but the African myth is also contaminated. Unprogressive, unreconstructed, self-born Pilate is unimpressed by Solomon's flight and knocks Milkman down when, made new by his appropriation of his own family's fable, he returns to educate her with it. Upon hearing all he has to say, her only interest is filial. "Papa? . . . I've been carryin' Papa?" And her longing to hear the song, finally, is a longing for balm to die by, not a submissive obedience to history—anybody's.

The opening sentence of *Tar Baby,* "He believed he was safe," is the second version of itself. The first, "He thought he was safe," was discarded because "thought" did not contain the doubt I wanted to plant in the reader's mind about whether or not he really was—safe. "Thought" came to me at once because it was the verb my parents and grandparents used when describing what they had dreamed the night before. Not "I dreamt" or "It seemed" or even "I saw or did" this or that—but "I thought." It gave the dream narrative distance (a dream is not "real") and power (the control implied in "thinking" rather than "dreaming"). But to use "thought" seemed to undercut the faith of the character and the distrust I wanted to suggest to the reader. "Believe" was chosen to do the work properly. And the person who does the believing is, in a way, about to enter a dream world, and convinces himself, eventually, that he is in control of it. He believed; was convinced. And although the word suggests his conviction, it does not reassure the reader. If I had wanted the reader to trust this person's point of view I would have written "He was safe." Or, "Finally, he was safe." The unease about this view of safety is important because safety itself is the desire of each person in the novel. Locating it, creating it, losing it.

You may recall that I was interested in working out the mystery of a piece of lore, a folktale, which is also about safety and danger and the skills needed to secure the one and recognize and avoid the other. I was not, of course, interested in retelling the tale; I suppose that is an idea to pursue, but it is certainly not interesting enough to engage me for four years. I have said, elsewhere, that the exploration of the Tar Baby tale was like stroking a pet to see what the anatomy was like but not to disturb or distort its mystery. Folklore may have begun as allegory for natural or social phenomena; it may have been employed as a retreat from contemporary issues in art; but folklore can also contain myths that reactivate themselves endlessly through providers—the people who repeat, reshape, reconstitute, and reinterpret them. The Tar Baby tale seemed to me to be about masks. Not masks as covering what is to be hidden, but how masks come to life, take life over, exercise the tensions between themselves and what they cover. For Son, the most effective mask is none. For the others the construction is careful and delicately borne, but the masks they make have a life of their own and collide with those they come in contact with. The texture of the novel seemed to want leanness, architecture that was worn and ancient like a piece of mask sculpture: exaggerated, breathing, just athwart the representational life it displaced. Thus, the first and last sentences had to match, as the exterior planes match the interior, concave ones inside the mask. Therefore "He believed he was safe" would be the twin of "Lickety-split. Lickety-split. Lickety-lickety-lickety-split." This close is (1) the last sentence of the folktale, (2) the action of the character, (3) the indeterminate ending that follows from the untrustworthy beginning, (4) the complimentary meter of its twin sister (u u / u u / with u u u / u u u /), and (5) the wide and marvelous space between the contradiction of those two images: from a dream of safety to the sound of running feet. The whole mediated world in between. This masked and unmasked; enchanted, disenchanted; wounded and wounding world is played out on and by the varieties of interpretation (Western and Afro-American) the Tar Baby myth has been (and continues to be) subjected to. Winging one's way through the vise and expulsion of history becomes possible in creative encounters with that history. Nothing, in those encounters, is safe, or should be. Safety is the fetus of power as well as protection from it, as the uses to which masks and myths are put in Afro-American culture remind us.

"124 was spiteful. Full of a baby's venom."

In beginning *Beloved* with numerals rather than spelled out numbers, it was my intention to give the house an identity separate from the street or even the city; to name it the way "Sweet Home" was named; the way plantations were named, but not with nouns or "proper" names—with numbers instead because numbers have no adjectives, no posture of coziness or grandeur or the haughty yearning of arrivistes and estate builders for the parallel beautifications of the nation they left behind, laying claim to instant history and legend. Numbers here constitute an address, a thrilling enough prospect for slaves who had owned nothing, least of all an address. And although the numbers, unlike words, can have no modifiers, I give these an adjective—"spiteful" (there are two other modifiers of 124). The address is therefore personalized, but personalized by its own activity, not the pasted on desire for personality.

Also there is something about numerals that makes them spoken, heard, in this context, because one expects words to read in a book, not numbers to say, or hear. And the sound of the novel, sometimes cacophonous, sometimes harmonious, must be an inner-ear sound or a sound just beyond hearing, infusing the text with a musical emphasis that words can do sometimes even better than music can. Thus the second sentence is not one: it is a phrase that properly, grammatically, belongs as a dependent clause with the first. Had I done that, however ("124 was spiteful, full of a baby's venom," or "124 was full of a baby's venom"), I could not have had the accent on "full" (/ u u / u / u pause u u u u / u).

Whatever the risks of confronting the reader with what must be immediately incomprehensible in that simple, declarative authoritative sentence, the risk of unsettling him or her, I determined to take. Because the in medias res opening that I am so committed to is here excessively demanding. It is abrupt, and should appear so. No native informant here. The reader is snatched, yanked, thrown into an environment completely foreign, and I want it as the first stroke of the shared experience that might be possible between the reader and the novel's population. Snatched just as the slaves were from one place to another, from any place to another, without preparation and without defense. No lobby, no door, no entrance—a gangplank, perhaps (but a very short one). And the house into which this snatching—this kidnapping—propels one changes from spiteful to loud to quiet, as the sounds in the body of the ship itself may have changed. A few words have to be read before it is clear that "124" refers to a house (in most of the early drafts, "The women *in the house* knew it" was simply "The women knew it"; "house" was not mentioned for seventeen lines), and a few more have to be read to discover why it is spiteful, or rather the source of the spite. By then it is clear, if not at once, that something is beyond control, but is not beyond understanding since it is not beyond accommodation by both the "women" and the "children." The fully realized presence of the haunting is both a major incumbent of the narrative and sleight of hand. One of its purposes is to keep the reader preoccupied with the nature of the incredible spirit world while being supplied a controlled diet of the incredible political world.

The subliminal, the underground life of a novel is the area most likely to link arms with the reader and facilitate making it one's own. Because one must, to get from the first sentence to the next, and the next and the next. The friendly observation post I was content to build and man in *Sula* (with the stranger in the midst), or the down-home journalism of *Song of Solomon,* or the calculated mistrust of the point of view in *Tar Baby* would not serve here. Here I wanted the compelling confusion of being there as they (the characters) are; suddenly, without comfort or succor from the "author," with only imagination, intelligence, and necessity available for the journey. The painterly language of *Song of Solomon* was not useful to me in *Beloved.* There is practically no color whatsoever in its pages, and when there is, it is so stark and remarked upon, it is virtually raw. Color seen for the first time, without its history. No built architecture as in *Tar Baby;* no play with Western chronology as in *Sula;* no exchange between book life and "real" life discourse with printed text units rubbing up against seasonal black childtime units as in *The Bluest Eye.* No compound of houses, no neighborhood, no sculpture, no paint, no time, especially no time because memory, prehistoric memory, has no time. There is just a little music, each other, and the urgency of what is at stake. Which is all they had. For that work, the work of language is to get out of the way.

I hope you understand that in this explication of how I practice language is a search for and deliberate posture of vulnerability to those aspects of Afro-American culture that can inform and position my work. I sometimes know when the work works, when *nommo* has effectively summoned, by reading and listening to those who have entered the text. I learn nothing from those who resist it, except, of course, the sometimes fascinating display of their struggle. My expectations of and my gratitude to the critics who enter, are great. To those who talk about how as well as what; who identify the workings as well as the work; for whom the study of Afro-American literature is neither a crash course in neighborliness and tolerance, nor an infant to be carried, instructed, or chastised or even whipped like a child, but the serious study of art forms that have much work to do, and which are already legitimatized by their own cultural sources and predecessors—in or out of the canon—I owe much.

For an author, regarding canons, it is very simple: in fifty, a hundred, or more years his or her work may be relished for its beauty or its insight or its power, or it may be condemned for its vacuousness and pretension—and junked. Or in fifty or a hundred years the critic (as canon builder) may be applauded for his or her intelligent scholarship and powers of critical inquiry. Or laughed at for ignorance and shabbily disguised assertions of power—and junked. It's possible that the reputations of both will thrive, or that both will decay. In any case, as far as the future is concerned, when one writes, as critic or as author, all necks are on the line.

NOTES

1. See *"Race," Writing, and Difference,* ed. Henry Louis Gates (Chicago: University of Chicago Press, 1986).
2. Among many examples, *They Came Before Columbus, The African Presence in Ancient America* by Ivan Van Sertima (New York: Random House, 1976), xvi–xvii.
3. Tzvetan Todorov, "'Race,' Writing, and Culture," translated by Loulou Mack, in Gates, *"Race," Writing, and Difference,* 370–80.
4. Terrence Rafferty, "Articles of Faith," *New Yorker,* May 16, 1988, 110–18.
5. Martin Bernal, *Black Athena: The Afroasiatic Roots of Classical Civilization,* vol. 1, *The Fabrication of Ancient Greece 1785–1985* (New Brunswick, NJ: Rutgers University Press, 1987), 2.
6. Ibid., 310.
7. Ibid., 337.
8. See Michael Paul Rogin, *Subversive Genealogy: The Politics and Art of Herman Melville* (Berkeley: University of California Press, 1985), 15.
9. Ibid., 107 and 142.
10. Ibid., 112.

Academic Whispers

AT SOME TIME in the late eighties, I began to feel an uneasiness about what seemed to me a whispered conversation taking place within the study of African American literature, between students and masters of its scholarship; it appeared to be a private agreement about the true purpose of the discourse. My unease about this sotto dialogue was exacerbated by another blatant one that attacked and suborned the legitimacy of African American literature as a field of study. Both dialogues—the covert one and the blatant one—drove the debates on canon formation.

Back in the eighties I was not eager to think through my anxiety about the shape the debate was taking—the politics of identity versus the politics of identitylessness, sometimes known as "universality"—because I was not willing to be distracted into that old and sad routine that African American artists and scholars so often believe themselves forced to undertake: the routine of defending, forever defending, their right to exist. It was such a tedious battle, so unoriginal, so enervating it left no time and no strength for the real work of artists and scholars, which is to refine its own creation and go about their own business. I did not want to watch the billow of another toreador's red cape designed to provoke and thereby trick a force from knowing its own power. I chose rather to focus on how to create nonracist, yet race-specific literature within an already race-inflected language for readers who have been forced to deal with the assumptions of racial hierarchy. I chose to write as though there was nothing to prove or disprove, as though an unraced world already existed. Not to transcend race, or to aspire to some fraudulent "universalism"—a code word that had come to mean "nonblack"—but to claim the liberty of my own imagination. For I have never lived, nor has anyone, in a world in which race did not matter. Such a world, a world free of racial hierarchy, is usually imagined or described as dreamscape, Edenesque, utopian—so remote are the possibilities of its achievement. In hopeful language it has been posited as ideal, a condition possible only if accompanied by the Messiah or located in a protected preserve, rather like a wilderness park, or in the forests of Faulkner's imagination, where hunting prowess trumps race and class. As an already and always raced writer I knew that I would not, could not, reproduce the master's voice along with its assumptions of the all-knowing law of the white father. I wanted to figure out how to manipulate, mutate, and control imagistic, metaphoric language (and its syntax) in order to produce something that could be called literature that is free of the imaginative restraints that the racially inflected language at my disposal imposes on me. I don't mean, of course, simply the avoidance of racial slurs, name-calling, or stereotyping. I mean first to recognize these linguistic strategies, then either to employ or deploy them to achieve a counter effect; to deactivate their lazy, unearned power, to summon other oppositional powers, and liberate what I am able to invent, record, describe, and transform from the straitjacket a racialized society can and does buckle us into. I insisted on writing outside the white gaze, not against it but in a space where I could postulate the humanity writers were always being asked to enunciate. Writing of, about, and within a world committed to racial dominances without employing the linguistic strategies that supported it seemed to me the most urgent, fruitful, challenging work a writer could take on. As I mentioned earlier, imagining a world minus racial dominance or hierarchy appears in literature as an impossible Eden or unreachable utopia, but it has also been described as "barbarism," as "the end of history," "futureless," or doomed to a future of rubbish and declared an already damaged, valueless experience. In other words catastrophe. A naïve, corrupt Jonestown culminating in ignorance, murder, insanity.

Perhaps I was nursing an incipient paranoia, the origin of which I traced to the unusually large number of inquiries to speak to university populations on the issue of racism, and even to address campuses on which some specific and especially craven racial incidents had taken place. I was not simply annoyed by the assumptions of these requests, I was angered to be asked to clarify an area (one of many) about which I know nothing. Of course, I have been a victim of such treatment, but why, I wondered, would anybody ask the victim to explain his torturer? Isn't such insight best sought from those familiar with its rationale? (Does a rape victim know best how to calm a rapist?) It seemed to me the problem of racism ought to be addressed first by those who know its ins and outs from the privileged seat of its origin. Being asked to spend my time that way (to heal and to be sick) may have disturbed me unduly, but it connected somehow to my perception that the study of African American literature had become, in several quarters (if high school and certain college curricula, syllabi, anthologies, prefaces, headnotes, afterwords, and forewords were an indication) an exercise in the achievement of neighborliness or tolerance *through* the study of its special kind of pathology, in which the survivor is assumed to be both patient and physician. And this was where the whispered discourse took place.

With the best intentions in the world, the encounter between African American art and students of literature had developed these subtexts (*The Bluest Eye,* read in elementary schools, was a case in point, as was its banning). And it was easy to see how two messages—African American art as explications of pathology; African American art as restorative balms to rashes of racism—had been formulated and why. First, the history of black people in the United States has been a brutal one, and its consequences still shake and inform contemporary life. Examining and acknowledging that brutality can and does lend itself to the interpretation of black presence in that history as our pathology and only ours; it can and did lead to the notion that, as a people, we are a problem (the "negro problem" that every black writer from Richard Wright to Ralph Ellison to James Baldwin to Zora Neale Hurston had to comment on—not to mention the verification of literacy that Phillis Wheatley and the authors of slave narratives were required to provide) and it was our job to solve ourselves.

Countering that interpretation of African American studies as vaccination against incipient white racism is another one: African American studies as a field naturally immune from racism. That black life was a cornucopia of treasures, contributions, and constructive indigenous mechanisms beneficial to its community and that these social mechanisms operated as an innocent alternative to the race-bound society surrounding it. It is an interpretation that captures the sense that most African Americans have, that their real life, their nurturing life, their interior life is someplace else—outside its deforming history. And that obstacle-ridden as that life may be, it was clearly one they would choose, if the choice were presented to them. That while many (perhaps even most) African Americans valued the perceived privilege and license of white Americans, very few wanted to trade places if it meant becoming them.

Yet articulating this valued and revered difference seldom failed to come across as anything but self-serving, defensive patterns of denial: the "prideful" rhetoric typical of the weakened. Taking the position that history is not the determining factor, that stability, beauty, creativity, brilliance are the real characteristics of black life, seemed to weight (and in some circumstances, sully) the study of black culture with an ennobling program, an agenda, that broke its back in its attempt to enforce it.

These postures: (1) African American culture as examination and diagnoses of the patient, (2) African American culture as inoculation against intolerance, and (3) African American culture as an insistent celebration and recognition of cultural health and beauty (which could, by association or osmosis, heal others) clashed, and in the debris that resulted the literature itself was often buried. It appeared to me, as a writer participating in and inhabiting the world of that literature, that the work itself had become another kind of houseboy, opening doors for guests to enter a party to which it had not been invited.

Well, that was what was on my mind in the late eighties. Yet I determined not to be distracted from creative work into defense work and remained silent on the employment of my work as social healer. But there was still another problem. I understood and indeed preferred the role of writer committed to the work and not its explication. I believed anything and everything I had to say on the subject of African American literature was in the books I had written. Participating in their critique was antithetical to what I wanted my work to do, which was to arrive without tags, labels, or final meanings identified by me and pinned to its lapel. I wanted it owned by whomever wanted to take possession of it. Requests by diligent, earnest scholars for a conversation or interview to accompany their research seemed inappropriate, somehow, a kind of journalistic glue to hold together conclusions already drawn from primary and secondary sources. In addition, nobody was really interested in my thoughts about my books. They were, naturally and correctly, more interested in their own thoughts about them. I was just there in the conversation to provide confirmation or, in some cases, to be wrong, to be unable to understand what I had actually written. It was a long time, I confess, before I took these interviews seriously, because I associated them, unfairly, with journalism, not scholarship.

Finally I found myself forced to step up to the problem. My intense interest in the development of African American literary criticism and pedagogy and my refusal to participate in that criticism except as amicus curiae were incompatible once I understood that at the heart of my problem was a question at the heart of my work: that informing all of these kinds of approaches to the study of African American culture (pathology, tolerance, celebrated difference, erased difference; the writer as his or her best explicator, worse explicator, or friend of the court—or in my case an idle mixture) was the question, *What constitutes African American literature?* Is it the writing of Americans who "happen" to be Afro? Has it rather some cultural characteristics that surface, inform, and would surface and inform even if the literature had been shaped in Mexico City, London, Istanbul? Is there a difference? And if so, is the difference different from all other differences?

It does not "go without saying" that a work written by an African American is automatically subsumed by an enforcing black presence. There is a clear flight from blackness in a great deal of African American literature. In some there is an antagonistic duel with blackness. And in other cases, as they say, you'd never know. If I were to participate in the critical discourse, I would need to clarify the question of what, other than melanin and subject matter, made me an African American writer. I didn't expect to arrive at some quintessential moment when the search was ended, even if that were possible. But I did want to be counted among those for whom the quest was seriously taken and seriously pursued. Thus I entered the debate not as an artist only nor as an academic only, but as both. I believed that dual position could help expand and deepen the arguments about the validity, necessity, and direction of African American scholarship. Already there was significant work recontextualizing such studies, repositioning their impact in humanistic disciplines. But my interest turned from examining what black intellectuals and artists were up to, to something else. I was unhappy with the possibility of resegregation in African American studies—of driving the scholarship into protected turf where its uniqueness, its exceptionalism, its radical or even traditional characteristics could be interrogated, but where its powerful singularity could render it sui generis: a thing apart, in a class by itself. My thoughts were that African American studies could, but need not, confine itself to itself because the project was like the so-called race problem itself. It was not a neighborhood thriving or struggling at the edge of town, at the edge of campuses, at the outer rim of intellectual thought, nor was it an exotic, anthropologically interesting minority pulsing at the extremities of the body politic. It was and is at the heart of the heart of the nation. No policy decision could be understood without the black topic at its center, even or especially when unmentioned. Not housing, not education, the military, economy, voting, citizenship, prisons, loan practices, health care—name it, the real subject was what to do with black people, which became a substitute term for poor people. Very few disciplines escape the impact of racial constructs. Law, science, theology, medicine, medical ethics, psychiatry, anthropology, history were all implicated. Furthermore, was there any public discourse in which a reference to black people did not exist? As I wrote in *Playing in the Dark*, "It exists in every one of this nation's mightiest struggles." From the framing of the Constitution, to the Electoral College, "the battle over enfranchising unpropertied citizens, women, the illiterate . . . is there in the construction of a free and public school system; the balancing of representation in legislative bodies; jurisprudence and legal definitions of justice; it is there in . . . the memoranda of banking houses; the concept of manifest destiny and the driving narrative of the Americanization of every immigrant who came ashore." I was convinced there was no race card—there was simply a deck, each one operating on a terrain much wider than previously thought, echoing its influence in the national culture. The consequences of this inquiry was a series of twelve lectures, three of which became the book *Playing in the Dark*. In it I tried to articulate the breadth of the project and its complexity. African American studies could interrogate a large area of the cultural production, West and East, and in the process enliven and expand a wide variety of disciplines. That is, after all, the goal of education: access to more knowledge. There may come a time when we—students, faculty, administrators, artists, and parents—will have to fight hard for education, fight hard for uncorrupted science (not the ideological or racist science); for sound social history, apolitical anthropology (not strategies of control); for the integrity of art (not its celebrity).

There may indeed come a time when universities may have to fight for the privilege of intellectual freedom.

Gertrude Stein
and the Difference She Makes

I HAVE READ somewhere that there are two responses to chaos: naming and violence. The naming is accomplished effortlessly when there is a so-called unnamed, or stripped-of-names population or geography available for the process. Otherwise one has to be content with forcible renaming. Violence is understood as an inevitable response to chaos—the untamed, the wild, the savage—as well as a beneficial one. When one conquers a land the execution of the conquest, indeed its point, is to control it by reshaping, moving, cutting it down or through. And that is understood to be the obligation of industrial and/or cultural progress. This latter encounter with chaos, unfortunately, is not limited to land, borders, natural resources. In order to effect the industrial progress it is also necessary to do violence to the people who inhabit the land—for they will resist and render themselves anarchic, *part* of the chaos, and in certain cases the control has included introducing new and destructive forms of hierarchy, when successful, and attempts at genocide when not.

There is a third response to chaos, which I have not read about, which is stillness. Stillness is what lies in awe, in meditation; stillness also lies in passivity and dumbfoundedness. It may be that the early Americans contemplated all three: naming, violence, and stillness. Certainly this latter surfaces (or seems to) in Emerson, Thoreau, and the observer quality of Hawthorne. It is traceable in the Puritan ethos as well. But unlike the indigenous population of America, and unlike the bulk of the populations brought to America from Africa, the American stillness was braced with, even mitigated by, pragmatism. There was always an aspect of preparing for heirs, a distant future unresponsive to the past, and the virtue of wealth as God's bounty—which it was a sin not to accumulate. This highly materialistic "stillness" as practiced by the clerical/religious immigrants was in marked contrast to the "take only what you need and leave the land as you found it" philosophy of preindustrial societies. One of the more interesting matters in the Christian formation of public and private responsibility is the negotiation between thrift and awe; religious solace and natural exploitation; physical repression and spiritual bounty; the sacred and the profane. That negotiation persists in the tension among these three responses to chaos: naming, violence, and stillness. Although the majority of settlers in America were by no means the panicked religionists or the kind but gloomy Plymouth Rock crowd of national reverence, convenient commodification, and nostalgic delusion. I believe some 16 percent were, but that leaves 84 percent "other," as they say on censorship forms. Yet even among that 16 percent it did not take long for that already ambivalent idea and complicitous stillness to dissipate in the wake of industrialization. With the abundant supply of free labor in the form of slaves, indentured servants, convicts, and term debtors, and of cheap labor in the form of poor immigrants fleeing from indebtedness, starvation, and death. Even as Twain privileged rural and village life, language, and humor, even as he endowed the Mississippi and the lanes and roads of nineteenth-century America with pastoral yearning, he invested in profit-making schemes himself, disastrously as it turned out, and clearly urged and enjoyed the search for gold and the cleverness of money-making schemes in his characters. And it was our retiring, transcendentalist scholar Ralph Waldo Emerson who wrote of the California gold rush that "it did not matter what immoral means were used: the function of the gold rush was to hasten the settlement and *civilizing* of the West." The underscoring of civilizing is mine.

Melville, of course, was preoccupied with the counterclaims of a blossoming capitalism as it mirrored or impaled itself upon the force of nature. And along with much else, *Moby-Dick, Billy Budd, White-Jacket,* and "Benito Cereno" address the impact of economic pressure on the "innocent," the naïf laborer, and his "captain." All within the context of that two-thirds of the globe that represents chaos: the sea, and which seems to illustrate most clearly all three responses: naming (charting, mapping, describing), violence (conquest, whaling, slave ship, the naval fleet, etc.), and stillness (soul searching, idle watches aboard ships that produce the most self-reflective passages). Poe responded to chaos with violence and naming. Violence in his attraction to the damned, the dying, the murderer's mind. Naming in his insistent "scientific" footnotes, editorializing, indexing of historical and geographical data. But there was an additional element available to these writers, indeed to all Americans, for the contemplation of chaos. Nature, the "virgin" West, space, the proximity of death—all these mattered. Yet it was the availability of a domestic chaos, an invented disorder, a presumed uncivilized, savage, eternal and timeless "Other" that gives American history its peculiar and special formulation. This "Other," as we have suggested, was the Africanistic presence. American colonialists and their heirs could and did respond to this serviceable, controllable "chaos" by naming, violence, and, very late in the day, tentatively, carefully, hesitantly, a measure of pragmatic stillness. Again it is to the literature, the writers that we turn for evidence and figurations of this meditation on dominance. There one sees stillness (in Melville, for example) in the refusal to name in order to contemplate the mystery, the message of chaos's own inscription. In the refusal to do violence to, the refusal to conquer, to exploit. But to confront, to enter, to discover, as it were, of what this presence was or could be made.

It is in this context that I wish to read Gertrude Stein: her dedicated investigation of the interior life of this Other, and the problems of nonintervention that it presented and fell victim to. The "modernism" of which Stein is generally understood to be precursor has many forms: if we consider modernism to have as its single most consistent characteristic the merging of forms, the raveling away of borders, of frontierlessness, the mixing of media, the blending of genres, the redefinition of gender, of traditional roles, the appropriation of various and formerly separate disciplines in the service of new or conventional ones, the combination of historical periods and styles in art—then we can trace the particular ways in which American literature made that journey. In America, the first mark and fearful sign of merging, of mixing and the dissolution of what was held to be "natural" borders, was racial merging. It was the best represented, most alarming, most legislated against, and most desired foray into forbidden, unknown, dangerous territory, for it represented the slide into darkness, the out-lawed and illicit; the provocative, shocking break with the familiar.

In terms of literary embraces of modernism, as is also true of the visual-arts move toward modernism, the imaginative terrain upon which this journey took place was and is in a very large measure the presence of the racial "Other." Explicit or implicit, this presence informs in significant, compelling, and inescapable ways the shape of American literature. Ready to hand for the literary imagination it constituted both a visible and invisible mediating force. So that even, and especially, when American texts are not "about" African-istic presences, the shadow hovers there, in implication, in sign, in line of demarcation. It is no accident and no mistake that immigrant populations understood their "Americanness" as an opposition to the resident black population—and still do. In fact race has become so metaphorical, and as a metaphor so much more necessary to Ameri-canness, it rivals the old pseudoscientific and class-informed racialism we are familiar with. As a metaphor, this Africanistic presence may be something the United States can do without. For in this part of the twentieth century, if Americans are to be different, if they are to be Americans in some way that Canadians are not, that Latin Americans are not, that Britons are not, then they must be white Americans, and that distinction depends on a constantly reliable darkness. Deep within the word "American" is its association with race. (One notes that to identify someone as a South African is to say very little; we need the adjective "white" South African or "black" South African. In the States it is quite the opposite: "American" *means* white, and Africanistic peoples struggle to make the term applicable to themselves with hyphens and ethnicity.) The Americans did not have a profligate, predatory nobility from which to wrest its identity while coveting its license. They seemed to have merged both the wrench and the envy in their self-conscious and self-reflexive contemplation of mythological Africanism.

For the intellectual and imaginative adventure of writers who have come to signify "modern" in literature, this convenient Africanist Other was body, mind, chaos, kindness and love, the absence of restraint, the presence of restraint, the contemplation of freedom, the problem of aggression, the exploration of ethics and morality, the obligations of the social contract, the cross of religion, and the ramifications of power. The authors, American, who escape this influence are the ones who left the country—but not all of them.

Some astute critical observers believe that individualism American style precluded the possibility of, any room for, an "Other" and that, in the case of sexism, it was an erasure of the other as significant, as a nonperson. I wonder whether it is quite the contrary; that individualism emanates from the positioning of a safely bound self, out there. That there could be no inside, no stable, durable, individual self without the careful plotting and fabrication of an extrinsic gender, and likewise, an extrinsic, external shadow. Both are connected, but only at the outer limits of the self, the body. That this was true of white males should be clear. And since the definition of an American is a white male who is different, and a good or successful American is a white male who is different and powerful, what makes the whole contraption work is blackness, femaleness, disfamiliarizing strategies, and oppression. Bernard Bailyn provides the most succinct and fascinating portrait of this classic self-perpetuating and self-defining process. Among the immigrants and settlers he traces in his extraordinary book *Voyagers to the West* is a well-documented personage named William Dunbar.

The striking conclusion of this cameo is that there are four desirable consequences to the successful formation of this particular American:

autonomy, authority, newness and difference, and absolute power. These benefits translate, in the nineteenth and twentieth century, into individualism, difference, and the wielding of power. Unsurprisingly, they are also the major characteristics of American literature. Newness and difference; individualist; heroically powerful. These terms translate, at least until World War II, as follows. Nineteenth-century "newness" becomes twentieth-century "innocence." "Difference" becomes the hallmark of the modern. "Individualism," the cult of the Lone Ranger, is fused with a solitary, alienated malcontent (who is nevertheless still innocent)—and of course there is the interesting digression, which we won't enter into here, of Tonto. My puzzlement used to be why is the Lone Ranger called "lone" if he is always with Tonto? Now, I see that given the racial and metaphorical nature of the relationship, he is able to be understood as "alone" precisely because of Tonto. Without him he would be, I suppose, simply "Ranger." The heroically powerful gives way, after the war, to the problems of using and abusing power. Each of these characteristics, I think, is informed by a complex awareness and employment of a constituted Africanism as the trained ground and stadia for its identity. What, one wonders, are Americans always being insistently *of*? What is the relationship of the modern to the actively creative presence of African Americans? (It has been pointed out to me, that whenever the film industry wishes to and does manifest some brand-new technology or scope it employs Africanistic characters, narrative, or idiom. The first full-scale speaking film was *The Jazz Singer;* the first box-office hit was *Birth of a Nation;* the first situation comedy on television was *Amos 'n' Andy;* and, although this does not quite fit, but it almost does, the first documentary was *Nanook of the North.* And there is probably no contest from any quarter that the informing scores of "modern" filmmakers have been what we call in the States "black music.") Back to the matter at hand, the final question is what is the individual alienated from, if not his "white" self in an abiding but somehow fraudulently maintained articulated pluralism? The final question focuses on the holding, withholding, and distributing of power.

I mentioned Gertrude Stein as a paradigm or precursor of modernism. Now I would like to look at one of her most admired works to illustrate what I take to be a fascinating display of literary American-ism, to try to establish its connection to her innovations, her newness, her representations of individuality, her perceptions of sexual power, and the privileges emanating from class and race.

The three lives Gertrude Stein renders in her novel of that name are decidedly unequal. Not only in treatment, as I hope to dem-onstrate, but also in various other ways. Of the three women that constitute this work (a work of three stories put together to make a novel or novella), one covers seventy-one pages, another requires forty pages, and another, the central and middle narrative, takes up twice the length of one and almost four times the space of the other. This unequal distribution of space, each of which focuses on one woman, is marked by a further differing inequality. The first part is called "The Good Anna," the last part is called "The Gentle Lena." Only the central, centered, and longest part has no adjective; it is called "Melanctha." Simply. As you will remember, Melanctha is a black woman (or as Miss Stein identifies her, a Negro). Sandwiched in between the two others, she appears framed, bounded by the others as though to foreground and underscore her difference while keeping it firmly under control. Before I get into the remarkable differences between Melanctha and the two women who stand to her right and to her left, I should perhaps identify the similarities—for there are some, although they seem to throw further into relief Melanctha's difference, and the difference Stein makes of her. All three women constituting this text are servants; all die in the end; all are mistreated in some fash-ion by men or the consequences of male-dominated society. All are at the line between abject poverty and deserving poverty. And although all were born in some country, the similarities end precisely at this point. The two white women have a nationality: German, first, and then, as immigrants, they can assume the category German American if they choose. Only Melanctha was born in the United States, and only Melanctha is given no national identification. She is a Negro, and therefore even in 1909, forty years after the proclamation freed all slaves, without a land, without a citizenship designation. She is never described as an American and certainly never labeled one by the narrator.

For Miss Stein, Melanctha is a special kind of Negro. An acceptable one, for she has light skin, and the point has power when we note that her section opens with the comparison between Melanctha and her very close friend, Rose, who is described repeatedly (insistently) as very black: "sullen, childish, cowardly, black Rosie grumbled and fussed and howled and made herself to be an abomination and like a simple beast." Within this collection of adjectives are all of the fetishes, forms of metonymic reduction, collapse of persons into animals to foreclose dialogue and identification and economical stereotyping that is pervasive in the implications, if not the explicit language, of most pre-1980 fictional descriptions of Africanistic characters. "Rose Johnson was a real black, tall, well built, sullen, stupid, childlike, good looking negress." "Rose Johnson was a real black negress *but* she had been brought up quite like their own child by white folks" (italics mine). We note at once that it is not necessary for Stein to describe or identify these white folks, to say whether they were good, or well educated, or poor, or stupid, or mean. It is enough apparently that they were white, the assumption being that whatever kind of white people they were, they were *that,* and therefore the instruction given to Rose would place her in a privileged position, a fact that Rose herself not only acknowledges but is grateful for. Melanctha, on the other hand, being light skinned, is described as "patient, submissive, soothing, and untiring." She is also a "graceful, pale yellow, intelligent negress" who has "not been raised like Rose by white folks but then she had been *half made with real white blood*" (italics mine). The point is redundantly clear. While Rose can claim the good fortune of being reared by white people, Melanctha has the higher claim, the blood claim. There is some carelessness here, for we are later made to understand that Melanctha's father was "very black" and "brutal" and her mother was a "sweet appearing and dignified and pleasant, pale yellow, colored woman." This does not suggest the "half-white" label. Although Stein calls Melanctha a "subtle, intelligent, attractive, half white girl," according to the racial genetics of the day, a half-white

person would have to have one white parent. I think this latter possibility would offer too much complexity for the author; she would
have had to explain how the white parent (in this case the mother,
since the father is pointedly black) happened to get together with the
black parent, and it is perhaps sufficient that Melanctha's white lover
is later on examined as pivotal to her destruction without having to
go into the ramifications of another mixed-blood relationship.

I am not repeating these routine racial lapses and linguistic short-
cuts aimlessly, but to stress the fact that the recourse Stein has to
them, in order to draw certain conclusions, is so necessary either she
is willing to make glaring errors in the finer points of racialism and to
risk losing the reader's trust or she loses control of her wayward and
insubordinate text. For example: Rose Johnson is repeatedly called
childlike and immoral. But she is the only one of Melanctha's friends
who sustains adult responsibility—a marriage, a house, some generosity. Stein asserts Rose's stupidity, but fails to dramatize it. We find no
evidence whatsoever of her being stupid. And in spite of Melanctha's
revered white blood, she spends most of her time in the streets, along
the docks, and railroad yards. One has to question the logic of this
blood fetish: perhaps it is her "white" blood rather than her black that
encourages this immorality that Stein does not remark upon.

Equally interesting is the role of African American men in Melanctha's story. That is, the place of fathers, husbands, friends of fathers,
as well as the beau in Melanctha's life. To Stein's credit, there is equal
distribution of virtue and malice among the white and black men;
to her discredit, she relies heavily on national stereotyping for them
all: Irish prejudices, German ones, and, as is clear from the obsessive
blood fetish mentioned earlier, conventional ones. Such pseudoscience ought to be surprising from one who attended medical school
for a couple of years. In any case, she abandons all responsibility for
particularizing her Africanistic characters by "explaining" and "justify-
ing" their behavior with the easy tools of metonymic reduction that
skin color provides, and the economy of stereotype that is companion
to it. Again, however, this strategy forces Stein into contradictions so
profound, the trust of the reader dissipates altogether. For example,

Melanctha's father is repeatedly described as "brutal and rough" to his daughter, and we are told that he is first a visitor to the household on an irregular basis, and then absents himself from them and the novel altogether. The evidence presented to us for his brutality and roughness is that he is "black" and "virile." When we look to see what this black, virile, brutal, and rough man is capable of we see that he protects his daughter from what he believed were advances made to her from a male friend and gets into a fight because of this protection. It is perhaps this contradiction that conveniently expels him from the text. Had he stayed, Melanctha would have had a fierce protector/ savior and not gotten into such deep trouble with men.

Most notably, however, are not the routine techniques of making the Africanist characters different *as blacks,* but what I believe is the reason for their inclusion in the first place, for the Melanctha section services Stein in a very specific way. The Africanism of that section becomes a means by which Stein can step safely into forbidden territory, articulate the illegal, the anarchic, ruminate upon the relations among women with and without men. Of all three of the women in the novel, only with Melanctha are sexual education and sexual relations central to the narrative and the fate of the characters. It may not have been thinkable, even for Gertrude Stein, to discuss, in 1909, explicit knowledge of carnal activities with white women—even if they were of a lower class. If we compare the sensuality/sexuality of Anna and Lena, we see that their lives are different from Melanctha's; they are chaste; their marriages arranged; their submission to the demands of patriarchy complete. It seems clear that, like other American writers, especially those we associate with modernism, Stein felt free to experiment with sexuality in narrative, felt the subject *palatable* if the object upon which these experiments are carried out is Africanistic. Like the French doctor who was able to develop the paradigm for his gynecological instruments after sustained experiments with his black servant woman, Gertrude Stein is comfortable advancing her "newness," safe in her choice of forbidden territory because she is operating on a body that appears to be offered up to her without protest, without restraint. Wholly available for the articulation of the illegal, the illicit, the dangerous, the new. Like the white entertainers who were able to garner huge audiences when, in blackface, they spoke *through* the Africanistic persona (*as*), they could say the unspeakable, the forthrightly sexual, the subversively political.

What are some of these new and illicit topics?

There are at least three: (1) the intricate bonding of women not for protection but for the resources of knowledge they provide; (2) the triangular formation of sexuality, freedom, and knowledge as principle to a modern woman; and (3) the dependency of the construction of an American on an Africanistic presence. There is a genuine, even desperate love between Melanctha and Jane and Melanctha and Rose (in spite of the difference in their skin color). The sufferance and wisdom Melanctha receives from these friends is far superior to the things she learns from her men friends, the black doctors, or black gamblers. All of the women in *Three Lives* come to a sad end, but it appears that only one, Melanctha, learns anything useful, and perhaps modern, about the world before her demise. It may be that in this respect, Stein's signal contribution to literature in her encounter with an Africanistic presence is to give this encounter the complexity and the modernity it had otherwise been denied by mainstream writers of that time. Although Stein's assumptions about white and black blood are traditionally racist, she provides an interesting variation on the theme by having Melanctha treasure the quality (if it can be called such) of blackness from her "unendurable" father; having the "very black" Rose advise Melanctha and persuade her not to commit suicide and be drawn as a "regularly" married woman with apparently very high standards of morality—denied by Stein's insistence that Rose "had the simple, promiscuous unmorality of the black people."

Key to Stein's exploration, however, is the question of the relationship of freedom for women to sexuality and knowledge. In this quest, we see again the difference she makes. *Three Lives* moves from the contemplation of an asexual spinster's life—the Good Anna—in its struggle for control and meaning, to and *through* the exploration of a quest for sexual knowledge (which Stein calls "wisdom") in the person and body of Melanctha, an Africanistic woman; to the presumably culminating female experience of marriage and birth—the Gentle Lena. That Stein chose a black woman for the examination of the erotic suggests and theatricalizes the uses of Africanism to represent and serve as license to address illicit sexuality.

Although Stein has her tongue in her own cheek for much of the text, has firm opinions that she puts in the mouths of others, and is forthrightly comic, even parodic in some passages, we are eager to follow her fairly radical look into the true lives of these women, but in only one of them (Melanctha) does the sexual repression of the other two not only disappear, but its repudiation becomes the central theme of Melanctha's and Stein's enterprise. The black woman alone provides access to a meditation on sexual knowledge, and it is of utmost importance that the author calls Melanctha's flirtations, her wanderings alone down to the docks and railroad depots to look at men, her promiscuity—all this she calls an eagerness for wisdom. The "very black" Rose is labeled promiscuous, but the half-white Melanctha is searching for knowledge. This difference in labels for presumably identical behavior is distancing and functions as a covert manner of giving dignity to one kind of inquisitiveness and discrediting another simply by marking a difference in the color of the inquirer's skin. Further differences are notable when the comparison is between the white servants and the black women. Neither Anna nor Lena is curious about sex. Good Anna never entertains the possibility of marriage or a love. Her "romance" is with her first close friend, Mrs. Lehntman. Gentle Lena is so terrified, dull, and uninquisitive, Stein does not have to speculate on the legal sexual intercourse that takes place between Lena and her husband, Herman. She simply delivers four children, dying with the last and leaving her husband quiet, content, and himself a nurturer. Only Melanctha has courage, feels the attractive power of her black father, and the weakness of her pale yellow mother, senses that her identification with her passive mother will give her no respect; she is free to roam the streets, stand on corners, visit the scene of black men at work on the railroad, at the docks; to compete with them in fearlessness, trade barbs with them, tease and escape from them—and to talk back to them. It is Melanctha's authorita-

tive voice that examines, articulates, and questions erotic heterosexual
love, which combats the middle class's ideal of domestic/romantic
union, and which boldly enters the field of male-female encounters
as a warrior—a militant. It is interesting to me that in her probe of
the value of carnal knowledge, Stein looks not toward the very black
Rose, the one she ascribes unmorality and promiscuity to, but to the
half-white, college-educated Melanctha. It is as though, fearless as she
was, Stein could not bear to investigate these very intimate matters
on the body of a very black woman—the risk of such an imaginative
association seems to have been too much for her. One feels her disdain
of Rose, but her admiration of Jane's loose behavior, like Melanctha's,
is ambivalent and rendered in clearly elevated and cynical language.
Jane Harden is identified as a "roughened woman. She had power
and she liked to use it, she had much white blood and that made her
see clear. . . . Her white blood was strong in her and she had grit and
endurance and a vital courage." There is no mistaking Stein's codified
values and opinions regarding race. She is identifying her own self
with the white blood that makes for clarity and strength and vital
courage, but is working its sexual expression out on the not-white
blood that courses through these bodies in apparently two separate
veins. The ludicrousness of these claims of what white blood is capable
of in its generic transfer of power, intelligence, and so on is, of course,
emphasized by the fact that in the same breath, if not paragraph, we
witness the behavior of completely white people, people with all-white
blood who are passive, stupid, and so on. If we were going to succumb
to the idiocy of scientific racialism, the logic of the opposite would be
unspeakable: that in *Three Lives* it is the black blood that provides the
"vital courage" and "endurance." There is tension and some readerly
distrust of these hierarchies and claims, because of the contradictions
that accompany them. Africanistic women, for example, are suffused
with loose immorality, but Mrs. L., the friend and major force in
Lena's tiny world, spends her professional life midwifing and likes
especially to deliver girls in trouble; she even seems to be involved in
abortions with her wicked doctor lover at one point. Why these white
girls in trouble are not also guilty of amorality and looseness as are

their dark sisters is part of the question these matters pose. That series of episodes is glazed over by pointing to the generosity of Mrs. L. and her skill. There is no lingering over the unmorality of her patients; they are not assumed to have a "promiscuous" nature because of their skin color, or even, it seems, to have been seeking the wisdom of the world down at the docks.

The last point to which I wish to direct attention is the one with which I began: that much of this business of imagining Africanistic people has to do with the careful, consistent construction of an American who gets his or her distinction in asserting and developing whiteness as a precondition to Americanness.

Three Lives centers on two immigrant women and one black woman who is never given a nationality, although she is the only natural-born citizen among the three. When a minor character in the Good Anna section visits Germany, her mother's birthplace, and becomes embarrassed by Anna's peasant manners, her remark is that her cousin is "no better than a nigger." Miss Stein, fascinated with her project *The Making of Americans* has indeed delivered up to us a model case in literature: (1) build barriers in language and body, (2) establish difference in blood, skin, and human emotions, (3) place them in opposition to immigrants, and (4) voilà! The true American arises!

Sandwiched between a pair of immigrants—her aggression and power contained by the palms of chaste but restraining white women—Melanctha is bold but discredited; free to explore but bound by her color and confined by the white women on her left and her right, her foreground and her background, her beginning and her end, who precede her and follow her. The format and its interior workings say what is meant. All of the ingredients that have an impact on Americanness are on display in these women: labor, class, relations with the Old World, forging an un-European new culture, defining freedom, avoiding bondage, seeking opportunity and power, situating the uses of oppression. These considerations are inextricable from any deliberation on how Americans selected, chose, constructed a national identity. In the process of choosing, the unselected, the unchosen, the detritus is as significant as the cumulative, built American. Among the explorations vital to the definition, one of the strongest is the rumination of Africanistic character as a laboratory experiment for confronting emotional, historical, and moral problems as well as intellectual entanglements with the serious questions of power, privilege, freedom, and equity. Is it not just possible that the union, the coalescence of what America is and was made of, is incomplete without the place of Africanism in the formulation of this so-called new people, and what implications such a formulation had for the claims of democracy and egalitarianism as far as women and blacks were concerned? Is not the contradiction inherent in these two warring propositions—white democracy and black repression—also reflected in the literature so deeply that it marks and distinguishes its very heart?

Just as these two immigrants are literally *joined* like Siamese twins to Melanctha, so are Americans joined to and defined by this Africanistic presence at its spine.

Hard, True, and Lasting

MANY STRANGERS TRAVERSE our land these days. They look on our lives with horror and quickly make means to pass on to the paradises of the north. Those who are pressed by circumstances and forced to tarry a while, grumble and complain endlessly. It is just good for them that we are inbred with habits of courtesy, hospitality, and kindness. It is good that they do not know the passion we feel for this parched earth. We tolerate strangers because the things we love cannot be touched by them." That's a paragraph from a short story called "The Green Tree" by Bessie Head, and I print all of it for you just to get to that one sentence: *We tolerate strangers because the things we love cannot be touched by them.* It suggests to me an attitude and a position that might be necessary for any artist and writer who finds himself not only in an alien culture, but vulnerable to it, and in some ways threatened by it.

There is nothing new or special about this condition of separateness—it is generally the first impression that an artist or a writer feels when he is compelled to write. And it may be even *out* of that feeling of separateness that he writes at all. The questions that all writers put are questions of value: identifying the values they feel worthy of preservation; or identifying the values they believe detrimental to some freer, or finer, or, at the least, steadier life.

Early national literatures all over the world concentrated on describing and, by implication, supporting the cultures that the writer found himself in. (The sagas, the lieder, the myths when they were recorded were precisely that.) Just as the early literature of expatriates, immigrants, or people in some form of diaspora concentrated on, and, frequently, condemned the new or alien culture the writers found themselves in. And the most assimilationist of them all brought something from his own culture to that assimilation. It is still rare to find massive flowerings of Joseph Conrads and Pushkins in national literature anthologies.

More recent literatures by both natives to and aliens in a culture are equally preoccupied with the problem. Indeed "alienation" became the password, the general catchall word for practically all post–World War II literature in the Western world. The writers view their own culture as alien: middle-class writers betrayed their own class and aspired toward the leisure-class values or the values of classes beneath them; working-class writers deplored the limitations of their own class; upper-class writers found inspiration among the poor, the "noble," the innocent, the untutored peasant; postwar writers separated themselves from everybody except veterans and war victims. Of course there were and are writers who felt something quite the opposite: that things were pretty much all right the way they were and their suspicion of feeling alien came not from too little change, but too much, and too soon, which is to say before they were ready for it.

That the world is an exquisitely unpleasant place is a familiar ode to writers. And it is usually just at the point of reconciliation to the world, just at the moment when it becomes probably a comfortable enough place, after all that the writer is confronted with the Last Great Isolation—the one that minces every other alienation he has known: and that is the premonition of his own death. Under the shadow of that wing, even the most hostile of alien cultures is preferable.

But both of those conditions (my own awareness of being a native of this country and as an alien in it) are of interest to me as a writer, and I'd like to talk about that expected and perhaps inevitable sense of separateness from the culture that pervades the country I live in. The remarks I have to make are applicable to probably every group that has ever existed. And I paraphrase Miss Head to say that I can tolerate the overweening culture that is not mine because the things I love cannot be touched by it. It sounds hostile, I know, and unsharing, I know; and ungenerous and defensive. I know that. But I am nevertheless convinced that clarity about who one is and what one's work is, is inextricably bound up with one's place in a tribe—or a family, or a nation, or a race, or a sex, or what have you. And the clarity *is* necessary for the evaluation of the self and it *is* necessary for any productive intercourse with any other tribe or culture. I am not suggesting a collection of warring cultures, just clear ones, for it is out of the clarity of one's own culture that life within another, near another, in juxtaposition to another is healthily possible. Without it, a writer lives on whatever pinnacle he achieves in loneliness and whatever road he walks on is finally a cul-de-sac. It is vital, therefore, to know what "the things we love" are, in order to care for and to husband them.

I have always myself felt most alive, most alert, and most sterling among my own people. All of my creative energy comes from there. My stimulation for any artistic effort at all originates there. The compulsion to write, even to *be,* begins with my consciousness of, experience with, and even my awe of black people and the quality of our lives as lived (not as perceived). And all of my instincts tell me that both as a writer and as a person any total surrender to another culture would destroy me. And the danger is not always from indifference; it is also from acceptance. It is sometimes called the fear of absorption, the horror of cultural embrace. But at the heart of the horror for me is what I know about what the history of the culture that pervades this country has been.

My instincts combine therefore with my intelligence to inform me that there are many aspects of that culture that are not trustworthy and are not supportive.

Every and each attempt I have made to write has centered on that assumption and this question: What is there of value in black culture to lose and how can it be preserved and made useful? I am not very good at the writing of tracts, so I frequently identify the things I love and find of value by showing them in danger; things in my novels are threatened and sometimes destroyed. It is my way of directing attention at sensitized readers in such a way that they will yearn for, miss, and, I hope, learn to care for certain aspects of that life that are worth the preservation.

Now in order for me to try even to identify those things, I need to know a lot or try to find out a lot about the civilization within the civilization in which I grew up. I mean the black civilization that functioned within the white one. And the questions I must put to it are: What was the hierarchy in my civilization? Who were the arbiters of custom? What were the laws? Who were the outlaws—not the legal outlaws, but the community outlaws? Where did we go for solace and for advice? Who were the betrayers of that culture? Who did we respect and why? What was our morality? What was success? Who survived? And why? And under what circumstances? What is deviant behavior? Not deviant behavior as defined by white people, but what is deviant behavior as defined by black people?

I have been for years, and it will probably be a fascination that lasts all my life, continually fascinated by the fact that no bestial treatment of human beings ever produces beasts. White marauders can force Native American Indians to walk from one part of the country to another and watch them drop like flies and cattle, but they did not end up as cattle; Jewish people could be thrown into ovens like living carcasses but Jews were not bestialized by it; black people could be enslaved for generation after generation and recorded in statistics along with lists of rice, tar, and turpentine cargo, but they did not turn out to be cargo. Each one of those groups civilized the very horror that oppressed it. It doesn't work, and I don't think it can. It never works; what preoccupies me is *why.* Why was the quality of my great-grandmother's life so much better than the circumstances of her life? How was it possible without the feminist movement, without a black arts movement, without any movement, how was it possible that the sheer integrity and quality of her life were so superior to its circumstances? I know that she was not atypical among the women of her day. She was as average a black woman as there ever was. And no amount of quisling scholarship, no amount of psychological tyranny, no number of black colonizers, who in their quest for jobs and national prominence join hands with those who would rape us cultur-ally, none of them will ever convince me otherwise. Because I knew her—and I knew the people she knew.

In my own writing, in order to reveal what seems to me the hard and the true and the lasting things, I am drawn to describing people under duress, not in easy circumstances, but backed up into a corner, people called upon to fish or cut bait. You say you are my friend? Let's see. You say you are a revolutionary? Let me see how it looks when I push you all the way out. You say you love me? Let's see. What hap-pens if you follow *your* course all the way through? What are the things you will give up? And, under duress, I know *who* they are, of what they are made, and which of their qualities is the last to go, and which of their qualities never go. It gives a melancholy cast to my work. I know. And it leads me to exceptional rather than routine characters. I know. And it leaves me wide open for criticism about bizarre char-acters and nonpositive images. I know. But I am afraid I will have to leave the "positive" images to the comic-strip artists and the "normal" black characters to some future Doris Day, because I believe it is silly, not to say irresponsible, to concern myself with lipstick and Band-Aid when there is a plague in the land. The so-called everyday life of black people is certainly lovely to live, but whoever is living it must know that each day of his "everyday" black life is a triumph of matter over mind and sentiment over common sense. And if he doesn't know that, then he doesn't know anything at all. As the young African poet Keorapetse Kgositsile put it, "The present is a dangerous place to live." Superficial literary cosmetics will not save us from that danger. As a matter of fact, literature will not save us at all. All it can do is point out the need perhaps for defense, but it is not itself that defense. What it can do is participate in the process of identifying what is of value, and once that surfaces, once black tradition can be extricated from black fashion, once black writing stops posturing and catering to the voyeurs of black life, once it stops doing an American version of airport art, then an even harder job presents itself.

Because it is relatively easy to recognize values in isolation. The problem gets complicated when those values are in conflict with other values. For then you have to figure out how to protect the very best of the group sensibilities; how to protect the noblest impulses. What are the nurturing structures worth keeping in the community? What are the culturgens that provide emotional safety, the customs that allow freedom without excessive risk or certain destruction, that allow courage minus recklessness, generosity without waste, support without domination, and in times of deep, deep trouble (as in some of the black countries abroad) a resource for survival that may very well include sustained and calculated ferocity.

Black writers who are committed to the renewal and refreshment of values can be identified by their taste, by their judgments, by their intellect, and by their work. They do not use black life as exotic ornament for pedestrian nonblack stories. The essence of black life is the substance, not the decoration, of their work. Their work turns on a moral axis that has been forged among black people. They do not impose alien moralities about broken homes, and house-bound fathers, and petite power, and what is or is not gainful employment on their characters.

They do not regard black language as dropping g's or as an exercise in questionable phonetics and inconsistent orthography. They know that it is much more complicated than that.

And they waste no time explaining, explaining, explaining away everything they feel and think and do—to the other culture. They are challenged by and concerned with the enlightenment of their own, even when the enlightenment includes painful information.

They do not view the habits and customs of their people with the eye of a charged-up ethnologist examining curios.

The writers who are also scholars in so-called black studies are unimpressed with standard cries of "lowering standards" when any change in curricula is recommended. They know their job doesn't have anything to do with maintaining standards. It has to do with reshaping the content of those standards in order to improve them and *raise* them.

Those black writers who are critics are not busy painting Bertolt Brecht black and relabeling his thoughts (which were perfectly suitable to his own cultural needs) as some sort of "new" black criticism. Any critical apparatus or critical system that is inappropriate to and foolish when applied to black music or non-Western black art is fraudulent when applied to black literature.

Once, when I first began to write, I didn't know a lot about how to dramatize and I was forced sometimes to use exposition as a way of saying something I could not properly show. And in the first book, *The Bluest Eye,* I wrote a passage at the end that is as close as I have ever gotten to sustained didacticism. It is a wholly unsatisfactory passage to me, and I had certainly hoped to read it to you in context, but I haven't got a copy of the book with me. But in the last two pages of *The Bluest Eye,* is, in essence, what I believe to be the dangers when one assumes that you can substitute license for freedom, when one assumes that you can use another's deficiency for one's own generosity, when one assumes that you can use another person's misery and nightmares in order to clarify your own dreams. When all of those things are done and completed, then the surrender and the betrayal of one's culture is also complete.

PART II

God's Language

James Baldwin Eulogy

Jimmy, there is too much to think about you, and much too much to feel. The difficulty is your life refuses summation—it always did—and invites contemplation instead. Like many of us left here, I thought I knew you. Now I discover that, in your company, it is myself I know. That is the astonishing gift of your art and your friendship: you gave us ourselves to think about, to cherish. We are like Hall Montana watching "with a new wonder" his brother sing, knowing the song he sang is us, "*he* is—*us*."

I never heard a single command from you, yet the demands you made on me, the challenges you issued to me were nevertheless unmistakable if unenforced: that I work and think at the top of my form; that I stand on moral ground but know that ground must be shored up by mercy; that "the world is before [me] and [I] need not take it or leave it as it was when [I] came in."

Well, the season was always Christmas with you there, and like one aspect of that scenario, you did not neglect to bring at least three gifts. You gave me a language to dwell in—a gift so perfect, it seems my own invention. I have been thinking your spoken and written thoughts so long, I believed they were mine. I have been seeing the world through your eyes so long, I believed that clear, clear view was my own. Even now, even here, I need you to tell me what I am feeling and how to articulate it. So I have pored (again) through the 6,895 pages of your published work to acknowledge the debt and thank you for the credit.

No one possessed or inhabited language for me the way you did. You made American English honest—genuinely international. You exposed its secrets and reshaped it until it was truly modern, dialogic, representative, humane. You stripped it of ease and false comfort and fake innocence and evasion and hypocrisy. And in place of deviousness was clarity; in place of soft, plump lies was a lean, targeted power. In place of intellectual disingenuousness and what you called "exasperating egocentricity," you gave us undecorated truth. You replaced lumbering platitudes with an upright elegance. You went into that forbidden territory and decolonized it, "robbed it of the jewel of its naïveté," and ungated it for black people, so that in your wake we could enter it, occupy it, restructure it in order to accommodate our complicated passion. Not our vanities, but our intricate, difficult, demanding beauty; our tragic, insistent knowledge; our lived reality; our sleek classical imagination. All the while refusing "to be defined by a language that has never been able to recognize [us]." In your hands language was handsome again. In your hands we saw how it was meant to be—neither bloodless nor bloody, and yet alive.

It infuriated some people. Those who saw the paucity of their own imagination in the two-way mirror you held up to them attacked the mirror, tried to reduce it to fragments that they could then rank and grade; tried to dismiss the shards where your image and theirs remained—locked but ready to soar. You are an artist, after all, and an artist is forbidden a career in this place; an artist is permitted only the commercial "hit." But for thousands and thousands of those who embrace your text, and who gave themselves permission to hear your language, by that very gesture they ennobled themselves, became unshrouded—civilized.

The second gift was your courage, which you let us share.
The courage of one who could go as a stranger in the village and
transform the distances between people into intimacy with the
whole world; courage to understand that experience in ways that
made it a personal revelation for each of us. It was you who gave
us the courage to appropriate an alien, hostile, all-white geography
because you had discovered that "this world [meaning history] is
white no longer, and it will never be white again." Yours was the
courage to live life in and from its belly as well as beyond its edges.
To see and say what it was; to recognize and identify evil but never
fear or stand in awe of it. It is a courage that came from a ruthless
intelligence married to a pity so profound it could convince anyone
who cared to know that those who despised us "need the moral
authority of their former slaves, who are the only people in the
world who know anything about them and who may be, indeed,
the only people in the world who really care anything about them."
When that unassailable combination of mind and heart, of intellect
and passion was on display, it guided us through treacherous
landscape, as it did when you wrote these words—words every
rebel, every dissident, revolutionary, every practicing artist from
Cape Town to Poland, from Waycross to Dublin, memorized: "A
person does not lightly elect to oppose his society. One would much
rather be at home among one's compatriots than be mocked and
detested by them. And there is a level on which the mockery of
the people, even their hatred, is moving because it is so blind: it is
terrible to watch people cling to their captivity and insist on their
own destruction."

The third gift was hard to fathom and even harder to accept.
It was your tenderness. A tenderness so delicate I thought it could
not last, but last it did and envelop me it did. In the midst of anger
it tapped me, lightly, like the child in Tish's womb: "Something
almost as hard to catch as a whisper in a crowded place, as light and

as definite as a spider's web, strikes below my ribs, stunning and astonishing my heart. . . . The baby, turning for the first time in its incredible veil of water, announces its presence and claims me; tells me, in that instant, that what can get worse can get better. . . . In the meantime—forever—it is entirely up to me." Yours was a tenderness, a vulnerability, that asked everything, expected everything, and, like the world's own Merlin, provided us with the ways and means to deliver. I suppose that is why I was always a bit better behaved around you, smarter, more capable, wanting to be worth the love you lavished, and wanting to be steady enough to witness the pain you had witnessed and were tough enough to bear while it broke your heart; wanting to be generous enough to join your smile with one of my own, and reckless enough to jump on in that laugh you laughed. Because our joy and our laughter were not only all right; they were necessary.

You knew, didn't you? How I needed your language and the mind that formed it? How I relied on your fierce courage to tame wildernesses for me? How strengthened I was by the certainty that came from knowing you would never hurt me? You knew, didn't you, how I loved your love? You knew. This then is no calamity. No. This is a jubilee. "Our crown," you said, "has already been bought and paid for. All we have to do," you said, "is wear it."

And we do, Jimmy. You crowned us.

The Site of Memory

MY INCLUSION in a series of talks on autobiography and memoir is not entirely a misalliance. Although it's probably true that a fiction writer thinks of his or her work as alien in that company, what I have to say may suggest why I'm not completely out of place here. For one thing, I might throw into relief the differences between self-recollection (memoir) and fiction, and also some of the similarities—the places where those two crafts embrace and where that embrace is symbiotic.

But the authenticity of my presence here lies in the fact that a very large part of my own literary heritage is the autobiography. In this country the print origins of black literature (as distinguished from the oral origins) were slave narratives. These book-length narratives (autobiographies, recollections, memoirs), of which well over a hundred were published, are familiar texts to historians and students of black history. They range from the adventure-packed life of Olaudah Equiano's *The Interesting Narrative of the Life of Olaudah Equiano, or Gustavus Vassa, the African, Written by Himself* (1769) to the quiet desperation of *Incidents in the Life of a Slave Girl: Written by Herself* (1861), in which Harriet Jacobs ("Linda Brent") records hiding for seven years in a room too small to stand up in; from the political savvy of Frederick Douglass's *Narrative of the Life of Frederick Douglass, an American Slave, Written by Himself* (1845) to the subtlety and modesty of Henry Bibb, whose voice, in *Narrative of the Life and Adventures*

of Henry Bibb, an American Slave, Written by Himself (1849), is surrounded by ("loaded with" is a better phrase) documents attesting to
its authenticity. Bibb is careful to note that his formal schooling (three
weeks) was short, but that he was "educated in the school of adversity,
whips, and chains." Born in Kentucky, he put aside his plans to escape
in order to marry. But when he learned that he was the father of a
slave and watched the degradation of his wife and child, he reactivated
those plans.

Whatever the style and circumstances of these narratives, they
were written to say principally two things. (1) "This is my historical
life—my singular, special example that is personal, but that also represents the race." (2) "I write this text to persuade other people—you,
the reader, who is probably not black—that we are human beings
worthy of God's grace and the immediate abandonment of slavery."
With these two missions in mind, the narratives were clearly pointed.

In Equiano's account, the purpose is quite up-front. Born in 1745
near the Niger River and captured at the age of ten, he survived the
Middle Passage, American plantation slavery, wars in Canada and
the Mediterranean; learned navigation and clerking from a Quaker
named Robert King; and bought his freedom at twenty-one. He lived
as a free servant, traveling widely and living most of his later life in
England. Here he is speaking to the British without equivocation: "I
hope to have the satisfaction of seeing the renovation of liberty and
justice, resting on the British government. . . . I hope and expect the
attention of gentlemen in power. . . . May the time come—at least
the speculation to me is pleasing—when the sable people shall grate-
fully commemorate the auspicious aera of extensive freedom." With
typically eighteenth-century reticence he records his singular and representative life for one purpose: to change things. In fact, he and his
coauthors did change things. Their works gave fuel to the fires that
abolitionists were setting everywhere.

More difficult was getting the fair appraisal of literary critics. The
writings of church martyrs and confessors are and were read for the
eloquence of their message as well as their experience of redemption,
but the American slaves' autobiographical narratives were frequently

scorned as "biased," "inflammatory," and "improbable." These attacks are particularly difficult to understand in view of the fact that it was extremely important, as you can imagine, for the writers of these narratives to appear as objective as possible—not to offend the reader by being too angry, or by showing too much outrage, or by calling the reader names. As recently as 1966, Paul Edwards, who edited and abridged Equiano's story, praises the narrative for its refusal to be "inflammatory."

"As a rule," Edwards writes, "he [Equiano] puts no emotional pressure on the reader other than that which the situation itself contains—his language does not strain after our sympathy, but expects it to be given naturally and at the proper time. This quiet avoidance of emotional display produces many of the best passages in the book." Similarly, an 1836 review of Charles Bell's "Life and Adventures of a Fugitive Slave," which appeared in the *Quarterly Anti-Slavery Magazine,* praised Bell's account for its objectivity. "We rejoice in the book the more, because it is not a partizan work. . . . It broaches no theory in regard to [slavery], nor proposes any mode of time of emancipation."

As determined as these black writers were to persuade the reader of the evil of slavery, they also complimented him by assuming his nobility of heart and his high-mindedness. They tried to summon up his finer nature in order to encourage him to employ it. They knew that their readers were the people who could make a difference in terminating slavery. Their stories—of brutality, adversity, and deliverance—had great popularity in spite of critical hostility in many quarters and patronizing sympathy in others. There was a time when the hunger for "slave stories" was difficult to quiet, as sales figures show. Douglass's *Narrative* sold five thousand copies in four months; by 1847 it had sold eleven thousand copies. Equiano's book had thirty-six editions between 1789 and 1850. Moses Roper's book had ten editions from 1837 to 1856; William Wells Brown's was reprinted four times in its first year. Solomon Northup's book sold twenty-seven thousand copies before two years had passed. A book by Josiah Henson (argued by some to be the model for the Tom of

Harriet Beecher Stowe's *Uncle Tom's Cabin*) had a prepublication sale of five thousand.

In addition to using their own lives to expose the horrors of slavery, they had a companion motive for their efforts. The prohibition against teaching a slave to read and write (which in many southern states carried severe punishment) and against a slave's learning to read and write had to be scuttled at all costs. These writers knew that literacy was power. Voting, after all, was inextricably connected to the ability to read; literacy was a way of assuming and proving the "humanity" that the Constitution denied them. That is why the narratives carry the subtitle "written by himself," or "herself," and include introductions and prefaces by white sympathizers to authenticate them. Other narratives, "edited by" such well-known antislavery figures as Lydia Maria Child and John Greenleaf Whittier, contain prefaces to assure the reader how little editing was needed. A literate slave was supposed to be a contradiction in terms.

One has to remember that the climate in which they wrote reflected not only the Age of Enlightenment but its twin, born at the same time, the Age of Scientific Racism. David Hume, Immanuel Kant, and Thomas Jefferson, to mention only a few, had documented their conclusions that blacks were incapable of intelligence. Frederick Douglass knew otherwise, and he wrote refutations of what Jefferson said in *Notes on the State of Virginia*: "Never yet could I find that a black had uttered a thought above the level of plain narration; never see even an elementary trait of painting or sculpture." A sentence that I have always thought ought to be engraved at the door to the Michael C. Rockefeller wing of the Met. Hegel, in 1813, had said that Africans had no "history" and couldn't write in modern languages. Kant disregarded a perceptive observation by a black man by saying, "This fellow was quite black from head to foot, a clear proof that what he said was stupid."

Yet no slave society in the history of the world wrote more—or more thoughtfully—about its own enslavement. The milieu, however, dictated the purpose and the style. The narratives are instructive, moral, and obviously representative. Some of them are patterned after the sentimental novel that was in vogue at the time. But whatever the level of eloquence or the form, popular taste discouraged the writers from dwelling too long or too carefully on the more sordid details of their experience. Whenever there was an unusually violent incident, or a scatological one, or something "excessive," one finds the writer taking refuge in the literary conventions of the day. "I was left in a state of distraction not to be described" (Equiano). "But let us now leave the rough usage of the field . . . and turn our attention to the less repulsive slave life as it existed in the home of my childhood" (Douglass). "I am not about to harrow the feelings of my readers by a terrific representation of the untold horrors of that fearful system of oppression. . . . It is not my purpose to descend deeply into the dark and noisome caverns of the hell of slavery" (Henry Box Brown).

Over and over, the writers pull the narrative up short with a phrase such as, "But let us drop a veil over these proceedings too terrible to relate." In shaping the experience to make it palatable to those who were in a position to alleviate it, they were silent about many things, and they "forgot" many other things. There was a careful selection of the instances that they would record and a careful rendering of those that they chose to describe. Lydia Maria Child identified the problem in her introduction to "Linda Brent's" tale of sexual abuse: "I am well aware that many will accuse me of indecorum for presenting these pages to the public; for the experiences of this intelligent and much-injured woman belong to a class which some call delicate subjects, and others indelicate. This peculiar phase of Slavery has generally been kept veiled; but the public ought to be made acquainted with its monstrous features, and I willingly take the responsibility of presenting them with the veil withdrawn."

But most importantly—at least for me—there was no mention of their interior life.

For me—a writer in the last quarter of the twentieth century, not much more than a hundred years after Emancipation, a writer who is black and a woman—the exercise is very different. My job becomes how to rip that veil drawn over "proceedings too terrible to relate." The exercise is also critical for any person who is black, or who belongs to any marginalized category, for, historically, we were seldom invited to participate in the discourse even when we were its topic.

Moving that veil aside requires, therefore, certain things. First of all, I must trust my own recollections. I must also depend on the recollections of others. Thus memory weighs heavily in what I write, in how I begin, and in what I find to be significant. Zora Neale Hurston said, "Like the dead-seeming, cold rocks, I have memories within that came out of the material that went to make me." These "memories within" are the subsoil of my work. But memories and recollections won't give me total access to the unwritten interior life of these people. Only the act of the imagination can help me.

If writing is thinking and discovery and selection and order and meaning, it is also awe and reverence and mystery and magic. I suppose I could dispense with the last four if I were not so deadly serious about fidelity to the milieu out of which I write and in which my ancestors actually lived. Infidelity to that milieu—the absence of the interior life, the deliberate excising of it from the records that the slaves themselves told—is precisely the problem in the discourse that proceeded without us. How I gain access to that interior life is what drives me and is the part of this talk that both distinguishes my fiction from autobiographical strategies and that also embraces certain autobiographical strategies. It's a kind of literary archaeology: on the basis of some information and a little bit of guesswork you journey to a site to see what remains were left behind and to reconstruct the world that these remains imply. What makes it fiction is the nature of the imaginative act: my reliance on the image—on the remains—in addition to recollection, to yield up a kind of a truth. By "image," of course, I don't mean "symbol"; I simply mean "picture" and the feelings that accompany the picture.

Fiction, by definition, is distinct from fact. Presumably it's the product of imagination—invention—and it claims the freedom to dispense with "what really happened," or where it really happened, or when it really happened, and nothing in it needs to be publicly verifiable, although much in it can be verified. By contrast, the scholarship of the biographer and the literary critic seems to us only trustworthy when the events of fiction can be traced to some publicly verifiable fact. It's the research of the "Oh, yes, this is where he or she got it from" school, which gets its own credibility from excavating the credibility of the sources of the imagination, not the nature of the imagination.

The work that I do frequently falls, in the minds of most people, into that realm of fiction called fantastic, or mythic, or magical, or unbelievable. I'm not comfortable with these labels. I consider that my single gravest responsibility (in spite of that magic) is not to lie. When I hear someone say, "Truth is stranger than fiction," I think that old chestnut is truer than we know, because it doesn't say that truth is truer than fiction; just that it's stranger, meaning that it's odd. It may be excessive, it may be more interesting, but the important thing is that it's random—and fiction is not random.

Therefore the crucial distinction for me is not the difference between fact and fiction, but the distinction between fact and truth. Because facts can exist without human intelligence, but truth cannot. So if I'm looking to find and expose a truth about the interior life of people who didn't write it (which doesn't mean that they didn't have it); if I'm trying to fill in the blanks that the slave narratives left—to part the veil that was so frequently drawn, to implement the stories that I heard—then the approach that's most productive and most trustworthy for me is the recollection that moves from the image to the text. Not from the text to the image.

Simone de Beauvoir, in *A Very Easy Death,* says, "I don't know why I was so shocked by my mother's death." When she heard her mother's name being called at the funeral by the priest, she says, "Emotion seized [me] by the throat. . . . 'Françoise de Beauvoir'; the words brought her to life; they summed up her history, from birth to marriage, to widowhood, to the grave; Françoise de Beauvoir—that retiring woman, so rarely named—became an important person." The book becomes an exploration both into her own grief and into the images in which the grief lay buried.

Unlike Mme. de Beauvoir, Frederick Douglass asks the reader's patience for spending about half a page on the death of his grandmother—easily the most profound loss he had suffered—and he apologizes by saying, in effect, "It really was very important to me. I hope you aren't bored by my indulgence." He makes no attempt to explore that death, its images or its meaning. His narrative is as close to factual as he can make it, which leaves no room for subjective speculation. James Baldwin, on the other hand, in *Notes of a Native Son,* says, in recording his father's life and his own relationship to his father, "All of my father's texts and songs, which I had decided were meaningless, were arranged before me at his death like empty bottles, waiting to hold the meaning which life would give them for me." And then his text fills those bottles. Like Simone de Beauvoir, he moves from the event to the image that it left. My route is the reverse: the image comes first and tells me what the "memory" is about.

I can't tell you how I felt when my father died. But I was able to write *Song of Solomon* and imagine, not him, not his specific interior life, but the world that he inhabited and the private or interior life of the people in it. And I can't tell you how I felt reading to my grandmother while she was turning over and over in her bed (because she was dying, and she was not comfortable), but I could try to reconstruct the world that she lived in. And I have suspected, more often than not, that I know more than she did, that I know more than my grandfather and my great-grandmother did, but I also know that I'm no wiser than they were. And whenever I have tried earnestly to diminish their vision and prove to myself that I know more, and when I have tried to speculate on their interior life and match it up with my own, I have been overwhelmed every time by the richness of theirs compared to my own. Like Frederick Douglass talking about his grandmother, and James Baldwin talking about his father, and Simone de Beauvoir talking about her mother, these people are my access to me; they are my entrance into my own interior life. Which is why the images that float around them—the remains, so to speak, at the archaeological site—surface first, and they surface so vividly and so compellingly that I acknowledge them as my route to a reconstruction of a world, to an exploration of an interior life that was not written, and to the revelation of a kind of truth.

So the nature of my research begins with something as ineffable and as flexible as a dimly recalled figure, the corner of a room, a voice. I began to write my second book, which was called *Sula,* because of my preoccupation with a picture of a woman and the way in which I heard her name pronounced. Her name was Hannah, and I think she was a friend of my mother's. I don't remember seeing her very much, but what I do remember is the color around her—a kind of violet, a suffusion of something violet—and her eyes, which appeared to be half closed. But what I remember most is how the women said her name: how they said "Hannah Peace" and smiled to themselves, and there was some secret about her that they knew, which they didn't talk about, at least not in my hearing, but it seemed loaded in the way in which they said her name. And I suspected that she was a little bit of an outlaw but that they approved in some way.

And then, thinking about their relationship to her and the way in which they talked about her, the way in which they articulated her name, made me think about friendship between women. What is it that they forgive each other for? And what is it that is unforgivable in the world of women? I don't want to know any more about Miss Hannah Peace, and I'm not going to ask my mother who she really was and what did she do and what were you laughing about and why were you smiling? Because my experience when I do this with my mother is so crushing: she will give you the most pedestrian information you ever heard, and I would like to keep all of my remains and my images intact in their mystery when I begin. Later I will get to the facts. That way I can explore two worlds—the actual and the possible.

What I want to do this evening is to track an image from picture to meaning to text—a journey that appears in the novel that I'm writing now, which is called *Beloved.*

I'm trying to write a particular kind of scene, and I see corn on the cob. To "see" corn on the cob doesn't mean that it suddenly hovers; it only means that it keeps coming back. And in trying to figure out "What is all this corn doing?" I discover what it is doing.

I see the house where I grew up in Lorain, Ohio. My parents had a garden some distance away from our house, and they didn't welcome me and my sister there, when we were young, because we were not able to distinguish between the things that they wanted to grow and the things that they didn't, so we were not able to hoe, or weed, until much later.

I see them walking, together, away from me. I'm looking at their backs and what they're carrying in their arms: their tools, and maybe a peck basket. Sometimes when they walk away from me they hold hands, and they go to this other place in the garden. They have to cross some railroad tracks to get there.

I also am aware that my mother and father sleep at odd hours because my father works many jobs and works at night. And these naps are times of pleasure for me and my sister because nobody's giving us chores, or telling us what to do, or nagging us in any way. In addition to which, there is some feeling of pleasure in them that I'm only vaguely aware of. They're very rested when they take these naps.

And later on in the summer we have an opportunity to eat corn, which is the one plant that I can distinguish from the others, and which is the harvest that I like the best; the others are the food that no child likes—the collards, the okra, the strong, violent vegetables that I would give a great deal for now. But I do like the corn because it's sweet, and because we all sit down to eat it, and it's finger food, and it's hot, and it's even good cold, and there are neighbors in, and there are uncles in, and it's easy, and it's nice.

The picture of the corn and the nimbus of emotion surrounding it became a powerful one in the manuscript I'm now completing.

Authors arrive at text and subtext in thousands of ways, learning each time they begin anew how to recognize a valuable idea and how to render the texture that accompanies, reveals, or displays it to its best advantage. The process by which this is accomplished is endlessly fascinating to me. I have always thought that as an editor for twenty years I understood writers better than their most careful critics, because in examining the manuscript in each of its subsequent stages I knew the author's process, how his or her mind worked, what was effortless, what took time, where the "solution" to a problem came from. The end result—the book—was all that the critic had to go on. Still, for me, that was the least important aspect of the work.

Because, no matter how "fictional" the account of these writers, or how much it was a product of invention, the act of imagination is bound up with memory. You know, they straightened out the Mississippi River in places, to make room for houses and livable acreage. Occasionally the river floods these places. "Floods" is the word they use, but in fact it is not flooding; it is remembering. Remembering where it used to be. All water has a perfect memory and is forever trying to get back to where it was. Writers are like that: remembering where we were, what valley we ran through, what the banks were like, the light that was there and the route back to our original place. It is emotional memory—what the nerves and the skin remember as well as how it appeared. And a rush of imagination is our "flooding."

Along with personal recollection, the matrix of the work I do is the wish to extend, fill in, and complement slave autobiographical narratives. But only the matrix. What comes of all that is dictated by other concerns, not least among them the novel's own integrity. Still, like water, I remember where I was before I was "straightened out."

Q. *I would like to ask about your point of view as a novelist. Is it a vision, or are you taking the part of the particular characters?*

A. I try sometimes to have genuinely minor characters just walk through, like a walk-on actor. But I get easily distracted by them, because a novelist's imagination goes like that: every little road looks to me like an adventure, and once you begin to claim it and describe it, it looks like more, and you invent more and more and more. I don't mind doing that in my first draft, but afterward I have to cut back. I have seen myself get distracted, and people have loomed much larger than I had planned, and minor characters have seemed a little bit more interesting than they need to be for the purposes of the book. In that case I try to endow them: if there are little pieces of information that I want to reveal, I let them do some of the work. But I try not to get carried away; I try to restrain it, so that, finally, the texture is consistent and nothing is wasted; there are no words in the final text that are unnecessary, and no people who are not absolutely necessary.

As for the point of view, there should be the illusion that it's the characters' point of view, when in fact it isn't; it's really the narrator who is there but who doesn't make herself (in my case) known in that role. I like the feeling of a told story, where you hear a voice but you can't identify it, and you think it's your own voice. It's a comfortable voice, and it's a guiding voice, and it's alarmed by the same things that the reader is alarmed by, and it doesn't know what's going to happen next either. So you have this sort of guide. But that guide can't have a personality; it can only have a sound, and you have to feel comfortable with this voice, and then this voice can easily abandon itself and reveal the interior dialogue of a character. So it's a combination of using the point of view of various characters but still retaining the power to slide in and out, provided that when I'm "out" the reader doesn't see little fingers pointing to what's in the text.

What I really want is that intimacy in which the reader is under the impression that he isn't really reading this; that he is participating in it as he goes along. It's unfolding, and he's always two beats ahead of the characters and right on target.

Q. *You have said that writing is a solitary activity. Do you go into steady seclusion when you're writing, so that your feelings are sort of contained, or do you have to get away, and go out shopping and . . . ?*

A. I do all of it. I've been at this book for three years. I go out shopping, and I stare, and I do whatever. It goes away. Sometimes it's very intense and I walk—I mean, I write a sentence and I jump up and run outside or something; it sort of beats you up. And sometimes I don't. Sometimes I write long hours every day. I get up at five thirty and just go do it, and if I don't like it the next day, I throw it away. But I sit down and do it. By now I know how to get to that place where something is working. I didn't always know; I thought every thought I had was interesting—because it was mine. Now I know better how to throw away things that are not useful. I can stand around and do other things and think about it at the same time. I don't mind not writing every minute; I'm not so terrified.

When you first start writing—and I think it's true for a lot
of beginning writers—you're scared to death that if you don't
get that sentence right that minute it's never going to show up
again. And it isn't. But it doesn't matter—another one will, and
it'll probably be better. And I don't mind writing badly for a
couple of days because I know I can fix it—and fix it again and
again and again, and it will be better. I don't have the hysteria
that used to accompany some of those dazzling passages that
I thought the world was just dying for me to remember. I'm a
little more sanguine about it now. Because the best part of it all,
the absolutely most delicious part, is finishing it and then doing
it over. That's the thrill of a lifetime for me: if I can just get done
with that first phase and then have infinite time to fix it and
change it. I rewrite a lot, over and over again, so that it looks like
I never did. I try to make it look like I never touched it, and that
takes a lot of time and a lot of sweat.

Q. *In* Song of Solomon, *what was the relationship between your
memories and what you made up? Was it very tenuous?*

A. Yes, it was tenuous. For the first time I was writing a book
in which the central stage was occupied by men, and that had
something to do with my loss, or my perception of loss, of a
man (my father) and the world that disappeared with him. (It
didn't, but I felt that it did.) So I was re-creating a time period
that was his—not biographically his life or anything in it; I use
whatever's around. But it seemed to me that there was this big
void after he died, and I filled it with a book that was about men
because my two previous books had had women as the central
characters. So in that sense it was about my memories and the
need to invent. I had to do something. I was in such a rage
because my father was dead. The connections between us were
threads that I either mined for a lot of strength or they were
purely invention. But I created a male world and inhabited it
and it had this quest—a journey from stupidity to epiphany,
of a man, a complete man. It was my way of exploring all that,
of trying to figure out what he may have known.

God's Language

ART OF THIS ESSAY is a substitute for an entry or series of entries in a journal or notebook that I have *never* kept. The kind of writer's journal, many of which I have read, which contains ideas for future work, sketches of scenes, observations and meditations. But especially the thoughts that undergird problems and solutions the writer encounters during a work in progress.

I don't keep such notebooks for a number of reasons, one of which is the leisure time unavailable to me, the other is the form my meditations take. Generally it is a response to some tangled, seemingly impenetrable dis-ease; an unquietness connected to a troubling image. (The images may be something seen in the material world or they might not be.) Other times I circle around an incident, a remark, or an impression that is peculiar enough to first provoke curiosity, then mysterious enough to keep recurring. With *The Bluest Eye* it was an exchange I had as a child with a friend that worried me on and off for years. In *Sula* it was a, to me, contradictory response my mother and her friends had to a woman in town. Another was a powerfully imagistic piece of male mythology inapplicable to women and dismissive of the consequences of the truth of that myth on women. In burrowing into those images or remarks or impressions questions surface: Suppose my childhood friend got what she prayed for? What were my mother's friends appreciating while they were disapproving? What was the real trick of the Tar Baby? Why was Margaret Garner so completely without remorse and what effect would her remorselessness have on the neighborhood and her family? These questions, obvious, even idle, when gentled along or nudged led to more nuanced ones. All the time I am ruminating on these things I am not searching for a theme or a novelistic subject; I am just wondering. Most of this wondering is wandering, and disappears sooner or later. But occasionally, within or among these wanderings, a larger question poses itself. I don't write it or my musings down because to do so would give them a gravity they may not deserve. I need to be or feel pursued by the question in order to be convinced that the further exploration is bookworthy. When that happens, at some point a scene or a bit of language arrives. It seems to me a waste of valuable time to sketch or record that when, if it is interesting enough to embellish, I could be tracking it by actually turning it directly into a fictional formulation. If I learn that I am wrong about its staying power or its fertility, I can always throw it away. So I get out the yellow legal pad and see what happens.

With the fiction project I followed the same procedure: waiting to see if certain images I had would wax or wane, yield or implode. One of those images was of a group of ladies standing on the steps of an African Methodist Episcopal church, three rows of them, in early-twentieth-century finery, posing as for a class or club photograph. They are exceptionally beautiful and they are earning a great deal of admiration, you can tell, from the eyes that watch them. Another image is also of women. Girls, rather. They are novices in habits running from the police who have come to arrest them. Both groups of women are associated with churches. The first group is an image—almost like a painting—that surfaced unsummoned; the second is a wholly unreliable piece of village gossip.

Two hundred and some pages later I feel certain this is a wane. Not a wax, although I am also certain that the project is impossible. While each novel I have written, other than the first two, seemed equally undoable, it still astonishes me how, the more work one does, the more difficult it becomes, the more impossible the task. In this instance I am trying to re-create, in the setting of the black towns of the West, a narrative about paradise—the earthly achievement of—its possibility, its dimensions, its stability, even its desirability. The novel's time frame, 1908 to 1976, and the history of its population, former and children of former slaves, require me to rely heavily on the characters' reserves of faith, their concept of freedom, their perception of the divine, and their imaginative as well as organizational/administrative prowess. For like many, but not all, deliberately, carefully constructed nineteenth-century communities, a deeply held and wholly shared belief system was much more vital to the enterprise than was physical endurance, leadership, and opportunity. In fact, faith in a system of belief—religious belief—enabled endurance, forged leadership, and revealed opportunity to be seized. Although for freed men and women prosperity, ownership, safety, and self-determination were thinkable, hungered-for goals, desire alone could not, did not animate the treacherous journey they took into unknown territory to build cities. The history of African Americans that narrows or dismisses religion in both their collective and individual life, in their political and aesthetic activity, is more than incomplete—it may be fraudulent. Therefore, among the difficulties before me is the daunting one of showing not just how their civic and economic impulses respond to their religious principles, but how their everyday lives were inextricably bound with these principles. If the polls taken in 1994, which indicate that 96 percent of African Americans believe in God, are correct I suspect the 4 percent who do not so believe are a recent phenomenon—unheard-of among slave and ex-slave populations. Assuming the religiosity of nineteenth-century African Americans is a given, then, and few texts, fiction or memorialist, have neglected this aspect. But this is 1996 and the solution for fictional representation that takes this in account is not to layer religiosity onto an existing canvas of migration and the quest for citizenship, or to tip one's hat to characters whose belief is unshakable. It is rather to construct a work in which religious belief is central to the narrative itself.

Thus the first problem with paradise: how to render expressive religious language credibly and effectively in postmodern fiction without having to submit to a vague egalitarianism, or to a kind of

late-twentieth-century environmental spiritualism, or to the modern-
ist/feminist school of the goddess-body adored, or to a loose, undis-
criminating conviction of the innate divinity of all living things, or to
the biblical/political scholasticism of the more entrenched and dictatorial wings of contemporary religious institutions—none of which,
it seems to me, represents the everyday practice of nineteenth-century
African Americans and their children, nor lends itself to postmodernist narrative strategies. The second problem then is part of the first:
how to narrate persuasively profound and motivating faith in and to
a highly secularized, contemporary, "scientific" world. In short, how
to reimagine paradise. (The question that surfaces immediately—Why
reimagine it at all, since the ablest geniuses have already and long ago
provided unsurpassed and unsurpassable language to describe it?—is
a question I will address in a moment.) Right now I want to outline
what my problem is and then tell you why I have it.

Paradise is no longer imaginable or, rather, it is overimagined—which
amounts to the same thing—and has thus become familiar, common,
even trivial. Historically, the images of paradise, in poetry and prose,
were intended to be grand but accessible, beyond the routine but
imaginatively graspable, seductive precisely because of our ability to
recognize them—as though we "remembered" the scenes somehow.
Milton speaks of "goodliest trees, loaden with fairest fruit, / Blossoms
and fruits at once of golden hue, / . . . with gay enameled colours
mixed"; of "Native perfumes"; of "that sapphire fount the crispèd
brooks, / Rolling on orient pearl and sands of gold"; of "nectar, visiting
each plant, and fed / Flowers worthy of Paradise . . ."; "nature boon /
poured forth profuse on hill and dale and plain"; "Groves whose rich
trees wept odorous gums and balm; / Others, whose fruit, burnished
with golden rind, / Hung amiable—Hesperian fables true, / . . . of
delicious taste; / Betwixt them lawns, or level downs, and flocks /
Grazing the tender herb"; "Flowers of all hue, and without thorn the
rose"; "caves / of cool recess, o'er which the mantling vine / Lays forth
her purple grape, and gently creeps / Luxuriant."

Such a beatific expanse, in this the last decade of the twentieth
century, we recognize as bounded real estate, owned by the wealthy,

viewed and visited by guests and tourists, or it is regularly on display for the rest of us in the products and promises sold by various media. Overimagined. Quite available if not in fact, then certainly as ordinary unexceptional desire. Let's examine the characteristics of physical paradise—beauty, plenty, rest, exclusivity, and eternity—to see how they are understood in 1996.

Beauty of course is a duplicate of what we already know, intensified, refined. Or what we have never known articulated. Beatific, benevolent nature combined with precious metals and jewelry. What it cannot be is beauty beyond imagination.

Plenty, in a world of excess and attending greed that tilts resources to the haves and forces the have-nots to locate bounty within what has already been acquired by the haves, is an almost obscene feature of paradise. In this world of tilted resources, of outrageous, shameless wealth squatting, hulking, preening itself before the dispossessed, the very idea of plenty, of sufficiency, as utopian ought to make us tremble. Plenty should not be regulated to a paradisiacal state, but to normal, everyday, humane life.

Rest, that is the superfluity of working or fighting for rewards of food or luxury, has dwindling currency these days. It is a desirelessness that suggests a special kind of death without dying.

Exclusivity, however, is still an attractive, even compelling, feature of paradise because certain people, the unworthy, are not there. Boundaries are secure; watchdogs, gates, keepers are there to verify the legitimacy of the inhabitants. Such enclaves are cropping up again, like medieval fortresses and moats, and it does not seem possible or desirable for a city to be envisioned in which poor people can be accommodated. Exclusivity is not just an accessible dream for the well-endowed, but an increasingly popular solution for the middle class. "Streets" are understood to be populated by the unworthy and the dangerous; young people are forced off the streets for their own good. Yet public space is fought over as if it were private. Who gets to enjoy a park, a beach, a mall, a corner? The term "public" is itself a site of contention. Paradise as exclusive terrain therefore has a very real attraction to modern society.

Eternity, since it avoids the pain of dying again, and, in its rejection of secular, scientific arguments, has probably the greatest appeal. And medical, scientific resources directed toward more life, and fitter life, remind us that the desire is for earthbound eternity, rather than eternal afterlife. The suggestion being this is all there is. Thus, paradise, as an earthly project, as opposed to a heavenly one, has serious intellectual and visual limitations. Aside from "Only me or us forever" it hardly bears describing anymore.

But that might be unfair. It is hard not to notice how much more attention has always been given to hell rather than heaven. Dante's *Inferno* beats out *Paradiso* every time. Milton's brilliantly rendered pre-paradise world, known as Chaos, is far more fully realized than his Paradise. The visionary language of antithesis reaches heights of linguistic ardor with which the thesis language seldom competes. There are many reasons why the images of the horrors of hell were meant to be virulently repulsive in the twelfth, fifteenth, and seventeenth centuries. The argument for avoiding it needed to be visceral, needed to reveal how much worse such an eternity was than the hell of everyday life. But the need has persisted, in our times, with a significant addition. There is an influx of books devoted to a consternation about the absence of a sense of evil—if not hell—of a loss of shame in contemporary life.

One wonders how to account for the melancholy that accompanies these exhortations about our inattention to, the mutedness, the numbness toward the decidedly anti-paradisiacal experience. Evil is understood, justifiably, to be pervasive, but it has somehow lost its awe-fullness. It does not frighten us. It is merely entertainment. Why are we not so frightened by its possibilities that we turn in panic toward good? Is afterlife of any sort too simple for our complex, sophisticated modern intelligence? Or is it that, more than paradise, evil needs costumes, constantly refurbished and replenished? Literary? Hell has always lent itself to glamour, headlines, a tuxedo, cunning, a gruesome mask or a seductive one. Maybe it needs blood, slime, roaring simply to get our attention, to tickle us, draw from us our wit, our imagination, our energy, our heights of performance. After which paradise is simply its absence, an edgeless and therefore unavailing lack full of an already perceived, already recognizable landscape: great trees for shade and fruit, lawns, palaces, precious metals, jewelry, animal husbandry. Outside fighting evil, waging war against the unworthy, there seems nothing for its inhabitants to do. A nonexclusionary, unbordered, come-one-come-all paradise, without dread, minus a nemesis, is no paradise at all.

Under these circumstances, then, the literary problem is harnessing contemporary language to reveal not only the intellectual complexity of paradise, but language that seizes the imagination not as an amicus brief to a naïve or psychotic life, but as sane, intelligent life itself. If I am to do justice to, bear witness to the deeply religious population of this project and render their profoundly held moral system affective in these alienated, uninspiring, and uninspired times—where religion is understood to run the gamut from scorned, unintelligible fundamentalism to literate, well-meaning liberalism, to televangelistic marketing to militaristic racism and phobophilia—I have serious problems.

Historically the language of religion (and I am speaking here of Christianity, but I am relatively certain this is true of all text-based religions) is dependent upon and gains its strength, beauty, and unassailability from biblical or holy texts. Contemporary religious language, that is the speech and the script that seeks to translate divine translations into "popular" or "everyday common" parlance, seems to work best in song, in anecdote, and in the apt rhetorical flourish. I understand that the reason for modernizing traditional language of the Bible is an effort to connect with and proselytize a population indifferent or unresponsive to the language that moved our ancestors. To compete for the attention of a constituency whose discourse has been shaped by the language of media and commerce and whose expectation of correlating images to accompany and clarify text is a difficult enterprise. And it appears reasonable to accommodate altering circumstances with alternate modes of discourse. While I can't testify to the success of such efforts, I suspect the "modernization" of God's language has been rewarding—otherwise these attempts would not be so plentiful.

Marketing religion requires new strategies, new appeals, and a relevance that is immediate, not contemplative. Thus modern language, while successful in the acquisition of converts and the spiritual maintenance of the confirmed, is forced to kneel before the denominator that is most accessible, to bankrupt its subtlety, its mystery in order to bankroll its effect. Nevertheless it seems a poor substitute for the language it seeks to replace, not only because it sacrifices ambiguity, depth, and moral authority, but also because its techniques are reinforcement rather than liberation.

I do not mean to suggest that there are no brilliant sermons, powerfully intelligent essays, revelatory poems, moving encomiums, or elegant arguments. Of course there are. Nor do I mean to suggest that there is no personal language, no prayer that is not stunning in its creativity, its healing properties, its sheer intellectual power. But these rhetorical forms are not suitable for sustained prose fiction. Modern narrative is devoid of religious language that does not glean most of its nourishment from allusions to or quotations from the King James Version of the Holy Bible. Two examples of fiction that deliberately and successfully merge modern and biblical language are Leon Forrest's novels and Reynolds Price's short narratives.

The questions I put to myself are: Is it possible to write religion-inflected prose narrative that does not rest its case entirely or mainly on biblical language? Is it possible to make the experience and journey of faith fresh, as new and as linguistically unencumbered as it was to early believers, who themselves had no collection of books to rely on?

I have chosen this task, this obligation partly because I am alarmed at the debasement of religious language in literature; its cliché-ridden expression, its apathy, its refusal to refuel itself with nonmarket vocabulary (or its insistence on refueling itself with marketing vocabulary), its substitution of the terminology of popular psychology for philosophical clarity; its patriarchal triumphalism, its morally opinionated dictatorial praxis, the unearned pleasure it takes in performability for its miracle rather than content; its low opinion of itself.

How can a novelist represent bliss in nonsexual, nonorgiastic terms? How can a novelist, in a land of plenty, render undeserved, limitless love, the one "that passeth all understanding," without summoning the consumer pleasure of a lotto win? How to invoke paradise in an age of theme parks?

The answer, unfortunately, is that, so far, I cannot.

I have chosen in the meantime something else, some other strategy to concretize these informing, old-fashioned passions and conflicts. Not to use paeanistic, rapturous, large words, etc., but to reveal their consequences.

Here I would like to do what I have always done when the questions becomes answerable only in the act of storytelling. Begin the story.

"They shoot the white girl first. With the rest they can take their time."

Grendel and His Mother

I AM HOPING that you will agree that the piece of literature I want to draw from is, as one of its translators says, "equal to our knowledge of reality in the present time." And discover in the lines of association I am making with a medieval sensibility and a modern one a fertile ground on which we can appraise our contemporary world.

I am going to tell you a story. First because narrative is probably the most effective way knowledge is structured and second because I am a storyteller. The practice of writing makes demands on me that nothing else does. The search for language, whether among other writers or in originating it, constitutes a mission. Delving into literature is neither escape nor a surefire route to comfort. It has been a constant, sometimes violent, always provocative engagement with the contemporary world, the issues of the society we live in. So you won't be surprised that I take my text from ancient but by no means remote sources. The story is this. As I tell it you may be reminded of the events and rhetoric and actions of many current militarized struggles and violent upheavals.

Once upon a time there lived a man-eating monster of unprecedented cruelty and unparalleled appetite, who ravaged generally at night and focused primarily on the people of one particular kingdom, but it was only because he chose to. Clearly he could slaughter whomever and wherever he decided to. His name was Grendel and he spent a dozen years dismembering, chewing, and swallowing the livestock, the thanes, the citizens of Scandinavia.

The leader of the besieged country lived in a great mead hall with his queen, his family, friends, guards, counsels, and a grand army of heroes. Each night when the leader retired, guards and warriors were stationed to protect the hall and its inhabitants from destruction and to try, if at all possible, to slay their nighttime enemy. And each night Grendel picked them off as though they were ripe cherries on an eternally fruited tree. The kingdom was sunk in mourning and helplessness; riven with sorrow for the dead, with regret for the past, and in fear of the future. They were in the same situation as the Finns of one of their sagas: "hooped within the great wheel of necessity, in thrall to a code of loyalty and bravery, bound to seek glory in the eye of the warrior world. The little nations are grouped around their lord, the greater nations spoil for war and menace the little ones, a lord dies, defenselessness ensues, the enemy strikes, vengeance for the dead becomes an ethic for the living, bloodshed begets further bloodshed, the wheel turns, the generations tread and tread and tread."

But what seemed never to trouble or worry them was who was Grendel and why had he placed them on his menu? Nowhere in the story is that question put. The question does not surface for a simple reason: evil has no father. It is preternatural and exists without explanation. Grendel's actions are dictated by his nature; the nature of an alien mind—an inhuman drift. He is the essence of the one who loathes you, wants you not just dead, but nourishingly so, so that your death provides gain to the slayer: food, land, wealth, water—whatever. Like genocide, ethnic cleansing, mass murder, or individual assault for profit. But Grendel escapes these reasons: no one had attacked or offended him; no one had tried to invade his home or displace him from his territory; no one had stolen from him or visited any wrath upon him. Obviously he was neither defending himself nor seeking vengeance. In fact no one knew who he was. He was not angry with the Danes; he didn't want to rule their land or plunder their resources or rape their women, so there could be no reasoning with him. No bribery, no negotiations, no begging, no trading could stop him. Humans, even at their most corrupt, selfish, and ignorant can be made available to reason, are educable, retrainable, and, most important, fathomable. Humans have words for madness, explanations for evil, and a system of payback for those who trespass or are judged outlaws. But Grendel was beyond comprehension, unfathomable. The ultimate monster: mindless without intelligible speech. In the illustrations that imagine him and the language that described him, Grendel is ugly: hairy, his body is folded in on itself, reeking, easy and most comfortable on all fours. But even without claws or rows of sharklike teeth, even if he had been beautiful, it would not have lessened the horror; his mere presence in the world was an affront to it.

Eventually, of course, a brave and fit hero named Beowulf volunteers to rid the kingdom of this pestilence. He and his task force of warriors enter the land, announce their purpose, and are welcomed with enthusiasm. On the first night, following a celebration to rally the forces and draw their courage, the war is won—or so it seemed. When the monster appears, they suffer only one casualty before Beowulf rips off Grendel's arm, sending him fatally bleeding, limping and moaning, slouching back home to his mother, where he dies.

Yes, mother. I suggested earlier that evil has no father, but it should not come as a surprise that Grendel has a mother. In true folkloric, epic fashion, the bearer of evil, of destruction is female. Monsters, it seems, are born after all, and like her sisters—Eve, Pandora, Lot's wife, Helen of Troy, and the female that sits at the gate of Milton's hell, birthing vicious dogs who eat one another and are replaced by more and more litters from their mother's womb—it turns out that Grendel's mother is more repulsive, more "responsible" for evil than her son is. Interestingly enough, she has no name and cannot speak (I would like to follow these images, but at some other time). In any case, this silent, repulsive female is a mother, and unlike her child, does have a motive for murder—therefore she sets out immediately to avenge her son. She advances to the mead hall, interrupts the warriors reveling at their victory, and fills the pouch she carries with their mangled bodies. Her vengeance instigates a second, even more determined foray by Beowulf, this time on the monster's territory and in his home. Beowulf swims through demon-laden waters, is captured, and, entering the mother's lair, weaponless, is forced to use his bare hands.

He fights mightily but unsuccessfully. Suddenly and fortunately, he grabs a sword that belongs to the mother. With her own weapon she cuts off her head, and then the head of Grendel's corpse. A curious thing happens then: the victim's blood melts the sword. The conventional reading is that the fiends' blood is so foul it melts steel, but the image of Beowulf standing there with a mother's head in one hand and a useless hilt in the other encourages more layered interpretations. One being that perhaps violence against violence—regardless of good and evil, right and wrong—is itself so foul the sword of vengeance collapses in exhaustion or shame.

Beowulf is a classic epic of good vanquishing evil; of unimaginable brutality being overcome by physical force. Bravery, sacrifice, honor, pride, rewards both in reputations and wealth—all come full circle in this rousing medieval tale. In such heroic narratives, glory is not in the details; the forces of good and evil are obvious, blatant, the triumph of the former over the latter is earned, justified, and delicious. As Beowulf says, "It is always better / to avenge dear ones than to indulge in mourning. / . . . So arise, my lord, and let us immediately / set forth on the trail of this troll-dam. / I guarantee you she will not get away, / not to dens under ground nor upland groves / nor the ocean floor. She'll have nowhere to flee to."

Contemporary society, however, is made uneasy by the concept of pure, unmotivated evil, by pious, unsullied virtue, and contemporary writers and scholars search for more.

One challenge to the necessary but narrow expectations of this heroic narrative comes from a contemporary writer, the late John Gardner, in his novel, titled *Grendel*. Told from the monster's point of view, it is a tour de force and an intellectual and aesthetic enterprise that comes very close to being the sotto-voiced subject of much of today's efforts to come to grips with the kind of permanent global war we now find ourselves engaged in. The novel poses the question that the epic does not: Who is Grendel? The author asks us to enter his mind and test the assumption that evil is flagrantly unintelligible, wanton, and undecipherable. By assuming Grendel's voice, his point of view, Gardner establishes at once that unlike the character in the poem, Grendel is not without thought, and is not a beast. In fact he is reflecting precisely on real true beasts the moment the reader is introduced to him. When the novel opens he is watching a ram, musing, "Do not think my brains are squeezed shut, like the ram's, by the roots of horns." And "Why can't these creatures discover a little dignity?"

Gardner's version has the same plot, characters, etc., as the original, and relies on similar descriptions and conventions: referring to women, for example, only queens have names. If Grendel's mother has a name it is as unspeakable as she is unspeaking. Seamus Heaney's introduction to his translation of *Beowulf* emphasizes the movement of evil from out there to in here, from the margins of the world to inside the castle, and focuses on the artistic brilliance of the poem, the "beautiful contrivances of its language"; Gardner, however, tries to penetrate the interior life—emotional, cognizant—of incarnate evil and prioritizes the poet as one who organizes the world's disorder, who pulls together disparate histories into meaning. We learn in Gardner's novel that Grendel distinguishes himself from the ram that does not know or remember his past. We learn that Grendel, in the beginning, is consumed by hatred and is neither proud nor ashamed of it. That he is full of contempt for the survivors of his rampages. Watching the thanes bury their dead, he describes the scene as follows: "On the side of the hill the dirge-slow shoveling begins. They throw up a mound for the funeral pyre, for whatever arms or legs or heads my haste has left behind. Meanwhile, up in the shattered hall, the builders are hammering, replacing the door . . . industrious and witless as worker ants—except that they make small, foolish changes, adding a few more iron pegs, more iron bands, with tireless dogmatism." This contempt extends to the world in general. "I understood that the world was nothing: a mechanical chaos of casual, brute enmity on which we stupidly impose our hopes and fears. I understood that, finally and absolutely, I alone exist. All the rest, I saw, is merely what pushes me, or what I push against, blindly—as blindly as all that is not myself pushes back. I create the whole universe, blink by blink."

But the fundamental theme of the novel lies in Grendel's possibilities—first, his encounter with shaped, studied, artistic language (as opposed to noise, groans, shouts, boasts) and, second, his dialogue with the dragon who sits atop the mountain of gold he has been guarding for centuries. Regarding the first, his encounter with the poet, who is called the Shaper, offers him the only possibility of transformation. Grendel knows the Shaper's song is full of lies, illusion. He has watched carefully the battles of men and knows they are not the glory the Shaper turns them into. But he succumbs to the Shaper's language nevertheless because of its power to transform, its power to elevate, to discourage base action. He defines the poet's potency this way: "He reshapes the world. . . . So his name implies. He stares strange-eyed at the mindless world and turns dry sticks to gold." It is because of this shaped, elevated, patterned language that Grendel is able to contemplate beauty, recognize love, feel pity, crave mercy, and experience shame. It is because of the Shaper's imagination that he considers the equation of quality with meaning. In short he develops a desperate hunger for the life of a completely human being. "My heart," he says, "was light with Hrothgar's goodness, and leaden with grief at my own bloodthirsty ways." Overwhelmed with these reflections on goodness and light, he goes to the mead hall weeping for mercy, aching for community to assuage his utter loneliness. "I staggered out into the open and up toward the hall with my burden, groaning out, 'Mercy! Peace!' The harper broke off, the people screamed. . . . Drunken men rushed me with battle-axes. I sank to my knees, crying, 'Friend! Friend!' They hacked at me, yipping like dogs." So he reverts to the deep wilderness of his hatred. Yet he is still in turmoil, torn between "tears and a bellow of scorn." He travels to the dragon for answers to his own cosmic questions: Why am I here? What is God? What is the world?

At the end of a long and fascinating argument, loaded with the dragon's cynicism, bitterness, and indifference, Grendel receives one word of advice from the dragon: "Get a pile of gold, and sit on it." Between Grendel's suspicion that noble language produces noble behavior (just as puny, empty language produces puny, empty behavior) and the dragon's view of man's stupidity, banality, and irrelevance, his own denial of "free will and intercession," right there, exactly there, lies the plane on which civic and intellectual life rests, rocks, and rolls.

Grendel's dilemma is also ours. It is the nexus between the Shaper and the dragon; between Saint Augustine and Nietzsche, between art and science; between the Old Testament and the New, between swords and ploughshares. It is the space for as well as the act of thought; it is a magnetic space, pulling us away from reaction to thinking. Denying easy answers, and violence committed because, in crisis, it is the only thing one knows how to do.

Absolute answers, like those Grendel wanted, cynically poised questions, like those the dragon offered, can dilute and misdirect the educational project. In this country, where competition is worshipped and crisis is the driving force of media-salted information, and where homogeneity and difference, diversity and conformity are understood to be the national ideal, we are being asked to both recoil from violence and to embrace it; to waver between winning at all costs and caring for our neighbor; between the fear of the strange and the comfort of the familiar; between the blood feud of the Scandinavians and the monster's yearning for nurture and community. It was the pull of those opposites that trounced Grendel and that trouble and disable national, educational, and personal discourse.

Crisis is a heightened, sometimes bloody, obviously dangerous, always tense confluence of events and views about those events. Volatility, theatricality, and threat swirl about in crisis. Crisis, like war, demands "final answers," quick and definitive action—to douse flames, draw blood, soothe consciences.

Sometimes the demand for quick and definitive action is so keen all energy is gathered to avoid the crisis of impending crisis. The effect of militarizing virtually every fluid situation and social problem has been encroaching inertia, if not established paralysis. It has also produced an increased appetite for ever more thrilling, intense presentations of crisis. (Note the plethora of televised entertainment devoted to ersatz, fake crises—survival in third-world countries among people for whom survival is an unremarkable condition of life.) This hunger is not different from numb insensitivity, is, in fact, a vivid expression of it. Once the taste for the blood images of conquest is introduced, it may not be easily slaked.

I have elaborated upon this media version of crisis in order to distinguish it from conflict. Conflict is the clash of incompatible forces, the Shaper versus the dragon; a disharmony calling for adjustment, change, or compromise. Conflict recognizes legitimate oppositions, honest but different interpretations of data, contesting theories. These oppositions may be militarized, may have to be, but in the academy they should, must not be. In fact, they must be embraced if education is to occur. Conflict in the halls of the academy is unlike conflict in the malls, arcades, or on a battlefield. In academic halls versus arcade malls, conflict is not a screen game to play for its own sake, nor a social gaffe to avoid at all costs. It has a bad reputation only because we have been taught to associate it with winning and losing, with the desperate need to be right, to be alpha. With violence. Conflict is not another word for crisis or for war or for competition. Conflict is a condition of intellectual life, and, I believe, its pleasure. Firing up the mind to engage itself is precisely what the mind is for—it has no other purpose. Just as the body is always struggling to repair itself from its own abuse, to stay alive, so is the mind craving knowledge. When it is not busy trying to know, it is in disrepair.

The mind really is a palace. Not only for its perception of symmetry and the outrageously beautiful, but also because it can invent, imagine, and, most important, it can delve.

I like to think that John Gardner's view will hold: that language—informed, shaped, reasoned—will become the hand that stays crisis and gives creative, constructive conflict air to breathe, startling our lives and rippling our intellect. I know that democracy is worth fighting for. I know that fascism is not. To win the former intelligent struggle is needed. To win the latter nothing is required. You only have to cooperate, be silent, agree, and obey until the blood of Grendel's mother annihilates her own weapon and the victor's as well.

The Writer Before the Page

I ONCE KNEW a woman named Hannah Peace. I say "knew," but nothing could be less accurate. I was perhaps four years old when she was in the town where I lived. I don't know where (or even if) she is now or to whom she was related then. She was not even a visiting friend. And I couldn't to this day describe her in a way that would make her known in a photograph, nor would I recognize her if she walked into this room. But I have a memory of her and it's like this: the color of her skin—the matte quality of it. Something purple around her. Also eyes not completely open. There emanated from her an aloofness that seemed to me kindly disposed. But most of all I remember her name—or the way people pronounced it. Never Hannah or Miss Peace. Always Hannah Peace—and more. Something hidden—some awe perhaps, but certainly some forgiveness. When they pronounced her name, they (the women and the men) forgave her something.

That's not much, I know: half-closed eyes, an absence of hostility, skin powdered in lilac dust. But it was more than enough to evoke a character—in fact any more detail would have prevented (for me) the emergence of a fictional character at all. What is useful—definitive—is the galaxy of emotion that accompanied the woman as I pursued my memory of her, not the woman herself.

In the example I have given of Hannah Peace it was the having-been-easily-forgiven that caught my attention, and that quality, that "easily forgiveness" that I believe I remembered in connection with a shadow of a woman my mother knew, is the theme of *Sula*. The women forgive each other—or learn to. Once that piece of the constellation became apparent, it dominated the other pieces. The next step was to discover what there is to be forgiven among women. Such things must now be raised and invented because I am going to tell about feminine forgiveness in story form. The things to be forgiven are grave errors and violent misdemeanors, but the point was less the thing to be forgiven than the nature and quality of forgiveness among women—which is to say friendship among women. What one puts up with in a friendship is determined by the emotional value of the relationship. But *Sula* is not (simply) about friendship between women but between black women, a qualifying term the artistic responsibilities of which are what goes on before I ever approach the page. Before the act of writing, before the clean yellow legal pad or the white bond are the principles that inform the idea of writing. I will touch upon them in a moment.

What I want my fiction to do is to urge the reader into active participation in the nonnarrative, nonliterary experience of the text. And to refuse him makes it difficult for him (the reader) to confine himself to a cool and distant acceptance of data. When one looks at a very good painting, the experience of looking is deeper than the data accumulated in viewing it. The same, I think, is true in listening to good music. Just as the literary value of a painting or a musical composition is limited, so too is the literary value of literature limited. I sometimes think how glorious it must have been to have written drama in sixteenth-century England, or poetry in Greece before Christ, or religious narrative in 1000 AD, when literature was need and did not have a critical history to constrain or diminish the writer's imagination. How magnificent not to have to depend on the reader's literary associations—his literary experience—which can be as much an impoverishment of the reader's imagination as it is of a writer's. It is important that what I write not be merely literary. I am most self-conscious about in my work being overcareful in making sure that I don't strike literary postures. I avoid, too studiously perhaps, name-dropping, lists, literary references, unless oblique and based on written folklore. The choice of a tale or of folklore in my work is tailored to the character's thoughts or actions in a way that flags him or her and provides irony, sometimes humor.

Milkman, about to meet the oldest black woman in the world, the mother of mothers who has spent her life caring for helpless others, enters her house thinking of a European tale, "Hansel and Gretel," a story about parents who abandoned their own children to a forest and a witch who made a diet of them. His confusion at that point, his racial and cultural ignorance and confusion, is flagged. Equally marked is Hagar's bed being described as Goldilocks's choice. Partly because of Hagar's preoccupation with hair, and partly because, like Goldilocks, a housebreaker if ever there was one, she is greedy for things, unmindful of property rights or other people's space, and Hagar is emotionally selfish as well as confused.

This deliberate avoidance of literary references has become a firm if boring habit with me, not only because it leads to poses, not only because I refuse the credentials it bestows, but also because it is inappropriate to the kind of literature I wish to write, the aims of that literature, and the discipline of the specific culture that interests me. (Emphasis on *me*.) Literary references in the hands of writers I love can be extremely revealing, but they can also supply a comfort I don't want the reader to have because I want him to respond on the same plane an illiterate or preliterature reader would have to. I want to subvert his traditional comfort so that he may experience an unorthodox one: that of being in the company of his own solitary imagination.

My beginnings as a novelist were very much focused on creating this discomfort and unease in order to insist that the reader rely on another body of knowledge. However weak those beginnings were in 1965, they nevertheless pointed me toward the process that engages me in 1982: trusting memory and culling from it theme and structure. In *The Bluest Eye* the recollection of what I felt and saw upon hearing a child my own age say she prayed for blue eyes provided the first piece. I then tried to distinguish between a piece and a part (in the way that a piece of a human body is different from a part of a human body).

As I began developing parts out of pieces, I found that I preferred them unconnected—to be related but not to touch—to circle, not line up, because the story of this prayer was the story of a shattered, fractured perception resulting from a shattered, splintered life. The novel turned out to be a composition of parts circling one another, like the galaxy accompanying memory. I fret the pieces and fragment aspect of memory because too often we want the whole thing. When we wake from a dream we want to remember all of it, although the fragment we are remembering may be—very probably is—the most important piece in the dream. Chapter and part designations, as conventionally used in novels, were never very much help to me in writing. Nor are outlines. (I permit their use for the sake of the designer and for ease in talking about the book. They are usually identified at the last minute.)

There may be play and arbitrariness in the way memory surfaces but none in the way the composition is organized, especially when I hope to re-create play and arbitrariness in the way narrative events unfold. The form becomes the exact interpretation of the idea the story is meant to express. Nothing more traditional than that—but the sources of the images are not the traditional novelistic or readerly ones. The visual image of a splintered mirror, or the corridor of split mirrors in blue eyes, is the form as well as the context in *The Bluest Eye*.

Narrative is one of the ways in which knowledge is organized. I have always thought it was the most important way to transmit and receive knowledge. I am less certain of that now—but if the fact that the craving for narrative has never lessened it is any indication, the hunger for it is as keen as it was on Mount Sinai or Calvary or in the middle of the fens. (Even when novelists abandon or grow tired of it as an outmoded memetic form, historians, journalists, and performing artists take up the slack.) Still, narrative is not and never has been enough, just as the object drawn on a canvas or a cave wall is never simply mimetic.

My compact with the reader is not to reveal an already established reality (literary or historical) that he or she and I agree upon beforehand. I don't want to assume or exercise that kind of authority. I regard that as patronizing, although many people regard it as safe and reassuring. And because my métier is black, the artistic demands of black culture are such that I cannot patronize, control, or pontificate. In the third-world cosmology as I perceive it, reality is not already constituted by my literary predecessors in Western culture. If my work is to confront a reality unlike that received reality of the West, it must centralize and animate information discredited by the West—discredited not because it is not true or useful or even of some racial value, but because it is information held by discredited people, information dismissed as "lore" or "gossip" or "magic" or "sentiment."

If my work is faithfully to reflect the aesthetic tradition of Afro-American culture, it must make conscious use of the characteristics of its art forms and translate them into print: antiphony, the group nature of art, its functionality, its improvisational nature, its relationship to audience performance, the critical voice that upholds tradition and communal values and that also provides occasion for an individual to transcend and/or defy group restrictions.

Working with those rules, the text, if it is to take improvisation and audience participation into account, cannot be the authority—it should be the map. It should make a way for the reader (audience) to participate in the tale. The language, if it is to permit criticism of both rebellion and tradition, must be both indicator and mask, and the tension between the two kinds of language is its release and its power. If my work is to be functional to the group (to the village, as it were) then it must bear witness and identify danger as well as possible havens from danger; it must identify that which is useful from the past and that which ought to be discarded; it must make it possible to prepare for the present and live it out; and it must do that not by avoiding problems and contradictions but by examining them; it should not even attempt to solve social problems but it should certainly try to clarify them.

Before I try to illustrate some of these points by using *Tar Baby* as an example, let me hasten to say that there are eminent and powerful, intelligent, and gifted black writers who not only recognize Western literature as part of their own heritage but who have employed it to such an advantage that it illuminates both cultures. I neither object to nor am indifferent to their work or their views. I relish it, in precisely the way I relish a world of literature from other cultures. The question is not legitimacy or the "correctness" of a point of view, but the difference between my point of view and theirs. Nothing would be more hateful to me than a monolithic prescription for what black literature is or ought to be. I simply wanted to write literature that was irrevocably, indisputably black not because its characters were, or because I was, but because it took as its creative task and sought as its credentials those recognized and verifiable principles of black art.

TAR BABY

Recollecting the told story.

Refusing to read a modern or Westernized version of it.

Selecting out the pieces that were disturbing or simply memorable: fear, tar, the rabbit's outrage at a failing in traditional manners (the Tar Baby does not speak). Why the Tar Baby was formed, to what purpose, what was the farmer trying to protect, and why did he think the doll would be attractive to the rabbit (what did he know and what was his big mistake)? Why does the Tar Baby cooperate with the farmer, do the things the farmer wishes to protect, wish to be protected? What makes his job more important than the rabbit's, why does the farmer believe that a briar patch is sufficient punishment, what does the briar patch represent to the rabbit, to the Tar Baby, and to the farmer?

CREATION

Putting the above pieces together in parts.

Concentrating on tar as a part. What is it and where does it come from; its holy uses and its profane uses, consideration of which leads to a guiding motif: ahistorical earth and historical earth. How that theme is translated into the structure.

1. Coming out of the sea (that which was there before earth) is both the beginning and the end of the book—in both of which Son emerges from the sea in a section that is not numbered as a chapter.

2. The earth that came out of the sea and its conquest by modern man; that conquest as viewed by fishermen and clouds. The pain it caused to the conquered life forms.
3. Movement from the earth into the household: its rooms, its quality of shelter. The activity for which the rooms were designed: eating, sleeping, bathing, leisure, etc.
4. The houses disrupted precisely as the earth was disrupted. The chaos of the earth duplicated in the house designed for order. The disruption is caused by the man born out of the womb of the sea accompanied by ammonia odors of birth.
5. The conflict that follows is between the ahistorical (the pristine) and the historical (or social) forces inherent in the uses of tar.
6. The conflict is, further, between two kinds of chaos: civilized chaos and natural chaos.
7. The revelation, then, is the revelation of secrets. Everybody with one or two exceptions has a secret: secrets of acts committed (as with Margaret and Son), and secrets of thoughts unspoken but driving nonetheless (as with Valerian and Jadine). And then the deepest and earliest secret of all: that just as we watch other life, other life watches us.

I apologize for using my own work as an illustration to those of you who may not be familiar with it. But had I chosen material from other writers, the possibility of its being unfamiliar would be equally as great.

My inability to consider the world in terms other than verbal means that I am not able to not think about writing. It is the "world coherent" for me. So I am perplexed by the dread and apprehension with which some writers regard the process. I am also bored by the type and space devoted to the death of fiction when the funeral is lasting longer than the life of the art itself; we can be safe in our assumption that the corpse is immortal. The "goodbye" is at least 110 years old.

What the fiction-obituary critics are responding to is the peril literature is in. Peril that can be categorized in three parts:

1. First is the suspicion (or fact—I am not sure which) that the best young minds are not being attracted to writing, that technology, postmodernist architecture, "new" music, film, etc., are much more demanding and exciting.
2. Second is the conviction (in the academy at any rate) that fiction as narrative is obsolete because it is dictatorial, bourgeois, and self-congratulatory in its attempt to maintain the status quo.
3. Third of the categories of peril is the growth requirement of publishers—the marketplace demands narrow the possibilities for new writers to find a publishing home.

There are, of course, some other perhaps more immediate perils (global stability, poverty, hunger, love, death), so it really is not a good time to write. To which observation one can only say: So what? When has it ever been a good time? Plague-ridden Britain for Chaucer? World War II for Eudora Welty? World War I for Virginia Woolf? South African brutality for Nadine Gordimer? The 94 percent slave population for Plato?

As writers, what we do is remember. And to remember this world is to create it. The writer's responsibility (whatever her or his time) is to change the world—improve his/her own time. Or, less ambitious, to help make sense of it. Simply in order to discover that it does make sense. Not *one* sense. What is the point of 2 billion people making *one* sense.

I am old enough to have seen the northern lights (1938?) and I remember that most shocking, most profound event in the sky over Lorain, Ohio. After that how could I be content with one simple color? Or a simple Hannah Peace?

The Trouble with Paradise

I WANT to begin my meditation on the trouble with paradise with some remarks on the environment in which I work and in which many writers also work. The construction of race and its hierarchy have a powerful impact on expressive language, just as figurative, interpretative language impacts powerfully on the construction of a racial society. The intimate exchange between the atmosphere of racism and the language that asserts, erases, manipulates, or transforms it is unavoidable among fiction writers, who must manage to hold an unblinking gaze into the realm of difference. We are always being compelled by and being pulled into an imaginary of lives we have never led, emotions we have never felt to which we have no experiential access, and toward persons never invited into our dreams. We imagine old people when we are young, write about the wealthy when we have nothing, genders that are not our own, people who exist nowhere except in our minds holding views we not only do not share but may even loathe. We write about nationalities with whom we have merely a superficial acquaintance. The willingness, the necessity, the excitement of moving about in unknown terrain constitute both the risk and the satisfaction of the work.

Of the several realms of difference, the most stubborn to imagine convincingly is the racial difference. It is a stubbornness born of ages of political insistence and social apparatus. And while it has an almost unmitigated force in political and domestic life, the realm of racial difference has been allowed an intellectual weight to which it has no claim. It is truly a realm that is no realm at all. An all-consuming vacancy, the enunciatory difficulty of which does not diminish with the discovery that one is narrating that which is both constitutive and fraudulent, both common and strange. Strong critical language is available clarifying that discovery of the chasm that is none, as well as the apprehension which that discovery raises. But it is quite one thing to identify the apprehension and quite another to implement it, to narrate it, to dramatize its play. Fictional excursions into these realms are as endlessly intriguing to me as they are instructive in the manner in which the power of racial difference is rendered. These imaginative forays can be sophisticated, cunning, thrillingly successful, or fragile and uninformed. But none is accidental. For many writers it is not enough to indicate or represent difference, its fault line and its solidity. It is rather more to the point of their project to use it for metaphoric and structural purposes. Often enhancing or decorating racial difference becomes a strategy for genuflecting before one's own race about which one feels unease.

I am deeply and personally involved in figuring out how to manipulate, mutate, and control imagistic, metaphoric language in order to produce something that could be called race-specific race-free prose: literature that is free of the imaginative restraints that the racially inflected language at my disposal imposes on me. The *Paradise* project required me first to recognize and identify racially inflected language and strategies, then deploy them to achieve a counter effect, to deactivate their power, summon other opposing powers, and liberate what I am able to invent, record, describe, and transform from the straitjacket a racialized society can, and frequently does, buckle us into.

It is important to remind ourselves that in addition to poetry and fictional prose, racial discourse permeates all of the scholarly disciplines: theology, history, the social sciences, literary criticism, the language of law, psychiatry, and the natural sciences. By this I mean more than the traces of racism that survive in the language as normal and inevitable, such as name-calling; skin privileges (the equation of black with evil and white with purity); the orthographic disrespect given the speech of African Americans; the pseudoscience developed to discredit them, etc., and I mean more than the unabashedly racist agendas that are promoted in some of the scholarship of these disciplines. I mean the untrammeled agency and license racial discourse provides intellectuals, while at the same time fructifying, closing off knowledge about the race upon which such discourse is dependent. One of the most malevolent characteristics of racist thought is that it seems never to produce new knowledge. It seems able merely to reformulate and refigure itself in multiple but static assertions. It has no referent in the material world. Like the concept of black blood, or white blood, or blue blood it is designed to create and employ a self-contained field, to construct artificial borders and to maintain them against all reason and against all evidence.

The problem of writing in a language in which the codes of racial hierarchy and disdain are deeply embedded was exacerbated when I began *Paradise*. In that novel I was determined to focus the assault on the metaphorical, metonymic infrastructure upon which such language rests and luxuriates. I am aware of how whiteness matures and ascends the throne of universalism by maintaining its powers to describe and to enforce its descriptions. To challenge that view of universalism, to exorcize, alter, and defang the white/black confrontation and concentrate on the residue of that hostility seemed to me a daunting project and an artistically liberating one. The material had been for some time of keen interest to me: the all-black towns founded by African Americans in the nineteenth century provided a rich field for an exploration into race-specific/race-free language. I assumed the reader would be habituated to very few approaches to African American literature: (1) reading it as sociology—not art, (2) a reading that anticipated the pleasure or the crisis—the frisson of an encounter with the exotic or the sentimentally familiar with romantic, (3) a reading that was alert to, familiar with, and dependent upon racial codes. I wanted to transgress and render useless those assumptions.

Paradise places an all-black community, one chosen by its inhabitants, next to a raceless one, also chosen by its inhabitants. The grounds for traditional black/white hostilities shift to the nature of exclusion, the origins of chauvinism, the sources of oppression, assault, and slaughter. The exclusively black community is all about its race: preserving it, developing powerful myths of origin, and maintaining its purity. In the Convent of women, other than the nuns, race is indeterminate. All racial codes are eliminated, deliberately withheld. I tried to give so full a description of the women that knowing their racial identity would become irrelevant.

Uninterested in the black/white tension that one expects to be central in any fiction written by an African American author, the book provides itself with an expanded canvas. Unconstrained by the weary and wearying vocabulary of racial domination, outside the boundaries of an already defined debate, the novel seeks to unencumber itself from the limits that figurations of a racialized language impose on the imagination while simultaneously normalizing a particular race's culture. For many American readers this was disturbing: some admitted to being preoccupied with finding out which was the white girl; others wondered initially and then abandoned the question; some never concerned themselves with the discovery either by reading them as all black or, the lucky ones, by reading them as all fully realized people. In American English eliminating racial markers is challenging. There are matters of physical description, of dialogue, of assumptions about background and social status, of cultural differences. The technical problems were lessened because the action took place in the seventies, when women wandered about on their own and when African American culture reached a kind of apogee of influence on American culture in general. Conflicts in the text are gender related; they are also generational. They are struggles over history: Who will tell and thereby control the story of the past? Who will shape the future? They are conflicts of value, of ethics. Of personal identity. What is manhood? Womanhood? And finally, most importantly, what is personhood?

Raising these questions seemed to me most compelling when augmented by yearnings for freedom and safety; for plenitude, for rest, for beauty; by contemplations on the temporal and the eternal; by the search for one's own space, for respect, for love, for bliss—in short, paradise. And that throws into relief the second trouble with *Paradise:* how to render expressive religious language credibly and effectively in postmodernist fiction without having to submit to a vague egalitarianism, or to a kind of late-twentieth-century environmental spiritualism, or to the modernist/feminist school of the goddess-body adored, or to the biblical/political scholasticism of the more entrenched and dictatorial wings of contemporary religious institutions—none of which, it seems to me, represents the everyday practice of nineteenth-century African Americans and their children, nor lends itself to postmodernist narrative strategies. How to express profound and motivating faith in and to a secularized, scientific world? How, in other words, to reimagine paradise?

Paradise is no longer imaginable or, rather, it is overimagined—which amounts to the same thing—and has thus become familiar, common, even trivial. Historically, the images of paradise, in poetry and prose, were intended to be grand but accessible, beyond the routine but imaginatively graspable, seductive precisely because of our ability to recognize them—as though we "remembered" the scenes somehow. Milton speaks of "goodliest trees, loaden with fairest fruit, / Blossoms and fruits at once of golden hue, / . . . with gay enameled colours mixed"; of "Native perfumes"; of "that sapphire fount the crispèd brooks, / Rolling on orient pearl and sands of gold"; of "nectar, visiting each plant, and fed / Flowers worthy of Paradise"; "nature boon / poured forth profuse on hill and dale and plain"; "Groves whose rich trees wept odorous gums and balm; / Others, whose fruit, burnished with golden rind, / Hung amiable—Hesperian fables true, / . . . of delicious taste; / Betwixt them lawns, or level downs, and flocks / Grazing the tender herb"; "Flowers of all hue, and without thorn the rose"; "caves / Of cool recess, o'er which the mantling vine / Lays forth her purple grape, and gently creeps / Luxuriant."

That scenario, in this the last decade of the twentieth century, we recognize as bounded real estate, owned by the wealthy, viewed and visited by guests and tourists, regularly on display for the rest of us in the products and promises sold by various media. Overimagined. Quite available if not in fact, then certainly as ordinary unexceptional desire. Let's examine the characteristics of physical paradise—beauty, plenty, rest, exclusivity, and eternity—to see how they stack up in 1995.

Beauty of course is a duplicate of what we already know, intensified by what we have never known articulated. Beatific, benevolent nature combined with precious metals and jewelry. What it cannot be is beauty beyond imagination.

Plenty, in a world of excess and attending greed that tilts resources to the haves and forces the have-nots to locate bounty within what has already been acquired by the haves, is an almost obscene feature of paradise. In this world of tilted resources, of outrageous, shameless wealth squatting, hulking, preening itself before the dispossessed, the very idea of plenty, of sufficiency, as utopian ought to make us tremble. Plenty should not be regulated to a paradisiacal state, but to normal, everyday, humane life.

Rest, that is the superfluity of working or fighting for rewards of food or luxury, has dwindling currency these days. It is a desirelessness that suggests a special kind of death without dying.

Exclusivity, however, is still an attractive, even compelling feature of paradise because some, the unworthy, are not there. Boundaries are secure; watchdogs, gates, keepers are there to verify the legitimacy of the inhabitants. Such enclaves are cropping up again, like medieval fortresses and moats, and it does not seem possible or desirable for a city to be envisioned in which poor people can be accommodated. Exclusivity is not just an accessible dream for the well-endowed, but an increasingly popular solution for the middle class. "Streets" are understood to be populated by the unworthy and the dangerous; young people are forced off the streets for their own good. Yet public space is fought over as if it were private. Who gets to enjoy a park, a beach, a mall, a corner? The term "public" is itself a site of contention. Paradise therefore has a very real attraction to modern society.

Eternity, since it holds the pain of dying again, and, in its rejection of secular, scientific arguments, has probably the greatest appeal. And medical, scientific resources directed toward more life, and fitter life, remind us of the desire for earthbound eternity, rather than eternal afterlife. The suggestion being this is all there is. Thus, paradise, as an earthly project, as opposed to heaven, has serious intellectual and visual limitations. Aside from "Only me or us forever" it hardly bears describing anymore.

But that might be unfair. It is hard not to notice how much more attention has always been given to hell rather than heaven. Dante's *Inferno* beats out *Paradiso* every time. Milton's brilliantly rendered pre-paradise world, known as Chaos, is far more fully realized than his Paradise. The visionary language of antithesis reaches heights of linguistic ardor with which the thesis language seldom competes. There are many reasons why the images of the horrors of hell were meant to be virulently repulsive in the twelfth, fifteenth, and seventeenth centuries. The argument for avoiding it needed to be visceral, needed to reveal how much worse such an eternity was than the hell of everyday life. But the need has persisted, in our times, with a significant addition. There is an influx of books devoted to a consternation about the absence of a sense of evil—if not hell—of a loss of shame in contemporary life.

One wonders how to account for the melancholy that accompanies these exhortations about our inattention to, the mutedness, the numbness toward anti-paradisiacal experience. Evil is understood, justifiably, to be pervasive, but it has somehow lost its awe-fullness. It does not frighten us. It is merely entertainment. Why are we not so frightened by its possibilities that we turn toward good? Is afterlife of any sort too simple for our complex, sophisticated modern intelligence? Or is it that, more than paradise, evil needs costumes, constantly refurbished and replenished? Hell has always lent itself to glamour, headlines, a tuxedo, cunning, a gruesome mask or a seductive one. Maybe it needs blood, slime, roaring simply to get our attention, to tickle us, draw from us our wit, our imagination, our energy, our heights of performance. After which paradise is simply its absence, an edgeless and therefore unavailing lack full of an already perceived, already recognizable landscape: great trees for shade and fruit, lawns, palaces, precious metals, jewelry, animal husbandry. Outside fighting hell, waging war against the unworthy, there seems nothing for its inhabitants to do.

278 THE SOURCE OF SELF-REGARD

A nonexclusionary, unbordered, come-one-come-all paradise, without dread, minus a nemesis, is no paradise at all.

The literary problem is harnessing contemporary language to reveal not only the intellectual complexity of paradise, but language that seizes the imagination not as an amicus brief to a naïve or psychotic life, but as sane, intelligent life itself. If I am to do justice to, bear witness to the deeply religious population of this project and render their profoundly held moral system affective in these alienated, uninspiring, and uninspired times—where religion is understood to run the gamut from scorned, unintelligible fundamentalism to literate, well-meaning liberalism, to televangelistic marketing to militaristic racism and phobophilia—I have serious problems.

Historically the language of religion (and I am speaking here of Christianity, but I am relatively certain this is true of all text-based religions) is dependent upon and gains its strength, beauty, and unassailability from biblical or holy texts. Contemporary religious language, that is the speech and the script that seeks to translate divine translations into "popular" or "everyday common" parlance, seems to work best in song, in anecdote, and in the occasional rhetorical flourish. I understand that the reason for modernizing the traditional language of the Bible is an effort to connect with and proselytize a population indifferent or unresponsive to the language that moved our ancestors. To compete for the attention of a constituency whose discourse has been shaped by the language of media and commerce and whose expectation of correlating images to accompany and clarify text is a difficult enterprise. And it appears reasonable to accommodate altering circumstances with alternate modes of discourse. While I can't testify to the success of such efforts, I suspect the "modernization" of God's language has been rewarding—otherwise these attempts would not be so plentiful.

Marketing religion requires new strategies, new appeals, and a relevance that is immediate, not contemplative. Thus modern language, while successful in the acquisition of converts and the spiritual maintenance of the confirmed, is forced to kneel before the denominator that is most accessible, to bankrupt its subtlety, its mystery in order to bankroll its effect. Nevertheless it seems a poor substitute for the language it seeks to replace, not only because it sacrifices ambiguity, depth, and moral authority, but also because its techniques are reinforcement rather than liberation.

I do not mean to suggest that there are no brilliant sermons, powerfully intelligent essays, revelatory poems, moving encomiums, or elegant arguments. Of course there are. Nor do I mean to suggest that there is no personal language, no prayer that is not stunning in its creativity, its healing properties, its sheer intellectual power. But these rhetorical forms are not suitable for sustained prose fiction. Modern narrative is devoid of religious language that does not glean most of its nourishment from allusions to or quotations from holy texts.

Is it possible to write religion-inflected prose narrative that does not rest its case entirely or mainly on biblical language? Is it possible to make the experience and journey of faith fresh, as new and as linguistically unencumbered as it was to early believers, who themselves had no collection of books to rely on?

I have chosen this task, this obligation partly because I am alarmed at the debasement of religious language in literature; its cliché-ridden expression, its apathy, its refusal to refuel itself with nonmarket vocabulary (or "its insistence on refueling itself with marketing vocabulary"), its substitution of the terminology of popular psychology for philosophical clarity; its patriarchal triumphalism, its morally bankrupt dictatorial praxis, the unearned congratulations it awards itself for performability rather than content; its low opinion of its mission.

How can a novelist represent bliss in nonsexual, nonorgiastic terms? How can a novelist, in a land of plenty, render undeserved, limitless love, the one "that passeth all understanding," without summoning the consumer pleasure of a lotto win? How to invoke paradise in an age of theme parks?

The answer, unfortunately, is that, so far, I cannot. I chose something else, some other means of freshening the inquiry. I chose not only to explore the idea of paradise, but to interrogate the narrow imagination that has conceived it.

But that, I think, is another essay entirely.

On *Beloved*

I BEGAN thinking about *Beloved* in 1983. As it had been since the beginning of my writing years, I was drawn to it by my complicated relationship with history. A relationship that was wary, alert, but ready to be persuaded away from doubt. It was a caution based on my early years as a student, during which time I was keenly aware of erasures and absences and silences in the written history available to me—silences that I took for censure. History, it seemed, was about them. And if I or someone representative of myself ever were mentioned in fiction, it was usually something I wished I had skipped. Not just in the works of Harriet Beecher Stowe and Mark Twain's unconscionable humiliation of a grown man at the hands of children; there was no respite in those years even in the encyclopedia or in history texts. While I maintain a cool eye while reading historical texts, it is an eye no cooler than the one historians maintain, and ought to maintain when reading fiction. Yet in spite of my wariness, my skepticism, there is a dependence, solid and continuous, that I have on history, partly for the data available to me there, but mostly for precisely those gaps, those erasures, that censure. It is in the interstices of recorded history that I frequently find the "nothing" or the "not enough" or the "indistinct" or "incomplete" or "discredited" or "buried" information important to me. For example, in 1963, my first novel, *The Bluest Eye,* was a consequence of being overcome by the wholesale dismissal of a certain part of the population (to which

I belonged) in history texts and literature. Of all the characters chosen for artistic examination, with empathy or contempt, vulnerable young black girls were profoundly absent. When they did appear, they were jokes or instances of pity—pity without understanding. No one it seemed missed their presence center stage and no one it seemed took them seriously except me. Now, I didn't blame literature for that. Writers write what they like and what interests them. And even African American writers (mostly men, but not all) made clear that, except as background, prepubescent black girls were unable to hold their interest or stimulate their curiosity. Nevertheless, writers' lack of curiosity was not the point. To me the enforced or chosen silence, the way history was written, controlled and shaped the national discourse.

However much historical analysis has changed (and it has changed enormously) and broadened in the last forty years, the silences regarding certain populations (minorities) when finally articulated are still understood to be supplementary accounts of a marginal experience, a supplemental record, unassociated with the mainstream of history; an expanded footnote, as it were, that is interesting but hardly central to the nation's past. Racial history, for example, remains very much parallel to main historical texts, but is seldom seen as either its warp or woof, and seldom threaded into the whole cloth. These ancillary and parallel texts are gaining wide readership while remaining the site of considerable controversy. (Debates about reading material swirled in many high schools.) Although the silences provoked virtually all of my work, inhabiting them with one's own imagination is easy to note, not so easy to do. I have to find the hook, the image, the newspaper article that produces sustained musing, a "what if?" or "what must it have been like?"

Beloved originated as a general question, and was launched by a newspaper clipping. The general question (remember, this was the early eighties) centered on how—other than equal rights, access, pay, etc.—does the women's movement define the freedom being sought? One principal area of fierce debate was control of one's own body—an argument that is as rife now as it was then. Many women were convinced that such rights extended to choosing to be a mother, suggesting that not being a mother was not a deficit and choosing motherlessness (for however long) could be added to a list of freedoms; that is, one could choose to live a life free of and from childbearing and no negative or value judgment need apply.

Another aspect of the women's movement involved strong encouragement of women to support other women. Not to have one's relationship to another woman be subordinate to a relationship with a man. That is, the time spent with a female friend was not downtime. It was real time.

The completion of the debate was more complicated than that (there was much class conflict roiling in it) but those were the issues surfacing with gusto. I addressed the second one (women being important friends) in *Sula*. But the first one—freedom as ownership of the body, childlessness chosen as a mark of freedom, engaged me deeply.

And here again the silences of historical accounts and the marginalizing of minority peoples in the debate claimed my attention and proved a rich being to explore. From the point of view of slave women, for example. Suppose having children, being called a mother, was the supreme act of freedom—not its opposite? Suppose instead of being required to have children (because of gender, slave status, and profit) one chose to be responsible for them; to claim them as one's own; to be, in other words, not a breeder, but a parent. Under U.S. slavery such a claim was not only socially unacceptable, it was illegal, anarchic. It was also an expression of intolerable female independence. It was freedom. And if the claim extended to infanticide (for whatever reason—noble or crazed) it could and did become politically explosive.

These lines of thought came together when I recalled a newspaper article I had read around 1970, a description of an abolitionist cause célèbre focused on a slave woman named Margaret Garner who had indeed made such claims. The details of her life were riveting. But I selected and manipulated its parts to suit my own purposes. Still my reluctance to enter the period of slavery was disabling. The need to reexamine and imagine it was repellent. Plus, I believed nobody else would want to dig deeply into the interior lives of slaves, except to summon their nobility or victimhood, to be outraged or self-righteously gripped by pity. I was interested in neither. The act of writing is a kind of act of faith.

Sometimes what is there—what is already written—is perfect and imitation is absurd and intolerable. But a perfect thing is not everything. Another thing, another different thing is required. Sometimes what is already there is simply not enough; other times it is indistinct, incomplete, even in error or buried. Sometimes, of course, there is nothing. And for a novelist that is the real excitement. Not what there is, but what there is not.

A tall door rises up into this nothing; its hardware is heavy, secure. No bell invites your hand. So you stand there, perhaps, or move away and, later, sticking your hand in your pocket, you find a key that you know (or hope) fits the lock. Even before the tumblers fall back you know you will find what you hoped to find: a word or two that turns the "not enough" into more; the line or sentence that inserts itself into the nothing. With the right phrase, this sense becomes murky, becomes lit, differently lit. Through that door is a kind of freedom that can frighten governments, sustain others, and rid whole nations of confusion. More important, however, is that the writer who steps through that door with the language of his or her own intellect and imagination enters uncolonized territory, which she can claim as rightfully her own—for a while at least.

The shared effort to avoid imagining slave life as lived from their own point of view became the subtheme, the structure of the work. Forgetting the past was the engine, and the characters (except for one) are intent on forgetting. The one exception being the one hungry for a past, desperate for being not just remembered, but dealt with, confronted. That character would be the only one in a position to accurately render judgment of her own murder: the dead child. Beloved. Thus, after following a number of trails trying to determine the structure, I decided that the single most uncontroversial thing one can say about the institution of slavery vis-à-vis contemporary time, is that it haunts us all. That in so many ways all our lives are entangled with the past—its manipulations and, fearful of its grasp, ignoring or dismissing or distorting it to suit ourselves, but always unable to erase it. When finally I understood the nature of a haunting—how it is both what we yearn for and what we fear, I was able to see the traces of a ghostly presence, the residue of a repressed past in certain concrete but also allusive detail. Footprints particularly. That disappear and return only to disappear again. The endings of my novels have to be clear in my mind before I begin. So I was able to describe this haunting even before I knew everything that would lead up to it.

Chinua Achebe

I TAKE great pleasure in having this opportunity to say some things in public that I have never said to the person who is the subject of these comments—Chinua Achebe. My debt to Mr. Achebe is the best kind. Large, minus repayment schedule, and interest-free. Let me describe it to you.

In 1965 I began reading African literature, devouring it actually. It was a literature previously unavailable to me, but by then I had discovered a New York bookstore called Africa House, which offered among other things back issues of *Transition, Black Orpheus,* and works by a host of African writers from all over the continent. Amos Tutuola, Ayi Kwei Armah, Ezekiel Mphahlele, James Ngugi, Bessie Head, Christina Ama Ata Aidoo, Mongo Beti, Léopold Senghor, Camara Laye, Ousmane Sembène, Wole Soyinka, John Pepper Clark: the jolt these writers gave me was explosive. The confirmation that African literature was not limited to Doris Lessing and Joseph Conrad was so stunning it led me to secure the aid of two academics who could help me anthologize this literature. At that time African literature was not a subject to be taught in American schools. Even in so-called world literature courses it had no reputation and no presence. But I was determined to funnel the delight, the significance, and the power of that literature into my work as an editor. The publication of *Contemporary African Literature* in 1972 was the beginning of my love affair.

But the more profound and more personal consequence was the

impact Chinua Achebe's novels had on my own beginnings as a writer. I had read his essay in *Transition,* on the struggle with definitions of African literature, and knew its ramifications for African American writers. In that essay, Achebe quoted James Baldwin's comments on the subject of language choice and manipulation in defining national and cultural literatures and its resonance with marginalized writers. "My quarrel," said Baldwin, "with the English language has been that the language reflected none of my experience. . . . Perhaps . . . I had never attempted to use it, had only learned to imitate it. If this were so, then it might be made to bear the burden of my experience if I could find the stamina to challenge it, and me, to such a test." But theorizing a definition is one thing. Executing a theory is another. Achebe's "answer," so to speak, was in his work. He (along with Camara Laye, Bessie Head, and others) constituted a complete education for me. Learning how to disassemble the gaze that I was wrestling with (the habitual but self-conscious writing toward a nonblack reader that threatened and coated much African American literature); discovering how to eliminate, to manipulate the Eurocentric eye in order to stretch and plumb my own imagination; I attribute these learned lessons to Chinua Achebe. In the pages of *Things Fall Apart* lay not the argument but the example; in the pages of *No Longer at Ease, Anthills of the Savannah* the assumption of the authenticity, the force, the valleys of beauty were abundant. Achebe's work liberated my artistic intelligence as nothing else had ever done. I became fit to reenter and reinhabit my own milieu without the services of a native guide.

So in fact that was not a debt in 1965. It was a gift.

Introduction of Peter Sellars

P ETER SELLARS WARNED me against any ideas I might be forming about this introduction. He strongly suggested two and
only two sentences: "Thank you for coming." And "Here's Peter
Sellars."

I defy him at my peril, but I appeal to what Peter might be stunned
to learn is "a higher authority."

I happen to know Peter Sellars's mother. Have met her several
times in several countries. She is, in a word, lovely. And suspecting
the difficult joy of rearing sons—whether in Pennsylvania, where Peter
was born, or Denver, Colorado, where he directed Beethoven from
the podium his father built for him, or Phillips Andover, or Harvard
directing *Coriolanus,* collecting a Phi Beta Kappa key and an invitation to direct at the American Repertory Theater at the Loeb; or
studying in Japan, China, and India; or being director of the Boston
Shakespeare Company, the American National Theater, the Kennedy
Center; or receiving a MacArthur award. I say—suspecting a mother's
difficult joy, I am certain she would take the same pleasure I do in
hearing an introduction of one's son a bit more expansive. So, out of
affection for Mrs. Sellars, an English professor, I am going to bow to
her authority and I hope her desire and add a few sentences to the two
her son seriously recommended to me.

We go to art sometimes for safety, for a haven of order, serenity; for
recognizable, even traditional beauty; for anticipation with certainty

that the art form will take us past our mundane selves into a deepness where we also reside.

We go, sometimes, to art for danger; to be riveted by experiencing the strange, by understanding suddenly how uncanny the familiar really is. We go to be urged, shaken into reassessing thoughts we have taken for granted; to learn other ways of seeing, hearing. To be excited. Stirred. Disturbed.

Fortunately for us, among contemporary artists, Peter Sellars is rare: he never asks us to make those choices; he does not require us to select the red/green, food/no food buttons of mice in a laboratory, the one of two oppositional kinds of pleasure or power or genius we want. His work has always displayed both safety and danger; both the haven of the recognizable and the unchartered terrain of the disfamiliarized.

His almost pious devotion to the original score, the complete script, the uncommercial length (which pays a public the compliment of assuming its attention span—its memory bank—is longer than that of a housefly). In his fidelity, his respect for the work itself, we find safety, reassurance.

His deeply held conviction that profound art—whatever its date of origin—is always contemporary permits us fresh access to that nostrum when he chips away the encrustations of time and use to expose its truth. Whether it is Mozart's *Le Nozze de Figaro, Don Giovanni, Così fan Tutti;* Handel's *Julius Caesar in Egypt;* Kurt Weill's *Seven Deadly Sins;* Shakespeare's *Merchant of Venice;* Wagner's *Ring;* Gogol's *Inspector General*—whatever. By collapsing these otherwise mutually exclusive approaches to art's work—fidelity and resuscitation; safety and danger; thorough scholarship with outrageously innovative stagecraft; astonishingly incisive personal interpretation with an almost impertinent trust in actors' instincts. Because of his ability to embrace both approaches, we are made aware of how irresistible art is. We are made aware of his reverence for its possibilities—to keep us sane or make us so. His absolute love of it. His total faith in it. And in us.

Thank you for coming. Here's Peter Sellars.

Tribute to Romare Bearden

I N ORDER to get to the crux of my views on the art of Romare Bearden, on the discourse of African American art in general, I have to go back a bit, for my own sake, if not yours, to put my remarks in context.

Extraordinary things were happening in the sixties among African Americans. The realm of political change during that period has received, as it should, minute, even exhaustive attention. Yet in spite of some singular critiques of African American art at the moment of origin and some more expansive ones later on, the exploration of visual art as it relates to other genres in African American culture seems tentative. (I was not able to attend Saturday's panel on Bearden and other arts and disciplines, so the comments that follow may very well be inoperative.) Where analysis of this cross-genre aspect does exist, it relies on terms like "inspiration," "similarities," "spirit," "vibrancy," "intensity," "drama," "liveliness," shared cultural values. There are a number of reasons for this rather vague emotional vocabulary: artists are notoriously evasive about their creative process; it takes a certain amount of nerve, if not faith, for a scholar to assert connections, echoes across disciplines if she or he does not feel expert within them; aesthetic ramifications are very difficult to iterate.

More importantly, the early attention of scholars on African American literary and other art was engaged in canon formation—taking its cue from the mainstream's established format for the ranking of art production. The alternative canon that the new black critics urged had several goals (nationalism, revolutionary success, cultural hegemony), among which was an aesthetic put to the service of a strong political agenda and/or a cohesive cultural flowering. Aesthetics were understood to be a "corrective" to "polluted American mainstream"; a "sister" to the black power movement. Artists were encouraged and judged by the nation-building "uses" to which their work could be put. The groundswell of those who understood this to be the work of their work is legend—as any review of sixties poetry will reveal. And there is no question that matters of "authenticity"—of representing the lived life and concerns of black people—are still the sine qua non of virtually all African American art from rap music to film to novels to visual arts. How successfully, distorted or even triumphantly, this authenticity expresses itself is still much of the drive of criticism.

Although the explosion of creative energy was overwhelming in the sixties, its criticism did not, perhaps could not, refuse to wrestle with the eternal and eternally irrelevant argument about how and whether the art of a black artist could be, should be considered "universal," meaning "mainstream," "race transcendent," "agenda-free," and so on. The heart of the argument implied that if what was produced was merely political it was not art; if it was merely beautiful it was not relevant. Thus the critiques focused on the accuracy of the sociology and/or the inspirational, "self-help" value of the work. Some work was championed as representative, authentic; other was deemed unacceptable if it was less than uplifting; other work was dismissed as crude protest or propaganda. Virtually every African American writer in the near and distant past—James Baldwin, Zora Neale Hurston, Ralph Ellison, Richard Wright, Gwendolyn Brooks, Phillis Wheatley—has been called upon or felt called upon to explain what it meant to be a Negro or black artist. The sheer idiocy of that call has been enough to force artists (angrily, or with annoyance, I suspect) to respond to it. Romare Bearden was working long before the sixties and had traveled widely, studied carefully the ancient and the new. His homes included the South, the North, Europe, the Caribbean, country landscapes, porches, urban streets, clubs, churches. So it was with some delight that I read a comment by him on the subject of race or social factors in his work.

"I am afraid," he said, "despite my intentions, that in some instances commentators have tended to overemphasize what they believed to be the social elements in my work. But while my response to certain human elements is as obvious as it is inevitable, I am also pleased to note that upon reflection many persons have found that they were as much concerned with the aesthetic implications of my paintings as with, what may possibly be, my human compassion."

The operative words, for me, are "my response to certain human elements is as obvious as it is inevitable." How, he is asking, can a human artist not be responsive to human things, which are by their nature social things? He takes for granted the humanity of his subject matter, and as has been said, this in itself is a radical act in a country with a history of purposefully and consistently dehumanizing the black population. Bearden is also pleased to refer to "aesthetic implications." That is to say, there is information, truth, power, and beauty in his choice of color, form, in the structural and structured placement of images, in fragments built up from flat surfaces, rhythm implicit in repetition and in the medium itself—each move determining subsequent ones, enabling the look and fact of spontaneity, improvisation. This is the appropriate language employed to delineate his work, and to suggest its relationship to another genre—music. Which is very interesting since whatever the view of aesthetics in criticism, it has traditionally confined itself to explorations with an art form, not among them. It is odd, considering how affected artists are by other disciplines, that this approach, which so closely resembles traditional critique, maintains in spite of the insistence of the art itself on its wider sources and its far more interdisciplinary dialogue. The cross-fertilization among artists within a genre is a subject well examined. Less so are instances where the lines between genres are implicit.

The influence and representation of African American music is a mainstay in commentary on Romare Bearden's work as is the relationship between the plays and sensibility of August Wilson. The influence of and alignment with music is also a common observation in criticism of my own work—as well as my own acknowledgments on the subject. What I want to describe this evening are other ways in which artists of disparate disciplines fold into, energize, and transfer the aesthetics of one another.

Let me linger for a moment on some aspects of my own process that are, indeed, responsive to the work of Romare Bearden. I must say I have been generous to myself in getting ideas from painters other than Bearden, although they are usually scenes or figurative arrangements on canvas. With Bearden I am struck by the tactile sensuality of his work, the purity of gesture, and especially the subtext of the aggressive, large-as-life humanity of his subject matter. This latter is no small thing when the urgency of destereotyping is so strong it can push one easily into sentimentality. The edge of the razor embedded in Bearden's work prevents or ought to prevent easy, self-satisfying evaluations of his subject matter. Among the aspects of his work that appeal to me, that one is primary: lack of condescension.

Another aspect of my own process involves the composition of the text. A layered exercise that I consistently undergo that has more elements in common with painting than literature.

I need three kinds of information to complete, sometimes even start, a narrative. Once I've settled on an idea and the story through which to examine it, I need the structure, the sound, the palette. Not necessarily in that order. The sound of a text clearly involves the musical quality of the dialogue and the language chosen to contextualize it. Elsewhere I have written about my choices for the opening of *Beloved*, and I repeat those comments here: in reference to that opening—"124 was spiteful. Full of a baby's venom."—I was careful to illustrate the rhythm I thought necessary, and the quality of a spoken text: "There is something about numerals that makes them spoken, heard, in this context, because one expects words to read in a book, not numbers to say, or hear. And the sound of the novel, sometimes cacophonous, sometimes harmonious, must be an inner-ear sound or a sound just beyond hearing, infusing the text with a musical emphasis that words can do sometimes even better than music can." I go on to explain why the second sentence is not one—is instead a dependent clause given the status of a sentence just to mandate a stress on the world "full." In an effort to understate the strangeness of an infant ghost so the reader will understand its presence as normal as the household does. The remarkable thing being its power ("full") rather than its existence. In describing at such length the crucial nature of sound to my work, I hoped to focus attention not on a kind of forced poetry or lyricism, but rather on what meaning can be gleaned and communicated from sound, from the aural quality of the text. I only want to suggest that this is more than being influenced by blues or jazz. It is plumbing the music for the meaning that it contains. In other words, the "aesthetic implications" of which Romare Bearden spoke ought to include what is usually absent from aesthetic analysis. Most often the analysis is about how successful the technique is in summoning pleasure, a shocking or moving or satisfying emotional response.

Seldom does it center on the information, the meaning the artist is communicating by his style, via his aesthetics. It can be said, has been said, that the collage techniques, employed by several modernist artists (Matisse, for example) were taken to new levels by Bearden and reflect the "fractured" life he depicts—an intervention into the flat surface that repudiates as it builds on the cubism of earlier periods. And that collage was representative of the modernist thrust of African American life as well as its insurgency. Both structure and improvisation inform this choice—the essence of African American music. The attraction to me in this technique is how abrupt stops and unexpected liquidity enhance the narrative in ways that a linear "beginning, middle, and end" cannot. Thus I recognize that my own abandonment of traditional time sequence (and then, and then) is an effort to capitalize on these modernist trends. And to say something about the layered life—not the fractured or fragmented life of black society, but the layered life of the mind, the imagination, and the way reality is actually perceived and experienced.

The third, palette, or color, is one of the last and most crucial of my decisions in developing a text. I don't use color to "prettify" or please, or provide atmospherics, but to imply and delineate the themes within the narrative. Color says something directly or metaphorically.

The red, white, and blue strokes at the beginning of *Song of Solomon* should lie quietly in the mind of the reader as the American flag background the action is commenting on. The withholding of color in *Beloved,* its repudiation of any color at all until it has profound meaning to the character: Baby Suggs hankering for some; Sethe's startle when she is able to let it come into view; the drama of one patch of orange in a quilt of bleak greys. These studied distributions of color or its absence, the careful placement of white for its various connotations (the white, rather bridal dress of the figure praying next to Sethe; the dresses of the church ladies at the pie table in *Tar Baby*), the repetition of a collection of colors chosen to direct the reader to specific and related scenes in *Paradise,* do not mimic the choices of a Romare Bearden, but are clearly aligned with the process.

I am convinced that among the reasons Bearden must be widely viewed in galleries, should occupy the burgeoning attention of scholars to African American art, is only partly canon formation; is only minimally the quenching of nationalistic desire; is supplementally a tribute to his genius. The more significant reason in the exploration of the resonances, alignments, the connections, the intergenre sources of African American art is the resounding aesthetic dialogue among artists. Separating art forms, compartmentalizing them, is convenient for study, instruction, and institutions. But it is hardly representative of how artists actually work. The dialogue between Bearden and jazz music and musicians is an obvious beginning. The influence writers acknowledge is a further step. The borders established for the convenience of study are, I believe, not just porous, they are liquid. Locating instances of this liquidity is vital if African American art is to be understood for the complex work that it is and for the deep meaning it contains.

Romare Bearden sat in an airplane seat once and told me he would send me something. He did. An extraordinary, completely stunning portrait of a character in one of my books. Not his Pilate of 1979, but the Pilate in *Song of Solomon*—part of a series, I gather. Imagine my surprise at what he saw. Things I had not seen or known when I invented her. What he made of her earring, her hat, and her bag of bones—far beyond my word-bound description, heavy with the life that both energized and muted her; solitary, daring anyone to deprive her of her symbols, her history, her purpose. I had seen her determination, her wisdom, and her seductive eccentricity, but not the ferocity he saw and rendered.

Later on I acquired a watercolor of his, a row of Preservation Hall–type musicians standing before a riverboat, all in white with their traditional sashes of color. For the first time in a representation of black jazz musicians I saw stillness. Not the active, frenetic, unencumbered physical movement normally seen in renderings of musicians—but the quiet at the center. It was, in a word, sacred, contemplative. A glance into an otherwise obscured aspect of their art.

That kind of insight is rare indeed. Displaying it, underscoring it, analyzing it is far more compelling than merely enjoying it. The legacy enjoins us all to think deeply about what Romare Bearden has given us, and what African American art is imploring us to discover.

Faulkner and Women

I'M AMBIVALENT about what I'm about to do. On the one hand, I want to do what every writer wants to do, which is to explain everything to the reader first so that, when you read it, there will be no problems. My other inclination is to run out here and read it, then run off so that there would be no necessity to frame it. I have read from this manuscript three or four times before, and each time I learned something in the process of reading it, which was never true with any other book that I wrote. And so when I was invited to come to Oxford and speak to this conference about some aspect of "Faulkner and Women," I declined, saying that I really couldn't concentrate enough to collect remarks on "Faulkner and Women" because I was deeply involved in writing a book myself and I didn't want any distractions whatsoever. And then very nicely the conference directors invited me to read from this manuscript that had me so obsessed, so that I could both attend the conference and associate myself in some real way with the Center for the Study of Southern Culture and also visit Mississippi and "spend the night," as they say. So, on the one hand, I apologize for reading something that is not finished but is in process, but this was a way to satisfy my eagerness to visit the campus of the University of Mississippi, and I hope there will be some satisfaction rippling through the audience once I have finished. My other hesitation is simply because some of what I read may not appear in print, as a developing manuscript is constantly changing. Before reading to a group gathered to discuss "Faulkner and Women," I would also like to add that in 1956 I spent a great deal of time thinking about Mr. Faulkner because he was the subject of a thesis that I wrote at Cornell. Such an exhaustive treatment of an author makes it impossible for a writer to go back to that author for some time afterward until the energy has dissipated itself in some other form. But I have to say, even before I begin to read, that there was for me not only an academic interest in Faulkner, but in a very, very personal way, in a very personal way as a reader, William Faulkner had an enormous effect on me, an enormous effect.

The title of the book is *Beloved,* and this is the way it begins:

[The author read from her work-in-progress and then answered questions from the audience.]

MORRISON: I am interested in answering questions from those of you who may have them. And if you'll stand up and let me identify you before you ask a question, I'll do the best I can.

QUESTION: *Ms. Morrison, you mentioned that you wrote a thesis on Faulkner. What effect did Faulkner have on your literary career?*

MORRISON: Well, I'm not sure that he had any effect on my work. I am typical, I think, of all writers who are convinced that they are wholly original and that if they recognized an influence they would abandon it as quickly as possible. But as a reader in the fifties and later, of course (I said 1956 because that's when I was working on a thesis that had to do with him), I was concentrating on Faulkner. I don't think that my response was any different from any other student at that time, inasmuch as there was in Faulkner this power and courage—the courage of a writer, a special kind of courage. My reasons, I think, for being interested and deeply moved by all his subjects had something to do with my desire to find out something about this country and that artistic articulation of its past that was not available in history, which is what art and fiction can do but sometimes history refuses to do. I suppose history can humanize the past also, but it frequently refuses to do so for perfectly logically good reasons. But there was an articulate investigation of an era that one or two authors provided and Faulkner was certainly at the apex of that investigation. And there was something else about Faulkner that I can only call "gaze." He had a gaze that was different. It appeared, at that time, to be similar to a look, even a sort of staring, a refusal-to-look-away approach in his writing that I found admirable. At that time, in the fifties or the sixties, it never crossed my mind to write books. But then I did it, and I was very surprised myself that I was doing it, and I knew that I was doing it for some reasons that are not writerly ones. I don't really find strong connections between my work and Faulkner's. In an extraordinary kind of memorable way there are literary watersheds in one's life. In mine, there are four or five, and I hope they are all ones that meet everybody's criteria of who should be read, but some of them don't. Some books are just awful in terms of technique but nevertheless they are terrific: they are too good to be correct. With Faulkner there was always something to surface. Besides, he could infuriate you in such wonderful ways. It wasn't just complete delight—there was also that other quality that is just as important as devotion: outrage. The point is that with Faulkner one was never indifferent.

QUESTION: *Ms. Morrison, would you talk a little bit about the creation of your character Sula?*

MORRISON: She came as many characters do—all of them don't—rather full-fleshed and complete almost immediately, including her name. I felt this enormous intimacy. I mean, I knew exactly who she was, but I had trouble trying to make her. I mean, I felt troubled trying to make her into the kind of person that would upset everybody, the kind of person that sets your teeth on edge, and yet not to make her so repulsive that you could not find her attractive at the same time—a nature that was seductive but off-putting. And playing back and forth with that was difficult for me because I wanted to describe the qualities of certain personalities that can be exploited by conventional people. The outlaw and the adventuress, not in the sense of somebody going out to find a fortune, but in the way a woman is an adventuress, which has to do with her imagination. And people such as those are always memorable and generally attractive. But she's troublesome. And, by the time I finished the book, *Sula,* I missed her. I know the feeling of missing characters who are in fact, by that time, much more real than real people.

QUESTION: *Ms. Morrison, you said earlier that reading a work in progress is helpful to you as a writer. Could you explain how reading helps you?*

MORRISON: This whole business of reading my own manuscript for information is quite new for me. As I write I don't imagine a reader or listener, ever. I am the reader and the listener myself, and I think I am an excellent reader. I read very well. I mean I really know what's going on. The problem in the beginning was to be as good a writer as I was a reader. But I have to assume that I not only write books, I read them. And I don't mean I look to see what I have written; I mean I can maintain the distance between myself the writer and what is on the page. Some people have it, and some people have to learn it. And some people don't have it; you can tell because if they had read their work, they never would have written it that way. The process is revision. It's a long sort of reading process, and I have to assume that I am also this very critical, very fastidious, and not-easily-taken-in reader who is smart enough to participate in the text a lot. I don't like to read books when all the work is done and there's no place for me there. So the effort is to write so that there is something that's going on between myself and myself—myself as writer and myself as reader. Now, in some instances, I feel content in doing certain kinds of books without reading them to an audience. But there are others where I have felt—this one in particular because it's different—that what I, as a reader, am feeling is not enough, and I needed a wider slice, so to speak, because the possibilities are infinite. I'm not interested in anybody's help in writing technique—not that. I'm just talking about shades of meaning, not the score but the emphasis here and there. It's that kind of thing that I want to discover, whether or not my ear on this book is as reliable as I have always believed it to be with the others. Therefore, I agree quickly to reading portions of this manuscript. Every other book I wrote I didn't even negotiate a contract until it was almost finished because I didn't want the feeling that it belonged to somebody else. For this book I negotiated a contract at a very early stage. So, I think, probably some of the business of reading is a sort of repossession from the publisher. It has to be mine, and I have to be willing to not do it or burn it, or do it, as the case might be. But I do assume that I am the reader, and, in the past, when I was in doubt, if I had some problems, the people I would call on to help me to verify some phrase or some word or something would be the people in the book. I mean I would just conjure them up and ask them, you know, about one thing or another. And they are usually very cooperative if they are fully realized and if you know their name. And if you don't know their names, they don't talk much.

QUESTION: *Ms. Morrison, could you discuss the use of myth and folklore in your fiction?*

MORRISON: This is not going to sound right, but I have to say it anyway. There is infinitely more past than there is future. Maybe not in chronological time, but in terms of data there certainly is. So in each step back there is another world, and another world. The past is infinite. I don't know if the future is, but I know the past is. The legends—so many of them—are not just about the past. They also indicate how to function in contemporary times and they hint about the future. So that for me they were not ever simple, never simple. I try to incorporate those mythic characteristics that for me are very strong characteristics of black art everywhere, whether it was in music or stories or paintings or what have you. It just seemed to me that those characteristics ought to be incorporated into black literature if it was to remain that. It wasn't enough just to write about black people, because anybody can do that. But it was important to me as a writer to try to make the work irrevocably black. It required me to use the folklore as points of departure—as, for example in this book, *Beloved*, which started with a story about a slave, Margaret Garner, who had been caught with her children shortly after she escaped from a farm. And rather than subject them to what was an unlivable and unbearable life, she killed them or tried to. She didn't succeed, and abolitionists made a great deal out of her case. That story, with some other things, had been nagging me for a long, long time. Can you imagine a slave woman who does not own her children? Who cares enough to kill them? Can you imagine the daring and also the recriminations and the self-punishment and the sabotage, self-sabotage, in which one loves so much that you cannot bear to have the thing you love sullied? It is better for it to die than to be sullied. Because that is you. That's the best part of you, and that was the best part of her. So it was such a serious matter that she would rather they not exist. And she was the one to make that reclamation. That's a very small part of what this is about, but that's what was in my brainpan—as they say—when I got started. So that in this instance, I began with historical fact and incorporated it into myth instead of the other way around.

QUESTION: *Ms. Morrison, earlier you said you had no intention of becoming a writer when you started to write. Could you explain what you meant by this?*

MORRISON: I was in a place where I didn't belong, and I wasn't going to be there very long so I didn't want to make it any nicer than it was. And I didn't want to meet anybody, and I didn't like anybody and they didn't like me either; and that was fine with me; and I was lonely. I was miserable. My children were small, and so I wrote this story. I had written a little story before, in

the time I could spare to work it up in the evening. (You know
children go to bed, if you train them, at seven. Wake up at four
but go to bed at seven.) And so after I put them to bed, I would
write, and I liked it. I liked thinking about it. I liked making
that kind of order out of something that was disorderly in my
mind. And also I sensed that there was an enormous indifference
to these people, to me, to you, to black girls. It was as if these
people had no life, no existence in anybody's mind at all except
peripherally. And when I got into it, it just seemed like writing
was absolutely the most important thing in the world. I took
forever to write that first book: almost five years for just a little
book. Because I liked doing it so much, I would just do a little
bit, you know, and think about that. I was a textbook editor at
that time. I was not even trying to be a writer, and I didn't let
anybody know that I was writing this book because I thought
they would fire me, which they would have. Maybe not right
away, but they didn't want me to do that. They felt betrayed
anyway. If you're an editor, what you're supposed to do is acquire
books, not produce them. There is a light adversarial relationship
between publishers and authors that I think probably works
effectively. But that's why I was very quiet about writing. I don't
know what made me write it. I think I just wanted to finish
the story so that I could have a good time reading it. But the
process was what made me think that I should do it again, and I
knew that that was the way I wanted to live. I felt very coherent
when I was writing that book. But I still didn't call myself a
writer. And it was only with my third book, *Song of Solomon*,
that I finally said—not at my own initiative I'm embarrassed to
tell you but at somebody else's initiative—"This is what I do."
I had written three books. It was only after I finished *Song of
Solomon* that I thought, "Maybe this is what I do *only*." Because
before that I always said that I was an editor *who* also wrote
books or a teacher *who* also wrote. I never said I was a writer.
Never. And it's not only because of all the things you might
think. It's also because most writers really and truly have to give

themselves permission to win. That's very difficult, particularly for women. You have to give yourself permission, even when you're doing it. Writing every day, sending books off, you still have to give yourself permission. I know writers whose mothers are writers, who still had to go through a long process with somebody else—a man or editor or friend or something—to finally reach a point where they could say, "It's all right. It's okay." The community says it's okay. Your husband says it's okay. Your children say it's okay. Your mother says it's okay. Eventually everybody says it's okay, and then you have all the okays. It happened to me: even I found a moment after I'd written the third book when I could actually say it. So you go through passport and customs and somebody asks, "What do you do?" And you print it out: WRITE.

The Source of Self-Regard

I WANT TO TALK about two books in a way in which I understand a kind of progression to have taken place in my work, to talk a little bit about *Beloved* and a little bit about a new novel, and to suggest to you some of the obstacles that I created for myself in developing these books, and perhaps to talk, and illustrate by very short examples in the books, ways in which I approached the work.

I was told by somebody at a very, very large state university, "You know that *you*," meaning me, "are taught in twenty-three separate classes on this campus." Not twenty-three separate groups of students, but twenty-three different subject-matter classes. And I was very flattered by that, and very interested in that, but a little bit overwhelmed, because I thought, well, outside of, say, African American literature or women's studies, or who knows, maybe even English departments and places like that, how could there be twenty-three? Well, some of them were legal studies, and some of them were courses in history, and some of them courses in politics, some of them were in psychiatry, in all sorts of things. And aside from some obvious things that I could claim about *Beloved*, it did seem to me that it had become a kind of an all-purpose, highly serviceable source for some discourse in various disciplines and various genres and various fields.

And I thought, well then, there is not only perhaps a hunger for the information, maybe the book is a kind of substitute and a more intimate version of history, and in that way becomes serviceable in a way in which, perhaps, other novels that I have written have never become. *Song of Solomon* is not read that way, *Sula*'s not read that way, but *Beloved* is read that way and perhaps that's why it was distributed so widely on a campus that could accommodate many, many disciplines and genres and approaches. So my feeling was that it was kind of intimate but perhaps also kind of a shortcut to history. So I want to talk about how history is handled, or I had to handle it, in the writing of *Beloved*. And then segue from the impact of history on this fictional form, for me, into the culture of a later period, the twenties, and how that influenced my construction of the new book, *Jazz*.

In trying to think through how one deals with something as formidable and as well researched as history, and how one can convert it, or ignore it, or break its bounds or what have you in order to develop the novel, I was talking a couple of years ago to an audience in Tulsa, Oklahoma, and that audience was made up of librarians and people from the community and students and many teachers, high school teachers and private school teachers, and during the question-and-answer period following my reading and talk, one of the teachers asked me a question. She wanted to know whether as the author of *Beloved,* I could give her any information on how to teach that novel when, as she said, there were no CliffsNotes available. Well, I was a little astonished by her question. I mean, I would not have been astonished if a student had asked me, but I was a little astonished because she did, and so I said, "Well, I don't really know how to teach *Beloved,* and I certainly don't know how to tell *you* how to teach it, but since you say there are no CliffsNotes, maybe one of the ways to teach it is to have your students make some." And she sort of smiled and looked as though I had not treated her question seriously, but it was the best I could do under the circumstances.

But what's interesting is that later, six or seven months later, I got a large package from her, and in that package were three issues or editions, I guess you could call them, of CliffsNotes. And what she had done is taken my answer to heart and given her honors students the assignment of producing CliffsNotes for the novel. She divided them into three teams, and each team produced a booklet with a cover and preface and acknowledgments and table of contents and then that long, so-called analysis that you see in CliffsNotes. And each one had received a prize—one through three—and the students sent me their pictures of their team, holding their names up. And they wrote letters.

Clearly, in order to do that, they had to read the book very carefully, they had to do secondary source readings, they had to make literary references and cross-references and so on. So it turned out, I'm sure, to be a very interesting project. I read their letters very carefully, and most of them were complimentary, but you know the nice thing about high school students is that they are not *obliged* to be complimentary, and particularly after they have done all that work they feel very authoritative and they don't have to compliment you at all. And so they asked me questions that they had not been able to answer sufficiently to satisfy themselves. I am leading up to what I found to be one of the principal complaints they had. The consistent one, the one that if you took all the complaints and rolled them into one, that they were really expressing, was that they were either alarmed or offended by explicit sexuality in *Beloved* and the candor with which some of those scenes were described, and they didn't understand the necessity for the use of that kind of candor. On the one hand, it was reassuring to find students still shockable in terms of sexuality being described, so I felt pretty good about that, but on the other hand it was very disturbing to me because nobody was offended or confused or unable to understand the context in which the story is set, which is slavery. The sexuality troubled them. But the violence and the criminality and the license in that institution did not alarm or offend them.

I thought this pointed to one of the problems of writing novels that have a historical basis: that is, you don't question the history. Or really analyze it or confront it in some manner that is at odds with the historian or even the novelist's version of it. One sort of takes it, swallows it, agrees with it. Nothing is aslant. Although in fact, the reason I had written the book was to enter into that historical period from some point of view that was entirely different from standard history, not in terms of data or information but in terms of what it was able to elicit from the reader. It seemed that everything came under review in the text by these very clever students, *except* the major assumptions of the text. So either I did it very well, or I did it very badly.

But in truth, the problem lay in the nature of the beast itself—in the nature of trying to marry a certain kind of terribly familiar but at the same time estranging history. The question being, how to elicit critical thinking and draw out some honest art form from the silences and the distortions and the evasions that are in the history as received, as well as the articulation and engagement of a history that is so fraught with emotion and so fraught and covered with a profound distaste and repugnance. Because I would assume that everybody would either understand it, rationalize it, defend it, or be repelled by that history. So my job as a novelist was to try to make it palatable and at the same time disenfranchise the history, in a sense. The embrace of history and fiction is what I was concerned with, or rather the effort to disentangle the grip of history while remaining in its palm, so to speak. Especially this particular piece of history and this particular novel.

For the purposes of the rest of this talk I want us to agree that in all of our education, whether it's in institutions or not, in homes or streets or wherever, whether it's scholarly or whether it's experiential, there is a kind of a progression. We move from data to information to knowledge to wisdom. And separating one from the other, being able to distinguish among and between them, that is, knowing the limitations and the danger of exercising one without the others, while respecting each category of intelligence, is generally what serious education is about. And if we agree that purposeful progression exists, then you will see at once how dispiriting this project of drawing or building or constructing fiction out of history can be, or that it's easy, and it's seductive, to assume that data is really knowledge. Or that information is, indeed, wisdom. Or that knowledge can exist without data. And how easy, and how effortlessly, one can parade and disguise itself as another. And how quickly we can forget that wisdom without knowledge, wisdom without any data, is just a hunch.

In writing *Beloved,* all of that became extremely acute. Because I resisted the data at my disposal and felt that I was quite fully informed.

I didn't have to know small things, I could invent them easily—I'd read all the same books you have about slavery, the historical books, the *Slavery to Freedom* and *Roll, Jordan, Roll* and *Slavery and Social Death* and the Aptheker collections of documents, etc. I'd read Gutman's *Black Family in Slavery and Freedom,* but particularly I had read the autobiographies of the slaves themselves and therefore had firsthand information from people who were there. You add that to my own intuition, and you can see the shape of my confidence and the trap that it would lead me into, which would be confusing data with information and knowledge with hunches and so on. I thought I knew a great deal about it. And that arrogance was the first obstacle.

What I needed was imagination to shore up the facts, the data, and not be overwhelmed by them. Imagination that personalized information, made it intimate, but didn't offer itself as a substitute. If imagination could be depended on for that, then there was the possibility of knowledge. Wisdom, of course, I would leave alone, and rely on the readers to produce that.

So here I am appropriating a historical life—Margaret Garner's life—from a newspaper article, which is sort of reliable, halfway unreliable, not doing any further research on her, but doing a lot of research around her. What things were like from 1865 to 1877 within Reconstruction and so on in that part of the country, so that all of the details would be there. But also realizing that part of the imaginative process in dealing with history was that in the article this preacher who was interviewing her and telling her story with a great deal of shock refused to make any judgments about her. He withheld judgment. And this was sort of the way everybody was, although they all wrote these powerful editorials that were anti–Fugitive Slave Law and so on, there was this sort of refusal to judge. And that little scrap of information seemed key to me—the inability to judge what this woman had done. The withdrawal from judgment, the refusal, not to know, but to conclude. And there seemed just a little kernel of something in that.

Why not judge her? Everybody else had. It was clearly terrible. That was a judgment. It was obviously unconscionable. It was harrowing, what she had done. It was monstrous. But the interesting thing was, harrowing as it was, monstrous as it was, outrageous and inhuman as it was, it was not illegal. It was everything but that. The law did not recognize the relationship, so there was no legal language to hold it. Margaret Garner wasn't tried for murder; she was tried for what the law could accommodate, what the law could judge, what the law deemed "outlaw," which was the theft of property.

The question for me then became, well, if the law is unwilling to judge, and her mother-in-law can't judge, who can? Who is in a position to condemn her, absolutely, for the thing the courts would not even admit susceptible to litigation? The accusing finger would have to have a lot of weight if it were to be a finger that Margaret Garner pays some attention to. And that would only be, of course, her daughter, the one she managed to kill—successfully, if that term is applicable—before they stopped her. While I wasn't anxious or eager to get into those waters, I thought, well, if she could do it, then I could sort of imagine it, or think about it, and see what would happen when the dead daughter was introduced into the text. And of course what it did do was it destabilized everything, reformulated its own history, and then changed language entirely.

The other problem—that is, in addition to the history, the actual outline or plot of Margaret Garner's life, and my alteration of it to suit my own purposes—in trying to do this, is the problem of slavery. It would have been wonderful for me if she had done this some other time, like ten years ago, and then I could deal with it, but it happened in slavery. So the question is how does one handle it? How do you inhabit it without surrendering to it? Without making *it* the major focus of the novel, rather than the slaves themselves. The problem is how to take the imaginative power, the artistic control away from the institution of slavery and place it where it belongs—in the hands of the individuals who knew it, certainly as well as anybody, and that would be the slaves. And at the same time, not to dismiss it or denigrate its horror. Because the problem is always pornography. It's very easy to write about something like that and find yourself in the position of a voyeur, where actually the violence, the grotesqueries and the pain and the suffering, becomes its own excuse for reading. And there's a kind of relish in the observation of the suffering of another. I didn't want to go into that area, and it was difficult to find out—difficult and important to find out where those lines were, where you stop and how you can effect a kind of visceral and intellectual response without playing into the hands of the institution and making it its own excuse for being. I didn't want to chew on that evil and give it an authority that it didn't deserve, give it a glamour that it didn't really have; I wanted to return the agency into the hands of the slaves, who had always been fairly anonymous, or flat, it seemed to me, in much, although not all, of the literature.

Now of course here's three to four hundred years to peruse, and it is indeed a humbling experience. You find that the sheer documentation—the history—is too long. It's too big, it's too awful, too researched, too ancient, too recent, too defended, it's too rationalized, it's too apologized for, it's too resisted, it's too known, and it's too unknown, and it's too passionate, and it's too elusive. And, in order to explain other kinds of oppression, such as women's oppression, it was also very much appropriated.

So I'm dealing in an area that I know is already overdone and underdone—attractive in an unhealthy sense, and repulsive and hidden and repressed in another. What I needed then, to deal with what I thought was unmanageable, was some little piece, some concrete thing, some image that came from the world of that which was concrete. Something that was domestic, something that you could sort of hook the book on to, that would say everything you wanted to say in very human and personal terms. And for me that image, that concrete thing became the bit.

I had read references to this thing people put in their mouths. Slave narratives were very much like nineteenth-century novels, there were certain things they didn't talk about too much, and also because they were writing for white people whom they wanted to persuade to be abolitionists or to do abolitionist-type work, did not dwell on, didn't spend a lot of time telling those people how terrible all this was. They didn't want to call anybody any names, they needed their money, so they sort of created an upbeat story: I was born, it was terrible, I got out, and other people are still there and you should help them get out. They didn't stay and talk a great deal; there was a lot of hinting and a lot of reference but nothing explicit that you could see. So sometimes you might read that Equiano goes into a kitchen in New England and he sees a woman cooking, and she has this thing in her mouth and he says, "What is that?" And somebody says, "Oh, that's a brake," *b-r-a-k-e*, and he said, "I have never seen anything so awful in my life," and he leaves and doesn't talk about it anymore. And then I had seen many references, such as some entries, very selective entries, from William Byrd, in Virginia, in the early part of the eighteenth century, 1709, 1712—and his editors describe him, quote, as "Virginia's most polished and ornamental gentleman, a kindly master, who inveighed in some of his letters against brutes who mistreated their slaves."

> February the eighth: *Jenny and Eugene were whipped.* April: *Anna was whipped.* May: *Mrs. Byrd whips the nurse.* May: *Ma was whipped.* June: *Eugene* [who was a little child] *was whipped for running away and had the bit put on him.* September: *I beat Jenny.* September: *Jenny was whipped.* September: *I beat Anna.* November: *Eugene and Jenny were whipped.* December: *Eugene was whipped for doing nothing.* Then the next year in July: *The Negro woman ran away again with the bit on her mouth.* July again: *The Negro woman was found, and tied, but ran away again in the night.* Five days later: *My wife, against my will, caused little Jenny to be burned with a hot iron.* Next month: *I had a severe quarrel with little Jenny and beat her too much, for which I was sorry.* Same month: *Eugene and Jenny were beaten.* October: *I whipped three slave women.* November: *The Negro woman ran away.*

And there are three or four more pages of that. And it is true that taken into consideration with other kinds of behavior, this was not all that bad. But the two references to the bit, none of which he explains or describes, were similar to many others I had read. I had a lot of trouble trying to find descriptions of this contraption, pictures, what did it look like, what did it do, and so on. And it was very, very difficult, though I did end up being very lucky, in a way—I found some pictures.

But I felt, ultimately, that it wasn't something that really needed to be described. If I had described it exactly the way it was, and found language to say exactly what those things looked like, it would have defeated my purpose. It was enough to know that you couldn't order them from a large warehouse, that you had to make them yourself. It was enough to know that they—these handmade things—were not restrictive in the sense that they were not like docks, which made it so you couldn't work. You were supposed to go on and continue to work. It was important that it was not only used for slaves, it was also used a lot for white women, who sometimes, I suppose, needed, or someone felt that they needed, the same sort of thing, because the bit is just something that goes in your mouth and it hurts, I suppose, it's inconvenient, but you know what it does? It makes you shut up. You can't move your tongue. And for women, we know, that would be a torture instrument that would be primary.

Not describing it technically, physically, became more important because I wanted it to remain indescribable but not unknown. So the point became to render not what it looked like, but what it felt like and what it meant, personally. Now that was the parallel of my attitude toward the history, toward the institution of slavery, that is, I didn't want to describe what it *looked* like, but what it *felt* like and what it meant. So I eliminated all the data from the inquisition records that I read—São Paulo and *Harper's Weekly* and Equiano and slave owners' diaries—and tried to form language that would help me and, I hope, the reader, to know it. Just know it. Nowhere in *Beloved* is this contraption described. But this is what I ended up with when I tried to make it completely known or convey a sense of how it felt and what it meant.

At this point, in this short little passage, Sethe has found out that probably her husband never left that farm, Sweet Home, and that he probably saw what happened to her, because Paul D thinks so. And she's angry when she hears it, because she wants to know of Paul D, why didn't he, if he saw her husband collapsed in this way, why didn't he help him, and why didn't he say something to him, why did he just walk away without saying anything, and he said he couldn't because he had this thing in his mouth. And eventually she asks him to tell her not about what she's feeling about her husband, her ex-husband, but what that must have been like for him.

He wants to tell me, she thought. He wants me to ask him about what it was like for him—about how offended the tongue is, held down by iron, how the need to spit is so deep you cry for it. She already knew about it, had seen it time after time in the place before Sweet Home. Men, boys, little girls, women. The wildness that shot up into the eye the moment the lips were yanked back. Days after it was taken out, goose fat was rubbed on the corners of the mouth but nothing to soothe the tongue or take the wildness out of the eye.

Sethe looked up into Paul D's eyes to see if there was any trace left in them.

"People I saw as a child," she said, "who'd had the bit always looked wild after that. Whatever they used it on them for, it couldn't have worked, because it put a wildness where before there wasn't any. When I look at you, I don't see it. There ain't no wildness in your eye nowhere."

"There's a way to put it there and there's a way to take it out. I know em both and I haven't figured out yet which is worse." He sat down beside her. Sethe looked at him. In that unlit daylight his face, bronzed and reduced to its bones, smoothed her heart down.

"You want to tell me about it?" she asked him.

"I don't know. I never have talked about it. Not to a soul. Sang it sometimes, but I never told a soul."

"Go ahead. I can hear it."

"Maybe. Maybe you can hear it. I just ain't sure I can say it. Say it right, I mean, because it wasn't the bit—that wasn't it."

"What then?" Sethe asked.

"The roosters," he said. "Walking past the roosters looking at them look at me."

Sethe smiled. "In that pine?"

"Yeah." Paul D smiled with her. "Must have been five of them perched up there, and at least fifty hens."

"Mister, too?"

"Not right off. But I hadn't took twenty steps before I seen him. He come down off the fence post there and sat on the tub."

"He loved that tub," said Sethe, thinking, No, there is no stopping now.

"Didn't he? Like a throne. Was me took him out the shell, you know. He'd a died if it hadn't been for me. The hen had walked on off with all the hatched peeps trailing behind her. There was this one egg left. Looked like a blank, but then I saw it move so I tapped it open and here come Mister, bad feet and all. I watched that son a bitch grow up and whup everything in the yard."

"He always was hateful," Sethe said.

"Yeah, he was hateful all right. Bloody too, and evil. Crooked feet flapping. Comb as big as my hand and some kind of red. He sat right there on the tub looking at me. I swear he smiled. My head was full of what I'd seen of Halle a while back. I wasn't even thinking about the bit. Just Halle and before him Sixo, but when I saw Mister I knew it was me too. Not just them, me too. One crazy, one sold, one missing, one burnt and me licking iron with my hands crossed behind me. The last of the Sweet Home men.

"Mister, he looked so . . . free. Better than me. Stronger, tougher. Son a bitch couldn't even get out the shell by hisself but he was still king and I was . . ." Paul D stopped and squeezed his left hand with his right. He held it that way long enough for it and the world to quiet down and let him go on.

"Mister was allowed to be and stay what he was. But I wasn't allowed to be and stay what I was. Even if you cooked him you'd be cooking a rooster named Mister. But wasn't no way I'd ever be Paul D again, living or dead. Schoolteacher changed me. I was something else and that something was less than a chicken sitting in the sun on a tub."

Sethe put her hand on his knee and rubbed.

Paul D had only begun, what he was telling her was only the beginning when her fingers on his knee, soft and reassuring, stopped him. Just as well. Just as well. Saying more might push them both to a place they couldn't get back from. He would keep the rest where it belonged: in that tobacco tin buried in his chest where a red heart used to be. Its lid rusted shut. He would not pry it loose now in front of this sweet sturdy woman, for if she got a whiff of its contents it would shame him. And it would hurt her to know that there was no red heart bright as Mister's comb beating in him.

When I moved away from that project, which I thought was sort of incomplete, I began to think about another important point in American life that was also an extremely important point in African American life that I wanted to write about, but this time my problem was not how to deal with the *history,* but rather how to deal with the *culture.* There wasn't a great deal of history that had been written about the twenties, the period I call jazz, or we call jazz. There'd been lots and lots of books, lots and lots of movies, lots and lots of images, lots and lots of everything, but there was still this huge, powerful, amorphous kind of understanding of what that culture was.

If I say the word "jazz," I'm sure something comes to mind, something very concrete or maybe something that's unspecific, maybe just the music, a certain kind of music. And if I pursue that image of jazz music, you know, a sample might surface or a musician or arrangement or a song or something, or maybe just clubs, radio, whatever comes to mind. And places where that particular kind of music we call jazz is played. Or maybe just your own like of it or your dislike of it or your indifference to that particular music. But whatever you're thinking about that music, in the background of the word "jazz" is the recollection, if not the main feature of your memory, or your association, that jazz is music black people play, or originated, or shaped. But that it's not exclusively played or even enjoyed by them, now, or for even a long, long time. And also the fact that the appreciation of jazz is one of the few places where a certain kind of race transcendence or race-transcendent embrace is possible. Which doesn't mean there was no exploitation, but even the exploitation was possible only because of the interest in it, and the passion for it, and the embrace that did take place interracially, so to speak.

The dictionary definitions of "jazz" list usually three or four entries relating to the music—where it originated in New Orleans around the beginning of the twentieth century, and then they usually go on to characterize the music in very interesting words. "Compulsive," for example, is used a lot. "Intricate." "Freely improvised." And then they sometimes chart the course of jazz from diatonism to grammaticism to atonality, and then they go on to list some other entries in which jazz is not music, it's a kind of dance done to such music and having some of the characteristics of the music. But it's distinguished by *violent* bodily gestures and motions. And then following those definitions are slang definitions, including "vigorous," "liveliness," "spirited," and "insincerity," "exaggeration," or "pretentiousness." *All that jazz. Don't give me all that jazz.* You know, something you don't have to pay any attention to because it's overstatement. But something that is jazzy is highly energetic and wildly active.

I don't think anybody really needs those dictionary definitions to clarify because one of the attractions of the term is its loose association of energy and sensuality. And freedom. And release. And intricacy. All that. All of it backgrounded by a recognizable music black people originated and shaped. I don't myself usually think of music first. But of the many images that might surface, one would be a sort of recent history period, the twenties, the period known as the Jazz Age. And attached to that term may be the sound of the music as it affected or backgrounded an era or generation of people whom we associate with that period. "Jazz Age" elicits more detailed imagery—Prohibition, a change in fashion that was alarming and sort of exciting in some places, short hair and skirts in which women could actually walk and work and move. And dance. But it also suggested a kind of recklessness and license and sexuality.

But if you bend the Jazz Age the way I've just described it to suit more literary interests, then we make the association with writers who reached their maturity or started out and did something wonderful or had some influence or fame during the twenties and early thirties, and we begin to think of that wonderful poetry and drama and the novels of a whole group of post–World War I American artists: Dos

Passos and Fitzgerald and Hemingway and Stein and Pound, and well, you know that list and it's a familiar one, but familiar too is the whole constellation of things and people, the tone, the music, and the history that the word "jazz" evokes, and all of it is understood to be uniquely American. It's a uniquely American posture. And it suggests an American modernism that lingered on and on and on until there was something after modernism, and then of course something after that, and then something after that.

It is an American cultural phenomenon, and as such, it's more than any of the definitions or connotations that I have mentioned. It's really a concept. And it's interesting to me as a writer because it's so full of contradictions. It's American, indisputably American, *and* ethnically marginal. It's black *and* free. It's intricate *and* wild. It's spontaneous *and* practiced. It's exaggerated *and* simple. It's constantly invented, always brand-new, but somehow familiar and known. Wherever you go in the world, if you say, "Jazz," people say, "Oh yes, yes. I remember." Or "I understand." Or "I know." And I don't know if they're thinking about Josephine Baker or what, but it's "Oh yes, yes. Jazz. I know." It's immediately understood and all explanations become redundant.

Now these contradictions have been very much on my mind because I was trying to think through some other concepts that had to do with this very, very important transition, I think, and transformation in the history of African Americans and very much a transformation in the history of this country. So my attempt then was to take not the history but the culture of jazz, which is much more ineffable and vaporous, and I wanted to demystify and revalorize the jazz idea. And to do that from a viewpoint that precedes its appropriation—you know, when it becomes anybody's and everybody's—and that reculturizes and deculturizes this idea.

It is a part, this view, looking at that period in black life, of a rather sustained investigation I began with *Beloved,* which was that I'm really looking at self-regard in both racial and gendered terms, and how that self-regard evolves or is distorted or flourishes or collapses, and under what circumstances. In *Beloved,* I was interested in what contributed most significantly to a slave woman's self-regard. What was her self-esteem? What value did she place on herself? And I became convinced, and research supported my hunch, my intuition, that it was her identity as a mother, her ability to be and to remain exactly what the institution said she was not, that was important to her. Moving into Reconstruction and beyond it, as difficult as it was to function as a mother with control over the destiny of one's children, it still became then, certainly, a legal responsibility after slavery. So this is where the sources of self-regard came for Margaret Garner or Sethe. And it is exaggerated because it's that important and that alien and that strange and that vital. But when Sethe asks, "Me? Me?" at the end of *Beloved*, it's a real movement toward a recognition of self-regard.

But the answer to her question seemed to me to come or be available a generation or two later, when the possibility of personal freedom, and interior, imaginative freedom—not political or economic freedom, those were still distant, although there had been some changes—could be engaged. So it seemed to me that while the history, the data of traditional historians, both documented and denied this change in black life and in the culture, the information available to me in the cultural signs suggested there were alterations in the formulations and the sources of self-regard. Music, its lyrics, its performers held the first signs, for me, of this change in the culture. Movement, migration from rural areas to urban ones, held other kinds of information. The literature, the language, the custom, the posture, all of this was what I would look at.

It seemed to me that the twenties, with its sort of nascent and overwhelming jazz idiom, was as distinct as it was because, precisely, of this change. That period, the Jazz Age, was a period when black people placed an indelible hand of agency on the cultural scene. And this agency—unremarked in economic and political terms—informs my project. And all the terms I cited earlier—"defiance," "violence," "sensuality," "freedom," "intricacy," "invention," and "improvisation"—were intimated in the major figuration of that term. Subjective, demanding, deeply personal love relationships. The one place African Americans could command and surrender by choice. Where they did not marry who was chosen for them, or who lived down the road, or who was next door. Where they could effect the widest possible choice—by deciding to fall in love. Claiming another as the beloved. Not because of filial blood relationships or proximity, but precisely because it was ad hoc and accidental and fated but not predictable.

And this assertiveness, this creative agency, seemed to be most clear in the music, the style, the language of this—that post-Reconstruction era that represented both transition and transformation. You know, like life lived in flour sacking or plain, dull cotton gives you a hunger, a desperation for color and patterns and powerful, primary colors, in the same way that hundreds of years of being mated off or ordered whom to marry, of needing permission to join with another, of having to take these extraordinary, drastic measures to keep a family together and to behave like a family, and all of this under the greatest stress, with so little evidence that anything would ever change. You could get slaves to do anything at all, bear anything, if you gave them any hope that they could keep their children. They'd do anything. Every impulse, every gesture, everything they did was to maintain their families.

Well, under those historical pressures, the desire for choice in partners, the desire for romantic love, operate as a place, a space, away, for individual reclamation of the self. That is a part, maybe the largest part, certainly an important part, of the reconstruction of identity. Part of the "me" so tentatively articulated in *Beloved*. That's what she needs to discover. It will account for the satisfaction in the blues lyric and the blues phrase whether or not, and mostly not, the relationship flourishes. They're usually, you know, somebody's gone and not coming back or some terrible thing has happened and you'll never see this person again. Whether or not the affection is returned, whether or not the loved one reciprocated the ardor, the lover, the singer, has achieved something, accomplished something in the act of being in love. It's impossible to hear that sort of blues cry without acknowledging in it the defiance, the grandeur, the agency that frequently belies the wail of disappointed love.

It may be through that agency, and the even more powerful assertiveness of what we call "jazz," which uses those gestures, that compromise becomes reconciliation. It's also the way in which imagination fosters real possibilities: you can't imagine it, you can't have it. And a third thing grows, where despair may have been, or even where the past lay whole and wouldn't let go. And it is this third thing that jazz creates and that creates itself in these spaces and intersections of race and gender that interest me and that informed and propel the writing of this book called *Jazz*. I want to read just a page or two, which is kind of an illustration of that gesture of choice and love:

It's nice when grown people whisper to each other under the covers. Their ecstasy is more leaf-sigh than bray and the body is the vehicle, not the point. They reach, grown people, for something beyond, way beyond and way, way down underneath tissue. They are remembering while they whisper the carnival dolls they won and the Baltimore boats they never sailed on. The pears they let hang on the limb because if they plucked them, they would be gone from there and who else would see that ripeness if they took it away for themselves? How could anybody passing by see them and imagine for themselves what the flavor would be like? Breathing and murmuring under covers both of them have washed and hung out on the line, in a bed they chose together and kept together, nevermind one leg was propped on a 1916 dictionary, and the mattress, curved like a preacher's palm asking for witnesses in His name's sake, enclosed them each and every night and muffled their whispering, old-time love. They are under the covers because they don't have to look at themselves anymore; there is no stud's eye, no chippie glance to undo them. They are inward toward the other, bound and joined by carnival dolls and the steamers that sailed from ports they never saw. That is what is beneath their undercover whispers.

But there's another part, not so secret. The part that touches fingers when one passes the cup and saucer to the other. The part that closes her neckline snap while waiting for the trolley; and brushes lint from his blue serge suit when they come out of the movie house into the sunlight.

I envy them their public love. I myself have only known it in secret, shared it in secret and longed, aw longed to show it—to be able to say out loud what they have no need to say at all: *That I have loved only you, surrendered my whole self reckless to you and nobody else. That I want you to love me back and show it to me. That I love the way you hold me, how close you let me be to you. I like your fingers on and on, lifting, turning. I have watched your face for a long time now, and missed your eyes when you went away from me. Talking to you and hearing you answer—that's the kick.*

But I can't say that aloud; I can't tell anyone that I have been waiting for this all my life and that being chosen to wait is the reason I can. If I were able I'd say it. Say make me, remake me. You are free to do it and I am free to let you because look, look. Look where your hands are. Now.

Rememory

I SUSPECT my dependency on memory as trustworthy ignition is more anxious than it is for most fiction writers—not because I write (or want to) autobiographically, but because I am keenly aware of the fact that I write in a wholly racialized society that can and does hobble the imagination. Labels about centrality, marginality, minority, gestures of appropriated and appropriating cultures and literary heritages, pressures to take a position—all these surface when I am read or critiqued and when I compose. It is both an intolerable and inevitable condition. I am asked bizarre questions inconceivable if put to other writers: Do you think you will ever write about white people? Isn't it awful to be called a black writer?

I wanted my imagination as unencumbered as possible *and* as responsible as possible. I wanted to carve out a world both culture specific and "race-free." All of which presented itself to me as a project full of paradox and contradiction. Western or European writers believe or can choose to believe their work is naturally "race-free" or "race transcendent." Whether it is or not is another question—the fact is the problem has not worried them. They can take it for granted that it is because Others are "raced"—whites are not. Or so the conventional wisdom goes. The truth, of course, is that we are all "raced." Wanting that same sovereignty, I had to originate my own fictional projects in a manner I hoped would liberate me, the work, and my ability to do it. I had three choices: to ignore race or try to altogether and write about World War II or domestic strife without referencing race. But that would erase one, although not the only, most impinging fact of my existence and my intelligence. Two, I could become a cool "objective" observer writing about race conflict and/or harmony. There, however, I would be forced to surrender the center of the stage to received ideas of centrality and the subject would always and forever be race. Or, three, I could strike out for new territory: to find a way to free my imagination of the impositions and limitations of race *and* explore the consequences of its centrality in the world and in the lives of the people I was hungry to write about.

First was my effort to substitute and rely on memory rather than history because I knew I could not, should not, trust recorded history to give me the insight into the cultural specificity I wanted. Second, I determined to diminish, exclude, even freeze any (overt) debt to Western literary history. Neither effort has been entirely successful, nor should I be congratulated if it had been. Yet it seemed to me extremely important to try. You will understand how reckless it would have been for me to rely on Conrad or Twain or Melville or Stowe or Whitman or Henry James or James Fenimore Cooper, or Saul Bellow for that matter, or Flannery O'Connor or Ernest Hemingway for insights into my own culture. It would have been equally dim-witted, as well as devastating, for me to rely on Kenneth Stampp or Lewis Mumford, or Herbert Gutman, or Eugene Genovese or Moynihan, or Emerson, or Jefferson or any of those sages in the history of the United States for research that would enlighten me on these matters. There was and is another source that I have at my disposal, however: my own literary heritage of slave narratives.

For imaginative entrance into that territory I urged memory to metamorphose itself into the kind of metaphorical and imagistic associations I described at the beginning of this talk with Hannah Peace.

But writing is not simply recollecting or reminiscing or even epiphany. It is doing; creating a narrative infused (in my case) with legitimate and authentic characteristics of the culture.

Mindful of and rebellious toward the cultural and racial expectations and impositions my fiction would encourage, it was important for me not to reveal, that is, reinforce, already established reality (literary or historical) that the reader and I agree upon beforehand. I could not, without engaging in another kind of cultural totalizing process, assume or exercise that kind of authority.

It was in *Beloved,* however, that all of these matters coalesced for me in new and major ways. History versus memory, and memory versus memorylessness. Rememory as in recollecting and remembering as in reassembling the members of the body, the family, the population of the past. And it was the struggle, the pitched battle between remembering and forgetting, that became the device of the narrative. The effort to both remember and not know became the structure of the text. Nobody in the book can bear too long to dwell on the past; nobody can avoid it. There is no reliable literary or journalistic or scholarly history available to them, to help them, because they are living in a society and a system in which the conquerors write the narrative of their lives. They are spoken of and written about—objects of history, not subjects within it. Therefore not only is the major preoccupation of the central characters that of reconstituting and recollecting a usable past (Sethe to know what happened to her and to not know in order to justify her violent action; Paul D to stand still and remember what has helped to construct his self; Denver to demystify her own birth and enter the contemporary world that she is reluctant to engage) but also the narrative strategy the plot formation turns on the stress of remembering, its inevitability, the chances for liberation that lie within the process.

[Read]

The final pages in which memory is insistent yet becomes the mutation of fact into fiction then folklore and then into nothing.

The novel I worked on following the completion of *Beloved* presented a different set of circumstances in this regard. Some of the circumstances surrounding the writing of *Song of Solomon* included access I believed the contemplation of my father made available to me. This project is dependent on the grabbing hold of another parent—my mother. It takes place in 1926, which is the time of my mother's girlhood. That is, her memory of that time as told to me is both a veil secreting certain parts and a rend her narrative tore into it. I believe this short section is to me the essence of memory turned to nostalgia and regret and moving forward finally toward a very thin, but not so frail, possibility of hope for the present.

Memory, Creation, and Fiction

> It is not enough for a work of art to have ordered planes and lines. If a stone is tossed at a group of children, they hasten to scatter. A regrouping, an action, has been accomplished. This is composition. This regrouping, presented by means of color, lines, and planes is an artistic and painterly motif.
>
> —EDVARD MUNCH

I LIKE that quotation, as I do many of the remarks painters make about their work, because it clarifies for me an aspect of creation that engages me as a writer. It suggests how that interior part of the growth of a writer (the part that is both separate and indistinguishable from craft) is connected not only to some purely local and localized sets of stimuli but also to memory: the painter can copy or reinterpret the stone—its lines, planes, or curves—but the stone that causes something to happen among children he must remember, because it is done and gone. As he sits before his sketchbook he remembers how the scene looked, but most importantly he remembers the specific milieu that accompanies the scene.

Along with the stone and the scattered children is an entire galaxy of feeling and impression—the motion and content of which may seem arbitrary, even incoherent, at first.

Because so much in public and scholarly life forbids us to take seriously the milieu of buried stimuli, it is often extremely hard to seek out both the stimulus and its galaxy and to recognize their value when they arrive. Memory is for me always fresh, in spite of the fact that the object being remembered is done and past.

Memory (the deliberate act of remembering) is a form of willed creation. It is not an effort to find out the way it really was—that is research. The point is to dwell on the way it appeared and why it appeared in that particular way.

I once knew a woman named Hannah Peace. I say "knew," but nothing could be less accurate. I was perhaps four years old when she was in the town where I lived. I don't know where (or even if) she is now, or to whom she was related then. She was not even a visiting friend. I couldn't describe her in a way that would make her known in a photograph, nor would I recognize her if she walked into this room. But I have a memory of her and it's like this: the color of her skin—the matte quality of it. Something purple around her. Also eyes not completely open. There emanated from her an aloofness that seemed to me kindly disposed. But most of all I remember her name—or the way people pronounced it. Never Hannah or Miss Peace. Always Hannah Peace—and more. Something hidden—some awe perhaps, but certainly some forgiveness. When they pronounced her name, they (the women and the men) forgave her something.

That's not much, I know: half-closed eyes, an absence of hostility, skin powdered in lilac dust. But it was more than enough to evoke a character—in fact any more detail would have prevented (for me) the emergence of a fictional character at all. What is useful—definitive—is the galaxy of emotion that accompanied the woman as I pursued my memory of her; not the woman herself. (I am still startled by the ability—even the desire—to "use" acquaintances or friends or enemies as fictional characters. There is no yeast for me in a real-life person, or else there is so much it is not useful—it is done bread, already baked.)

The pieces (and only the pieces) are what begin the creative process for me. And the process by which the recollections of these pieces coalesce into a part (and knowing the difference between a piece and a part) is creation. Memory, then, no matter how small the piece remembered, demands my respect, my attention, and my trust.

I depend heavily on the ruse of memory (and in a way it does function as a creative writer's ruse) for two reasons. One, because it ignites some process of invention, and two, because I cannot trust the literature and the sociology of other people to help me know the truth of my own cultural sources. It also prevents my preoccupations from descending into sociology. Since the discussion of black literature in critical terms is unfailingly sociology and almost never art criticism, it is important for me to shed those considerations from my work at the outset.

In the example I have given of Hannah Peace it was the having-been-easily-forgiven that caught my attention, not growing up black, and that quality, that "easily forgivenness" that I believe I remember in connection with a shadow of a woman my mother knew, is the theme of *Sula*. The women forgive each other—or learn to. Once that piece of the galaxy became apparent, it dominated the other pieces. The next step was to discover what there is to be forgiven among women. Such things must now be raised and invented because I am going to tell about feminine forgiveness in story form. The things to be forgiven are grave errors and violent misdemeanors, but the point is less the thing to be forgiven than the nature and quality of forgiveness among women—which is to say friendship among women. What one puts up with in a friendship is determined by the emotional value of the relationship. But *Sula* is not simply about friendship among women, but among black women, a qualifying term the artistic responsibilities of which I will touch upon in a moment.

I want my fiction to urge the reader into active participation in the nonnarrative, nonliterary experience of the text, which makes it difficult for the reader to confine himself to a cool and distant acceptance of data. When one looks at a very good painting, the experience of looking is deeper than the data accumulated in viewing it. The same, I think, is true in listening to good music. Just as the literary value of a painting or a musical composition is limited, so too is the literary value of literature limited. I sometimes think how glorious it must have been to have written drama in sixteenth-century England, or poetry in ancient Greece, or religious narrative in the Middle Ages, when literature was need and did not have a critical history to constrain or diminish the writer's imagination. How magnificent not to have to depend on the reader's literary associations—his literary experience—which can be as much an impoverishment of the reader's imagination as it is of a writer's. It is important that what I write not be merely literary. I am most self-conscious about making sure that I don't strike literary postures. I avoid, too studiously perhaps, name-dropping, lists, literary references, unless oblique and based on written folklore. The choice of a tale or of folklore in my work is tailored to the character's thoughts or actions in a way that flags him or her and provides irony, sometimes humor.

Milkman, about to meet the oldest black woman in the world, the mother of mothers who has spent her life caring for helpless others, enters her house thinking of a European tale, "Hansel and Gretel," a story about parents who abandon their children to a forest and a witch who makes a diet of them. His confusion at that point, his racial and cultural ignorance, is flagged. Equally marked is Hagar's bed, described as Goldilocks's choice, partly because of Hagar's preoccupations with hair, and partly because, like Goldilocks, a housebreaker if ever there was one, she is greedy for things, unmindful of property rights or other people's space, and Hagar is emotionally selfish as well as confused.

This deliberate avoidance of literary references has become a firm if boring habit with me, not only because they lead to poses, not only because I refuse the credentials they bestow, but also because they are inappropriate to the kind of literature I wish to write, the aims of that literature, and the discipline of the specific culture that interests *me*. Literary references in the hands of writers I love can be extremely revealing, but they can also supply a comfort I don't want the reader to have because I want him to respond on the same plane an illiterate or preliterate reader would. I want to subvert his traditional comfort so that he may experience an unorthodox one: that of being in the company of his own solitary imagination.

My beginnings as a novelist were very much focused on creating this discomfort and unease in order to insist that the reader rely on another body of knowledge. However weak those beginnings were in 1965, they nevertheless pointed me toward the process that engages me in 1984: trusting memory and culling from it theme and structure. In *The Bluest Eye* the recollection of what I felt and saw upon hearing a child my own age say she prayed for blue eyes provided the first piece. I then tried to distinguish between a piece and a part—in the sense that a piece of a human body is different from a part of a human body.

As I began developing parts out of pieces, I found that I preferred them unconnected—to be related but not to touch, to circle, not line up—because the story of this prayer was the story of a shattered, fractured perception resulting from a shattered, splintered life. The novel turned out to be a composition of parts circling one another, like the galaxy accompanying memory. I fret the pieces and fragments of memory because too often we want the whole thing. When we wake from a dream we want to remember all of it, although the fragment we are remembering may be, and very probably is, the most important piece in the dream. Chapter and part designations, as conventionally used in novels, were never very much help to me in writing. Nor are outlines. (I permit their use for the sake of the designer and for ease in talking about the book. They are usually identified at the last minute.)

There may be play and arbitrariness in the way memory surfaces but none in the way the composition is organized, especially when I hope to re-create play and arbitrariness in the way narrative events unfold. The form becomes the exact interpretation of the idea the story is meant to express. There is nothing more traditional than that—but the sources of the images are not the traditional novelistic or readerly ones. The visual image of a splintered mirror, or the corridor of split mirrors in blue eyes, is the form as well as the context of *The Bluest Eye*.

Narrative is one of the ways in which knowledge is organized. I have always thought it was the most important way to transmit and receive knowledge. I am less certain of that now—but the craving for narrative has never lessened, and the hunger for it is as keen as it was on Mount Sinai or Calvary or in the middle of the fens. Even when novelists abandon or grow tired of it as an outmoded mimetic form, historians, journalists, and performing artists take up the slack. Still, narrative is not and never has been enough, just as the object drawn on a canvas or a cave wall is never simply mimetic.

My compact with the reader is not to reveal an already established reality (literary or historical) that he or she and I agree upon beforehand. I don't want to assume or exercise that kind of authority. I regard that as patronizing, although many people regard it as safe and reassuring. And because my métier is black, the artistic demands of black culture are such that I cannot patronize, control, or pontificate. In the third-world cosmology as I perceive it, reality is not already constituted by my literary predecessors in Western culture.

If my work is to confront a reality unlike that received reality of the West, it must centralize and animate information discredited by the West—discredited not because it is not true or useful or even of some racial value, but because it is information held by discredited people, information dismissed as "lore" or "gossip" or "magic" or "sentiment."

If my work is faithfully to reflect the aesthetic tradition of Afro-American culture, it must make conscious use of the characteristics of its art forms and translate them into print: antiphony, the group nature of art, its functionality, its improvisational nature, its relationship to audience performance, the critical voice that upholds tradition and communal values and that also provides occasion for an individual to transcend and/or defy group restrictions.

Working with those rules, the text, if it is to take improvisation and audience participation into account, cannot be the authority—it should be the map. It should make a way for the reader (audience) to participate in the tale. The language, if it is to permit criticism of both rebellion and tradition, must be both indicator and mask, and the tension between the two kinds of language is its release and its power. If my work is to be functional to the group (to the village, as it were) then it must bear witness and identify that which is useful from the past and that which ought to be discarded; it must make it possible to prepare for the present and live it out; and it must do that not by avoiding problems and contradictions but by examining them; it should not even attempt to solve social problems but it should certainly try to clarify them.

Before I try to illustrate some of these points by using *Tar Baby* as an example, let me hasten to say that there are eminent and powerful, intelligent, and gifted black writers who not only recognize Western literature as part of their own heritage but who have employed it to such an advantage that it illuminates both cultures. I neither object to nor am indifferent to their work or their views. I relish it, in precisely the way I relish a world of literature from other cultures. The question is not legitimacy or the "correctness" of a point of view, but the difference between my point of view and theirs. Nothing would be more hateful to me than a monolithic prescription for what black literature is or ought to be. I simply wanted to write literature that was irrevocably, indisputably black not because its characters were, or because I was, but because it took as its creative task and sought as its credentials those recognized and verifiable principles of black art.

In the writing of *Tar Baby*, *memory* meant recollecting the told story. I refused to read a modern or Westernized version of the *told* story, selecting out instead the pieces that were disturbing or simply memorable: fear, tar, the rabbit's outrage at a failing in traditional manners (the tar baby does not speak). Why was the tar baby formed, to what purpose, what was the farmer trying to protect, and why did he think the doll would be attractive to the rabbit—what did he know and what was his big mistake? Why does the tar baby cooperate with the farmer, and do the things the farmer wishes to protect? What makes his job more important than the rabbit's, why does he believe that a briar patch is sufficient punishment, what does the briar patch represent to the rabbit, to the tar baby, and to the farmer?

"Creation" meant putting the above pieces together in parts, first of all concentrating on tar as a part. What is it and where does it come from? What are its holy uses and its profane uses—consideration of which led to a guiding motif: ahistorical earth and historical earth. That theme was translated into the structure in these steps:

1. Coming out of the sea (that which was there before earth) is both the beginning and the end of the book—in both of which Son emerges from the sea in a section that is not numbered as a chapter.

2. The earth that came out of the sea, its conquest by modern man, and the pain caused to the conquered life forms, as they are viewed by fishermen and clouds.

3. Movement from the earth into the household: its rooms, its quality of shelter. The activity for which the rooms were designed: eating, sleeping, bathing, leisure, etc.

4. The house disrupted precisely as the earth was disrupted. The chaos of the earth duplicated in the house designed for order. The disruption caused by the man born out of the womb of the sea accompanied by ammonia odors of birth.

5. The conflict that follows between the ahistorical (the pristine) and the historical (or social) forces inherent in the uses of tar.

6. The conflict, further, between two kinds of chaos: civilized chaos and natural chaos.

7. The revelation, then, is the revelation of secrets. Everybody with one or two exceptions has a secret: secrets of acts committed (as with Margaret and Son), and secrets of thoughts unspoken but driving nonetheless (as with Valerian and Jadine). And then the deepest and earliest secret of all: that *just as we watch other life, other life watches us.*

Goodbye to All That

Race, Surrogacy, and Farewell

SOME YEARS AGO, when I was invited to be interviewed on a television show, I asked whether it was possible for our conversation to avoid any questions or topics about race. I suspected that if such voluntary exclusion were in place, then other equally interesting subjects might surface and produce a rare media encounter—one free of the cant one is inevitably forced to resort to in such a venue, on such a subject. I thought the experiment would be a first for me and elicit my views on what constitutes my writing life; or the relationship between teaching and writing, between editing and teaching, how the pleasure and despair of being a mother influenced my work—loosened or limited it; my views on the problems of transcription and oral data in slave narratives, the compelling blend of vernacular, standard, street, and lyric language for an American writer, the importance of Gerard Manley Hopkins and Jean Toomer to me; how poverty, once a romanticized, sentimentalized figuration in American literature, has returned to its nineteenth-century predecessor as a metaphor for illness, crime, and sin; of my work on the letters of abolitionists James McCune Smith and Gerrit Smith. All of these are topics, or shreds of topics, that have had something to do with my thinking, writing life. The interviewer agreed, but when we met, a few minutes before the show, he changed his mind, saying that the race aspect was far too interesting to abandon. I am not at all sure that the sort of chat I wanted would have had any appeal whatsoever to anybody else. Probably not. The interviewer's judgment was accurate if predictable: racial difference is a very big seller. The point I am making, however, is that neither he nor his audience was interested in any aspects of me other than my raced ones. Disappointed and irked, I dragged out my kit of the media's version of racial dialogue: great-great-granddaughter of Africans, great-great-granddaughter of slaves; great-granddaughter of sharecroppers; granddaughter of migrants; beneficiary of the American Dream—I ended up sleepwalking through a wan, rambling, profoundly uninteresting dialogue.

I had such a yearning for an environment in which I could speak and write without every sentence being understood as mere protest or understood as mere advocacy. Now, in no way should this desire be misinterpreted as an endorsement of deracination, or the fashionable term, "race transcendence," nor as an example of the dwindling impact of racial politics. Even a glance at the U.S. 2000 census data, where more refined racial identifications are also more pronounced; even a light curiosity about recommendations for death-penalty moratoriums; a vague awareness of the bruising disenfranchisement of African Americans in the last presidential election; the record numbers of discrimination and racial profiling cases—none of these vectors of racial policy would lead one to the conclusion that racial politics is benign. I don't foresee, or want, a color-blind, race-neutral environment. The nineteenth century was the time for that. It's too late, now. Our race-inflected culture not only exists, it thrives. The question is whether it thrives as a virus or a bountiful harvest of possibilities.

From the beginning, I claimed a territory by insisting on being identified as a black woman writer exclusively interested in facets of African American culture. I made these unambiguous assertions to impose on all readers the visibility in and the necessity of African American culture to my work precisely in order to encourage a wider critical vocabulary than the one in which I was educated. I wanted this vocabulary to stretch to the margins for the wealth that lay there and thus, not abandon, but reconfigure what occupied the center. It seemed to me a way of enriching the dialogue between and among cultures. I wanted to make impossible the role of temporary or honorary white writer; to frustrate the label of the inconsequentially black writer. The "just happen to be black" writer. My project was to discover what the black topic did and could do to language practices. I sought language that could exist on at least two levels: the clearly raced identity right alongside the unraced one that had to function within an already coded racial discourse. But I was never very good at manifestos, so my attempts proved to be a tightrope, a balancing that confused some readers, delighted others, disappointed some, but provoked enough of them to let me know the work was not always in vain. It led me to try strategies, employ structures and techniques emanating from African American culture cheek by jowl with, and responsive to, other ones.

This effort to balance the demands of cultural specificity with those of artistic range is a condition, rather than a problem, for me. A challenge rather than a worry. A refuge rather than a refugee camp. Home territory, not foreign land. Inhabiting and manipulating that sphere has excited me like no other. Of course African American writers have contemplated, written about, struggled with, and have taken positions on this politics or art, race and/or aesthetics debate since Phillis Wheatley suggested that slavery did her a favor. Jean Toomer tried to escape its shackle altogether by inventing an American race. Langston Hughes, Zora Neale Hurston, James Baldwin, Ralph Ellison, Richard Wright, African American scholars, and a host of post–civil rights writers have weighed in on the subject. And it is or has been, since the nineteenth century, a keenly argued concern of every immigrant group of writers in the United States. From Henry James to Chang-rae Lee; from William Faulkner to Maxine Hong Kingston; from Isaac Bashevis Singer to Frank McCourt; from Herman Melville to Paula Marshall. Still it is hard for me to believe that the necessity of responding to a perceived "outsider" status has been demanded so loudly and so insistently of any group more than African American artists. To me the implied, even voiced question, "Are you a black writer or an American writer?" not only means "Are you subverting art to politics?" It also means "Are you a black writer or a universal writer?" suggesting that the two are clearly incompatible. Race awareness apparently can never be sundered from politics. It is the result of a shotgun wedding originally enforced by whites, while African American artists (in the public and academic domains) are faulted and flailed for dealing with the consequences of this marriage. Forced to shout endlessly to white criticism, "These are not my racial politics—they are yours." These battles against such a mind-set are exhausting and are especially debilitating since those who launched the fray have only to observe it, not participate in it. Have only to misunderstand the demands of cultural specificity as identity politics or assaults on the canon, or special pleading, or some other threatening gesture. And the people most invested in the argument are usually those who have already reaped its benefits.

I suppose I approached the politics versus art, race versus aesthetics debate initially the way an alchemist would: looking for that combination of ingredients that turns dross into gold. But there is no such formula. So my project became to make the historically raced world inextricable from the artistic view that beholds it, and in so doing encourage readings that dissect both. Which is to say I claimed the right and the range of authorship. To interrupt journalistic history with a metaphorical one; to impose on a rhetorical history an imagistic one; to read the world, misread it; write and unwrite it. To enact silence and free speech. In short to do what all writers aspire to do. I wanted my work to be the work of disabling the art versus politics argument; to perform the union of aesthetics and ethics.

I am impressed by the fruitfulness and importance of scholarly and literary challenges that search for more ways in which to both sign and defang race, acknowledge its import and limit its corrosive effect on language. That is, work that avoids the unnatural schism between the political realm in which race matters and the artistic one in which it is presumed not to.

Scholarship that abandons the enforcing properties of the false debate and welcomes the challenges in the liberating ones hidden at its center is becoming sensitive to the fact that things have changed. Language that requires the mutual exclusion of x and y, or the dominance of x over y, is slowly losing its magic, its force. But it is literature that rehearses and enacts this change in ways far in advance of and more probingly than the critical language that follows it. Perhaps it is because of my own farewell to all that art versus politics, culture against aesthetics quarrel that I find literary partings (moments of racial goodbyes) so promising a site in which to examine the sea change expressive language of racial encounter has undergone, a sea change yielding opportunities for richer and more nuanced explorations. Over time the rites of farewell between the races as represented in some selected examples in American literature have moved dramatically from blatant assumptions of racial hierarchy to less overt ones to coded representation to nuanced decodings of those assumptions; from control to dismissal to anxiety to a kind of informed ease. Now, I insist on not being misunderstood here—implying that neutralizing race is the work of literature, its job, so to speak. It is not. Nevertheless the shape of racial discourse can be located there. A shape that plays about and moves through literature and therefore in our imaginations when we read it. Although even this brief inquiry could and ought to be widened, I will limit my observations to women writers because intimacy and alienation and severance between women is more often free of the sexual competition implicit among male writers addressing the same subject, and anxieties about sexual dominance can blur as well as exacerbate the racial equation (as Shakespeare and Hollywood both knew). Saying goodbye is a moment ready-made for literary histrionics, for deep emotional revelations seething with meaning. I am interested in the farewell between black and white strangers who have, or might have, shared something significant; or who represent the end of something larger than themselves, where the separation symbolizes loss or renewal, for example. There are the partings between black and white women whose histories are permanently entangled. Many, if not most, of these are surrogate relationships: surrogate mothers in the nanny-child domain; surrogate mothers, aunts, and other relatives in the servant-mistress category; surrogate sisters in which the friendships become surrogate, illegal, precisely because the dynamics of power between employer and employee are inescapably raced; and sometimes, though rarely, there is the farewell between black and white adult women in which the equity is not race based. Alice Walker's *Meridian* is an early example.

Let me begin with a farewell scene in a fine and prolific writer who is not American, but who was herself a foreigner far from home and who was in a position to form opinions on racial relationships from close quarters, Isak Dinesen. There is a haunting scene in *Out of Africa* that exhibits standard racial discourse as well as the presumptions of the foreigner's home. The scene in which the author is leaving a place, Kenya, that has been her home for much of her adult life. The necessity of moving out of Africa and its melancholy surface in each moment of leave-taking.

A passage toward the end reads as follows:

Now the old women were sorry that I was leaving them. From this last time, I keep the picture of a Kikuyu woman, nameless to me, for I did not know her well, she belonged, I think, to Kathegu's village, and was the wife or widow of one of his many sons. She came towards me on a path on the plain, carrying on her back a load of the long thin poles which the Kikuyu use for constructing the roofs of their huts,—with them this is women's work. These poles may be fifteen feet long; when the women carry them they tie them together at the ends, and the tall conical burdens give to the people underneath them, as you see them traveling over the land, the silhouette of a prehistoric animal, or a Giraffe. The sticks which this woman was carrying were all black and charred, sooted by the smoke of the hut during many years; that meant that she had been pulling down her house and was trailing her building materials, such as they were, to new grounds. When we met she stood dead still, barring the path to me, staring at me in the exact manner of a Giraffe in a herd, that you will meet on the open plain, and which lives and feels and thinks in a manner unknowable to us. After a moment she broke out weeping, tears streaming over her face, like a cow that makes water on the plain before you. Not a word did she or I myself speak, and, after a few minutes, she ceded the way to me, and we parted, and walked on in opposite directions. I thought that after all she had some materials with which to begin her new house, and I imagined how she would set to work, and tie her sticks together, and make herself a roof.

Lots of other Kenyans wept and deplored Dinesen's exit: because of their affection for her, or perhaps the loss of paid employment and protection, the despair of having to find other shelter. But the above recollection bedevils me for other reasons. What does the phrase "barring the path to me" mean? Not barring the path, or barring me in the path, but barring the path to me. Is the path only to and for Dinesen? Is the woman out of place? The syntax is curious. Additionally there is the sustained speculation about the woman's errand—carrying wood to build, rebuild, or repair her roof. To make a home for herself in a land that is her home, but in which she (the Kikuyu woman) is made to feel the outsider. While the true foreigner, the author, is leaving a false home about which she has some misgivings. The description of Dinesen's African woman is instructive. The sticks on her head make Dinesen think of a "prehistoric animal." Furthermore, the quiet woman is staring at her with what emotions we cannot yet know because she is relegated to the animal kingdom, where emotions and thoughts and life itself cannot be known by us. The woman is like a giraffe in a herd, speechless, unknowable, and when she evinces some powerful emotion such as sorrow, or rage, or disgust, or loneliness, or even joy we cannot know it because her tears are like a cow voiding its urine in public. It is a picture, says Dinesen, that she keeps with her, this nameless unknown woman. Surely a surrogate, a symbol, of Kenya and what she thinks of the world she is leaving behind. In these passages, beautiful "aesthetic" language serves to undermine the terms: the native, the foreigner, home, homelessness in a wash of preemptive images that legitimate and obscure their racist assumptions while providing protective cover from a possibly more damaging insight.

If we leave 1930s Africa and move to 1940s America to another writer with claim to some intimate relations to blacks, there is further instruction.

In a classic tale of American womanhood, *Gone with the Wind,* the black woman/white woman connection is the one we have learned from Harriet Beecher Stowe and others: a ubiquitous mammy whose devotion and nursing skills are as fierce as they are loyal. These surrogate mothers are more serviceable than real mothers not only because of their constancy, but also because, unlike biological mothers, you can command them and dismiss them without serious penalty. Notwithstanding their presence in the text, there will always come a time when these surrogates leave—they either exit the narrative itself because they are no longer relevant to it, or they leave the life of their mistress because their value as teachers is reduced when the cared-for matures, or when circumstances have changed: moving away, insubordination, or death. Of interest to me is how this severance is played out. Is protective language summoned to make the black woman's disappearance palatable? Is there a dependence on a metaphoric equation with the unfeeling, unthinking animal world? Are there deep or awkward silences to accompany her dismissal? Are there tears or a stubborn insistence upon permanent attachment?

In spite of the very real difference in the level of literary accomplishment, Mitchell's mammy is like Dinesen's Kikuyu in important ways. Similes chosen to bring each into view are from the animal kingdom; both black women are speechless with grief when departure is imminent; the severance in both instances is seen as trauma, a devastating deprivation to the black woman and in Mitchell, to the white woman as well. The "not one word spoken" by the Kenyan woman becomes the garbled babble of a black woman (who in sixty years of dialogue with her mistress had never learned to pronounce the word "white") and a quiet begrudging while her young mistress weeps.

These early and classic relationships between women of different races, frequently maternal, friendly, loving, are echoed in Willa Cather's *Sapphira and the Slave Girl* in a mesmerizing deathbed scene with another surrogate, a woman named Jezebel with whom the mistress had a close and mutually satisfying friendship. The dialogue is revelatory.

"You must eat to keep up your strength."

"Don't want nothin', Missy."

"Can't you think of anything that would taste good to you? Now think a minute, and tell me. Isn't there something?"

The old woman gave a sly chuckle; one paper eyelid winked, and her eyes gave out a flash of grim humour. "No'm, I cain't think of nothin' I could relish, lessen maybe it was a li'l pickaninny's hand."

She turned back again to the bed, took up Jezebel's cold grey claw, and patted it. "Good-bye til another time, Auntie. Now you must turn over and have a nap."

Evocative as this scene is, rampant with pleasant memories and a shared view of the world, its serenity explodes with flashes of the serviceable but sinister language of racial antagonism. The hint of cannibalism (understood to be "natural" to Africans) and not the patting of a hand, the patting of "a cold grey claw."

But something else begins to take place in fiction: changes that are usually attributed to social climate; the signs of the times. In any case, speech permissible in the nineteenth and early twentieth century is crude in the late twentieth. But that may not be the whole story. Surely the entrance of post–Harlem Renaissance minority voices into the political and literary landscape has had a share in this alteration. Perhaps a readership and a critical community that is intolerant of the easy dismissal of others. In any case there are fewer instances of unreflective dismissals; deeper probes into these relationships; more exacting observations of these exits and disruptions in the relationships. In 1946 Carson McCullers published *The Member of the Wedding.*" Before that *The Heart Is a Lonely Hunter.*

In both novels black women exit the life of the protagonist. The scene between Berenice and Frankie in *The Member of the Wedding* is one of struggle for control in which we witness the jealousy of the surrogate mother at the flight of the child. Then there is Harper Lee's *To Kill a Mockingbird,* where it is clear Lee is working away from certain assumptions of unknowableness. Although Calpurnia has self-revealing conversations only with other blacks and children—never white adults—the grapple for language to deal with these complicated matters is apparent. There are no leave-taking moments in the novel, nor in Lillian Hellman's autobiographical work that has several recollections of her servant, Caroline Ducky. Yet the point is sustained by the reach of these authors for a seriousness not shown in earlier writers. There seems to be a blossoming suspicion among these white women writers that complex thought, ambiguity, nuance are actually possible in their black characters, and that their speech does not require the strange, creative spellings that no other character's speech needs.

Lucille Clifton opens her own lovely memoir, *Generations,* in 1976, with a conversation between strangers of each race—a conversation that rings with the sayable and the unsaid.

But two years before that Diane Johnson fills in those gaps that lie about in Clifton's memoir and in other works. Her 1974 *The Shadow Knows* digs deeply into these relationships. The narrator has two domestics critical to her life: one disruptive, vengeful, grotesque; another benevolent, supportive, cheerful. The reflective quality of the prose is worth quoting.

"But I'm trying to confess that I don't think I experience Osella as a human, not really." "And she had seemed dead on arrival, delivered lonely and bereaved and far from home to our zoo, like some insignificant common animal barely noticeable to the keeper, me, who was more preoccupied with the misery of the delicate gazelle—me." Here the animal characteristics are equally distributed and the more lyric "gazelle" is delivered with irony. Later she muses, "I notice that whenever I describe Osella or think of her, it is in metaphors of things not people, or of fat animals. It is as if I did not consider her human, this fellow woman with whom I shared my children and my home and many hours. . . . There was nothing in her that wouldn't sit down sisterly and share a recipe but there was something in me." This is no casual, lazy (Margaret Mitchell) language: Osella is impossibly if understandably lunatic. While the death of Ev, who follows Osella, is a subject of the narrator's deep personal mourning.

Language ricochets in these race-inflected farewell scenes. In *Beloved* also there is a leave-taking between a white girl and a black one. The scene moves toward the parting that must take place between them, yes, but the scene is also meant to enact a goodbye to the impediments of race right in the middle of highly racialized dialogue. Each one begins by speaking in the language of the period. The power relationships are manifest in the casually racist remarks of Amy and the deceitful acquiescence of Sethe. Following their joint venture in the birth of Denver, they speak, finally, not of farewell, but of memory; how to fix the memory of one in the mind of the other—or, as with Sethe, how to immortalize the encounter beyond her own temporal life. While the action is separation, the parting of ways, the language is meant to displace it, is meant to invite meditation on its necessity. Washing up on the bank of the Ohio River is our knowing that if both women had been of the same race (both white or both black) they could have, might have, would have stayed together and shared their fortune. Neither one felt she belonged anywhere. Both are traveling through unknown, strange territory looking for a home. So the language is designed to imply the solitude of their farewell is somehow shaming.

In the later decades of the twentieth century the dissolution of the restrictions imposed by race consciousness on expressive language begins to erode, as in Barbara Kingsolver's *The Poisonwood Bible*. Instead of suppressing, ignoring the possibilities in these relationships, instead of the comfort of stereotype and the safety of an indolent imagination, one begins to hear not Dinesen's silence or Mitchell's gabble, but verbal fencing; not the unmitigated devotion or disobedience of servants, but the wrestle over the meaning of home; the probing of subtle jealousies, complicated forms of resistance, hatred, love, anger; the learned and earned exchange of mutual perception.

I think I know why African American women writers ignored the temptation to widen the racial divide rather than understand it. I am not sure why white women writers felt compelled to do likewise. It could not have been a simple choice between aestheticizing politics or politicizing aesthetics. Nor could it have been a juvenile yearning to deserve the terms "humanitarian" and "universal." Those terms, so tainted with the erasure of race, are no longer adequate. I leave it to others to name the equipoise that now resides in literature, especially of/by women, if not in the public discourse that seeks to comprehend it.

There already exists the material from which a new paradigm for reading and writing about literature can arise. Writers have already said farewell to the old one. To the racial anchor that weighed down the language and its imaginative possibilities. How novel it would be if, in this case, life imitated art. If I could have had that television interview reflecting my life's real work. If, in fact, I was not a (raced) foreigner but a home girl, who already belonged to the human race.

Invisible Ink

Reading the Writing and Writing the Reading

I ONCE WROTE an article for a popular magazine that had a small irregular "arts" section. They wanted something laudatory about the value or perhaps just the pleasure of reading. This last noun, "pleasure," annoyed me because it is routinely associated with emotion: delight accompanied by suspense. Reading is fundamental—emphasis on the "fun." At the least, of course, it is understood, in popular discourse, to be uplifting, instructive; at its best encouraging deep thought.

Thoughts about the practice of reading engaged me early on as a writer/imaginer as well as an absorbent reader.

I began reading when I was three years old, but it was always difficult for me. Not difficult as in hard to do, but difficult in the sense of having a hard time looking for meaning in and beyond the words. The first grade primer sentence "Run, Jip, run" led me to the question, Why is he running? Is that a command? If so, where to? Is the dog being chased? Or is it chasing someone? Later on when I tackled "Hansel and Gretel" more serious questions flooded. As they did with nursery rhymes and games: "ring around the rosie, pocket full of posies." It was some time before I understood that the rhyme, the game was about death during the bubonic plague.

So I chose for this magazine an attempt to distinguish reading as a skill and reading as an art.

This is some of what I wrote:

"Mr. Head awakened to discover that the room was full of moonlight. He sat up and stared at the floor boards—the color of silver—and then at the ticking on his pillow, which might have been brocade, and after a second, he saw half of the moon five feet away in his shaving mirror, paused as if it were waiting for his permission to enter. It rolled forward and cast a dignifying light on everything. The straight chair against the wall looked stiff and attentive as if it were awaiting an order and Mr. Head's trousers, hanging to the back of it, had an almost noble air, like the garment some great man had just flung to his servant."

In those opening sentences by Flannery O'Connor, she chose to direct her readers to Mr. Head's fantasy, his hopes. The ticking on a pillow, minus a pillow slip, is like brocade, rich, elaborate. Moonlight turns a wooden floor to silver and "casts a dignifying light" everywhere. His chair is "stiff and attentive" and seems to await an order from him. Even his trousers hanging on the chair's back had "a noble air," like the garment some great man has flung to his servant. So, Mr. Head has strong, perhaps unmanageable dreams of majesty, of controlling servants to do his bidding, of rightful authority. Even the moon in his shaving mirror pauses "as if it were waiting for his permission to enter." We don't really have to wait (a few sentences on) to see his alarm clock sitting on an overturned bucket or to wonder why his shaving mirror is five feet away from his bed, to know a great deal about him—his pretension, his insecurity, his pathetic yearnings—and to anticipate his behavior as the story unfolds.

In my essay, I was trying to identify characteristics of flawless writing that made it possible to read fiction again and again, to step into its world confident that attentiveness will always yield wonder. How to make the work work while it makes me do the same.

I thought my illustration was fine as far as it went, but what I could not clearly articulate was the way in which a reader participates in the text—not how she interprets it, but how she helps to write it. (Very like singing: there are the lyrics, the score, and then the performance—which is the individual's contribution to the piece.)

Invisible ink is what lies under, between, outside the lines, hidden until the right reader discovers it. By "right" reader, I am suggesting that certain books are obviously not for every reader. It's possible to admire but not become emotionally or intellectually involved in Proust. Even a reader who loves the book may not be the best or right lover. The reader who is "made for" the book is the one attuned to the invisible ink.

The usual dyad in literary criticism is the stable text versus the actualized reader. The reader and his readings can change, but the text does not. It is stable. As the text cannot change, it follows that a successful relationship between text and reader can only come about through changes in the reader's projections. It seems to me that the question becomes whether those dormant projections are products of the reader or the writer. What I want to suggest is that may not always be so. While the responsibility of interpretation is understood to be transferred to the reader, the text is not always a quiet patient the reader brings to life. I want to introduce a third party into the equation—the author.

Some writers of fiction design their texts to disturb—not merely with suspenseful plots, provocative themes, interesting characters, or even mayhem. They design their fiction to disturb, rattle, and engage the entire environment of the reading experience.

Withdrawing metaphor and simile is just as important as choosing them. Leading sentences can be written to contain buried information that completes, invades, or manipulates the reading. The unwritten is as significant as the written. And the gaps that are deliberate, and deliberately seductive, when filled by the "right" reader, produce the text in its entirety and attest to its living life.

Think of "Benito Cereno" in this regard, where the author chooses the narrator's point of view to deliberately manipulate the reading experience.

There are certain assumptions about categories that are regularly employed to arouse this disturbance. I would like to see a book written where the gender of the narrator is unspecified, unmentioned. Gender, like race, carries with it a panoply of certainties—all deployed by the writer to elicit certain responses and, perhaps, to defy others.

Race, as the O'Connor, Coetzee, and Melville examples show, contains and produces more certainties. I have written elsewhere about the metaphorical uses to which racial codes are put—sometimes to clarify, sometimes to solidify assumptions readers may hold. Virginia Woolf with her gaps, Faulkner with his delays both control the reader and lead her to operate within the text. But is it true that the text does not formulate expectations or their modification. Or that such formulation is the province of the reader, enabling the text to be translated and transferred to his own mind?

I admit to this deliberate deployment in almost all of my own books. Overt demands that the reader not just participate in the narrative, but specifically to help write it. Sometimes with a question. Who dies at the end of *Song of Solomon* and does it matter? Sometimes with a calculated withholding of gender. Who is the opening speaker in *Love*? Is it a woman or a man who says "Women spread their legs wide open and I hum"? Or in *Jazz* is it a man or woman who declares "I love this city"? For the not right reader such strategies are annoying, like a withholding of butter from toast. For others it is a gate partially open and begging for entrance.

I am not alone in focusing on race as a non-signifier. John Coetzee has done this rather expertly in *Life & Times of Michael K.* In that book we make instant assumptions based on the facts that the place is South Africa, the character is a poor laborer and sometimes itinerant; that people tend to shy away from him. But he has a severe harelip that may be the reason for his bad luck. Nowhere in the book is Michael's race mentioned. As readers we make the assumption or we don't. What if we read the invisible ink in the book and found it to be otherwise—as the trials of a poor white South African (of which there are legion)?

Clearly, the opening sentence of *Paradise* is a blatant example of invisible ink. "They shot the white girl first, and took their time with the rest."

How much will the reader's imagination be occupied with sorting out who is the white girl? When will the reader believe she has spotted her? When will it be clear that while having that information is vital to the town vigilantes, does it really matter to the reader? If so, whatever the choice made it is the reader I force into helping to write the book; it is the reader whom I summon in invisible ink, destabilizing the text and reorienting the reader.

From "Are you afraid?" the opening sentence of *A Mercy*, calming the reader, swearing to do no harm, to the penultimate chapter's "Are you afraid? You should be."

Writing the reading involves seduction—luring the reader into environments outside the pages. Disqualifying the notion of a stable text for one that is dependent on an active and activated reader who is writing the reading—in invisible ink.

Let me close with some words from a book that I believe is a further example.

"They rose up like men. We saw them. Like men they stood."

Sources

"Peril": Remarks upon receipt of the 2008 PEN/Borders Literary Service Award. New York, New York, April 28, 2008.

"*The Dead of September 11*": Memorial Service. Princeton University, Princeton, NJ, September 13, 2001.

"The Foreigner's Home": Alexander Lecture Series, University of Toronto, Toronto, Ontario, Canada, May 27, 2002.

"Racism and Fascism": *The Nation*, May 29, 1995. Excerpt from Charter Day Speech, "The First Solution": Howard University, Washington, DC, March 3, 1995.

"Home": Convocation, Oberlin College, Oberlin, Ohio, April 23, 2009.

"Wartalk": Oxford University, Oxford, England, June 15, 2002.

"The War on Error": Amnesty International Lecture, Edinburgh, Scotland, August 29, 2004.

"A Race in Mind": Newspaper Association of America Conference, San Francisco, California, April 27, 1994.

"Moral Inhabitants": Response to "In Search of a Basis for Mutual Understanding and Racial Harmony" by James Baldwin, The Nature of a Humane Society: A Symposium on the Bicentennial of the United States of America, Lutheran Church of America, Pennsylvania Southeast Synod, University of Pennsylvania, October 29–30, 1976.

"The Price of Wealth, the Cost of Care": Nichols-Chancellor's Award, Vanderbilt University, Nashville, Tennessee, May 9, 2013.

"The Habit of Art": Introduction to Toby Devan Lewis, the ArtTable Award, New York, New York, April 16, 2010.

"The Individual Artist": National Council on the Arts, Washington, DC, February 14, 1981.

"Arts Advocacy": Author's personal archive.

"Sarah Lawrence Commencement Address": Sarah Lawrence College, Bronxville, New York, May 27, 1988.

"The Slavebody and the Blackbody": America's Black Holocaust Museum, Milwaukee, Wisconsin, August 25, 2000.

"Harlem on My Mind": Louvre Museum, Paris, France, November 15, 2006.

"Women, Race, and Memory": Queens College, Queens, New York, May 8, 1989.

"Literature and Public Life": Cornell University, Ithaca, New York, November 17, 1998.

"The Nobel Lecture in Literature": Nobel Prize Lecture, Stockholm, Sweden, December 7, 1993.

"Cinderella's Stepsisters": Barnard College Commencement Address, New York, New York, May 13, 1979.

"The Future of Time": The Twenty-Fifth Jefferson Lecture in the Humanities, Washington, DC, March 25, 1996.

"*Tribute to Martin Luther King Jr.*": *Time* Magazine Seventy-Fifth Anniversary Gala, New York, New York, March 3, 1998.

"Race Matters": Race Matters Conference keynote address, Princeton University, Princeton, New Jersey, April 28, 1994.

"Black Matter(s)": *Grand Street* 40 (1991): 204–25. Clark Lectures, 1990. Massey Lectures, 1990.

"Unspeakable Things Unspoken": The Tanner Lectures on Human Values, University of Michigan, Ann Arbor, Michigan, October 7, 1988.

"Academic Whispers": Johns Hopkins University, Baltimore, Maryland, March 10, 2004.

"Gertrude Stein and the Difference She Makes": Studies in American Africanism, Charter Lecture, University of Georgia, Athens, Georgia, November 14, 1990.

"Hard, True, and Lasting": Robert and Judi Prokop Newman Lecture, University of Miami, Miami, Florida, August 30, 2005.

"*James Baldwin Eulogy*": Cathedral of St. John the Divine, New York, New York, December 8, 1987.

"The Site of Memory": *Inventing the Truth: The Art and Craft of Memoir,* ed. William Zinsser (Boston: Houghton Mifflin, 1987).

"God's Language": Moody Lecture, University of Chicago, Chicago, Illinois, May 10, 1996.

"Grendel and His Mother": Alexander Lecture Series, University of Toronto, Toronto, Ontario, Canada, May 28, 2002.

"The Writer Before the Page": Generoso Pope Writers' Conference, Manhattanville College, Purchase, New York, June 25, 1983.

"The Trouble with Paradise": Moffitt Lecture, Princeton University, Princeton, New Jersey, April 23, 1998.

"On *Beloved*": Author's personal archive.

"Chinua Achebe": Africa America Institute Award, New York, New York, September 22, 2000.

"Introduction of Peter Sellars": Belknap Lecture, Princeton University, Princeton, New Jersey, March 14, 1996.

"Tribute to Romare Bearden": The World of Romare Bearden Symposium, Columbia University, New York, New York, October 16, 2004.

"Faulkner and Women": *Faulkner and Women,* ed. Doreen Fowler and Ann J. Abadie, Faulkner and Yoknapatawpha Series, University of Mississippi, Oxford, Mississippi, University Press of Mississippi, 1986.

"The Source of Self-Regard": Portland Arts: Lecture Series, Portland, Oregon, March 19, 1992.

"Rememory": Author's personal archive.

"Memory, Creation, and Fiction": Gannon Lecture, Fordham University, Bronx, New York, March 31, 1982.

"Goodbye to All That": Radcliffe Inaugural Lecture Series, Radcliffe Institute for Advanced Study, Cambridge, Massachusetts, April 3, 2001.

"Invisible Ink": Wilson College Signature Lecture Series, Princeton University, Princeton, New Jersey, March 1, 2011.